Chef interrupted

Delicious Chefs' Recipes That You Can Actually Make at Home

melissa clark

Photographs by Tina Rupp

CLARKSON POTTER/PUBLISHERS

NEW YORK

This book is for Robin, Ana, Abby, Zoe, April, Joseph, Josh, Tina, my sister Amy, and all my other home-cook friends who have called me in a panic over the years, cookbook in hand, confusing recipe under way. I hope this book answers all the questions that come up, though you know you can still call me anyway.

www.crownpublishing.com
www.clarksonpotter.com

CLARKSON N. POTTER is a trademark and POTTER and colophon
are registered trademarks of Random House, Inc.

Printed in the United States of America

Design by Jane Treuhaft

Library of Congress Cataloging-in-Publication Data
Clark, Melissa.
    Chef, interrupted : delicious chefs' recipes that you can
actually make at home / Melissa Clark.
    Includes index.
    1. Cookery.   I. Title.
TX714.C553   2005
641.5—dc22   2005001593

ISBN-13: 978-1-4000-5440-4
ISBN-10: 1-4000-5440-0

10 9 8 7 6 5 4 3 2 1

First Edition

contents

introduction

Chefs' cookbooks abound. Glossy, highly illustrated, intricate, and many times impossible to cook from, they populate the shelves of bookstores like poppy seeds on a bagel. Yet chefs still write them and people still buy them—although only a core group of committed foodies ever really use them to their full capacity. Most of these books are destined to be fantasy bedtime reading, rather than anything you'd risk splattering squab *jus* on—if anyone even gets that far.

I should know. I've coauthored several chefs' books myself. As a food writer for newspapers and magazines, a collaborator on chefs' cookbooks, a former caterer, and an avid restaurant-goer, I know firsthand how marvelous chefs' recipes can be. But I also know that many are an awful pain in the neck. Translating—essentially interrupting these recipes at the point at which they are still somewhat home-cook–friendly— is part of what I do for every cookbook I collaborate on, and for every article I write. I know when to interrupt the narrative flow of chef-speak. I know the questions to ask, and when to ask them. And I know how to interpret the answers. But there are times when, no matter how much I try to cajole chefs into simplifying their recipes and techniques, they are only willing to take it so far. And for most home cooks, that's just not far enough.

So why do people continue to collect chefs' cookbooks, even those that prove to be about as usable as that impulse-purchased mini crème brûlée torch? It's because although the recipes can be intimidating, the dishes themselves— and the combinations of ingredients that only a true master would venture to put together—can be brilliant. That is one reason we go to restaurants, to marvel at and be inspired by culinary genius, and to sample the kind of fashionable, trendy cuisine we'd never make at home. Chef Janos Wilder's Venison Loin Adobada with Black Bean Coulis, Sweet Potato–Mushroom Chilaquiles, Smoked Tomato Salsa, and Shiitake Escabeche is not the kind of recipe that home cooks would ever undertake. But it's still fun and exciting to see how the dish is put together. We can ogle, perhaps, at the mouthwatering photo. And a home cook with three free days and the determination of Lance Armstrong might try it. With any luck, at the end of it, the recipe will actually work.

But wouldn't it be ideal if there were a way to have a taste of that recipe that's both delicious *and* attainable? A way to re-create the venison that keeps the essence of the flavors but pares away all the extraneous garnishes? What if the recipe simply becomes Venison Loin Adobada with Chipotle Black Beans (page 194)? And what if there were no complicated, overly time-consuming steps? In other words, what about a cookbook that combines the creativity of justly famous celebrity chefs with the down-to-earth, practical mentality of a home cook? A book that bridges the gap between impossibly opulent, cutting-edge restaurant cuisine and the all-too-simple, humdrum food of our everyday lives?

This is that book.

Chef, Interrupted could be thought of as Chefs' Recipes Made Easy. I've called on some of the most stellar chefs across the country to find their best, most intriguing dishes. Then I've deconstructed the recipes and put them back together, nipping and tucking at the overly complicated parts, until all that remains is the brilliant essence of a dish, without all the hassle. I've removed the obstacles, employing the efficient kitchen tricks that I've learned as a food writer, and stripping the recipes, time-wise, to their bones. And whenever possible, I've tried to look behind the ingredients and techniques of a recipe, simplifying and explicating in equal measure until the result seems as limpid as the kind of consommé I'd never ask anyone to clarify. I wanted to make this book the next best thing to taking a cooking class with America's greatest chefs.

Every recipe here is a jewel in its own right—even those as simple as the salads. Why would anyone care about a chef's recipe for something as basic as a salad?

Because if the recipe has made it into this book, it means that it's not just any salad; I haven't included a recipe for Mesclun Salad with Mustard Vinaigrette because it's on some restaurant menu somewhere and it's home-cook accessible. Instead, my aim was to track down the most interesting, innovative, and delicious salads, ones that are truly unique. For example, Suzanne Goin's Arugula–Mint Salad with Apricots and Cumin (page 46) didn't need much interrupting, but the dish is easily one of the best plates of green you'll ever eat.

Of course, not every dish in this book needed the same level of interpreting and paring down. After all, there are some straightforward techniques and ingredients that chefs use every single day. For example, while every home cook in America knows what a filet mignon is, how many would ever try poaching it in a spiced red wine broth, as chef Guido Haverkock does in his recipe for Wine-Poached Filet Mignon with Aromatics and Olive Oil Mashed Potatoes (page 164)? There is nothing esoteric about this recipe, yet it is resolutely distinctive.

With my background of a little restaurant training and a lot of home-cooking experience, I have the viewpoint of the home cook with the understanding and general knowledge base of the professional chef. In this book I attempt to tame the wild, clarify the obscure, and whip the recipes into shape—into delicious, doable recipes that everyone can actually make at home.

Hors d'Oeuvres
and Appetizers

Fresh and Smoked Salmon Rillettes
ERIC RIPERT, Le Bernardin

Chicken Liver and Fennel Crostini
MARIO BATALI, Babbo Ristorante e Enoteca

Warm Gougères with Crunchy Sea Salt
BILL YOSSES, Joseph's

Turkish Red Pepper and Walnut Dip
PETER HOFFMAN, Savoy

Mushroom Tarte Tatin
TOM COLICCHIO, Craft

Chicken Samosas with Cilantro Sauce
MOHAN ISMAIL, Kalustyan's Café

Fried Mortadella Sandwich with
Ricotta and Capers
ZAK PELACCIO, 5 Ninth

Heirloom Pea Pancakes with
Smoked Salmon and Crème Fraîche
BILL TELEPAN, formerly of JUdson Grill

Spanish Tortilla
BOBBY FLAY, Bolo

Hand-Cut Tuna Tartare with
Avocado and Red Radish
MICHAEL CIMARUSTI, Providence

Warm Grape-Leaf–Wrapped Goat
Cheese with Olives and Grilled
Sourdough
MELISSA KELLY, Primo

Foie Gras Terrine with Asian Pear
Marmalade
BRYCE WHITTLESEY, Wheatleigh

Spicy Tasso Shrimp with Crystal Hot
Sauce–Beurre Blanc
JAMIE SHANNON, Commander's Palace

Grilled Calamari with Greens and Aioli
LYNN MCNEELY, Barbuto

Oyster Pan Roast with Chives and
Curried Crouton
TOM VALENTI, Ouest

Foie Gras BLT
LAURENT TOURONDEL, BLT Steak

Truffled Egg Toast
JASON DENTON, 'ino

ERIC RIPERT, Le Bernardin, New York

Fresh and Smoked Salmon Rillettes

Rillettes is a French word meaning a soft pâté, or a spread, generally eaten with crusty hunks of baguette, potent mustard, and tiny cornichon pickles. Rillettes are usually made from pork, rabbit, or goose products, but this version, from seafood master Eric Ripert, is based on two kinds of salmon: the fresh salmon gives the spread a vibrant ocean taste, while the smoked adds an earthy undertone. Eric, of course, whips up his own homemade mayonnaise for this, but jarred works nearly as well and makes it incredibly easy to put together. Or use the homemade mayo recipe on page 125 if you want to go all out. **PREPARATION TIME: 35 MINUTES, PLUS 1 OR MORE HOURS CHILLING**

SERVES 8

2 cups dry white wine

1 tablespoon chopped shallot

½ teaspoon salt, plus additional to taste

1 pound fresh salmon fillet, fat trimmed, cut into 1-inch cubes

3 ounces smoked salmon, diced (about ½ cup)

1 tablespoon minced chives

2 tablespoons freshly squeezed lemon juice (from 1 lemon)

⅓ cup mayonnaise, or to taste

¼ teaspoon freshly ground white pepper

Toasted baguette slices, for serving

MELISSA'S TIPS If you want to shorten this recipe even more, just buy poached **salmon** instead of raw. Then all you have to do is mix everything together.

For a Francophile presentation, serve with cornichons and spicy Dijon mustard.

CHEF'S TIP This recipe can be made up to 8 hours ahead and refrigerated, tightly wrapped. It's at its peak when served 2 to 4 hours after you make it, giving the flavors a chance to come together.

1. In a saucepan, bring the wine, shallot, and salt to a boil. Add the fresh **salmon** cubes and poach at a gentle simmer until just cooked through, about 2 minutes. Drain well, wrap in plastic, and refrigerate until cold, at least 1 hour and up to 24 hours.

2. In a bowl, stir together the smoked salmon and chives. Add the poached fresh salmon and use the side of a wooden spoon to flake the salmon as you mix. Stir in the lemon juice, then the mayonnaise and pepper. Season with salt to taste and refrigerate until ready to serve. Serve with the baguette slices.

MARIO BATALI, Babbo Ristorante e Enoteca, New York

Chicken Liver and Fennel Crostini

Chicken livers and fennel are a classic Tuscan flavor combination that Mario Batali uses as an out-of-the-ordinary topping for crostini. But while Mario's version is a multistep affair, I've condensed the recipe so it can all be made in one pan. And conveniently, you can serve it hot, warm, or at room temperature—just not cold. PREPARATION TIME: 1 HOUR

SERVES 8 TO 10

2 pounds chicken livers, rinsed and patted dry

Coarse sea salt or kosher salt and freshly ground black pepper

3 tablespoons extra-virgin olive oil, plus additional for the crostini

1 small red onion, thinly sliced

3 garlic cloves, minced

2 fennel bulbs, trimmed, halved lengthwise, cored, and thinly sliced crosswise

¾ teaspoon fennel seeds

3 tablespoons chopped fennel fronds

2 teaspoons sherry vinegar, or to taste

1 loaf country bread (preferably day-old), sliced ¼ inch thick

CHEF'S TIP: Chicken livers are extremely perishable, so either buy them frozen and defrost them just before cooking (in the fridge overnight is good), or use them the day you purchase them.

1. Place the **chicken livers** in a large bowl, sprinkle generously with salt and pepper, and toss with 1 tablespoon of the olive oil. Cover and let sit at room temperature.

2. In a large sauté pan over medium heat, warm the remaining 2 tablespoons oil. Add the onion and garlic and cook, stirring, for 30 seconds. Add the fennel slices and seeds and sauté until golden brown and caramelized, 20 to 25 minutes. Transfer the fennel to a bowl and return the pan to the stove.

3. Turn the heat to high and use a slotted spoon to transfer the chicken livers to the pan. Sear the livers on all sides, about 7 minutes, but be sure they remain pink at the center (take care not to overcook them!). Using the slotted spoon, transfer the cooked livers to the bowl with the fennel.

MELISSA'S TIP If you don't have **sherry vinegar** on hand, it's not essential; white wine vinegar is a fine substitute.

4. Using a knife and fork, roughly chop the livers and mix them into the fennel. Add the chopped fronds, **vinegar,** and a generous pinch of salt, and toss well.

5. To make the crostini, toast the bread on a grill or under the broiler until crisp. Brush liberally with olive oil, sprinkle with sea salt, and mound with the liver and fennel mixture.

BILL YOSSES, Joseph's, New York

Warm Gougères with Crunchy Sea Salt

The crunchy crystals of coarse sea salt on top of these addictive little cheese puffs make them seem like soft, cheesy pretzels—albeit in a far more elegant package. The quark (see Melissa's Tips) gives them a slightly softer texture than the usual gougère recipe, and a fuller, richer flavor. Eat them hot from oven, one after another. PREPARATION TIME: 45 MINUTES, PLUS 20 MINUTES BAKING

MAKES ABOUT 3 DOZEN PUFFS; SERVES 8

- 1 cup whole milk
- 1 cup (2 sticks) unsalted butter
- 2 teaspoons sugar
- 1 teaspoon salt or kosher salt
- 1 cup quark cheese or whole-milk yogurt (see Melissa's Tips)

- 1¾ cups all-purpose flour
- 6 large eggs
- 1 cup grated Parmesan or Gruyère cheese
- Coarse sea salt or kosher salt

MELISSA'S TIPS Quark is a German fresh white-curd cheese that vaguely resembles sour cream but has a firmer, dryer texture and a more complex, tangy taste. It's available here in gourmet shops and cheese stores. Or substitute whole-milk yogurt, which has a similar tang.

CHEF'S TIPS Pâte à choux doughs like this one are cooked on the stovetop to get rid of the **taste of raw flour.** We timed it, but I recommend tasting to be sure it has a rich, smooth, buttery flavor that is devoid of the dry, powdery, raw starch taste of flour. By the time you're done, there will be a slight film on the bottom of the pan, which you needn't bother scraping out with the dough.

1. Preheat the oven to 375°F. and line two baking sheets with parchment paper or nonstick liners. In a large saucepan over medium-high heat, combine the milk, butter, sugar, and salt, and bring to a boil. Stir in the **quark** or yogurt and reduce the heat to medium. Add the flour and stir until the mixture dries out slightly and no longer **tastes of raw flour,** 7 to 9 minutes.

2. Transfer the batter to the bowl of an electric mixer fitted with the paddle attachment and beat in the eggs one at a time until smooth. Beat in ½ cup of the grated cheese.

3. Use two spoons to drop 1¼-inch (walnut-size) blobs of batter onto the lined baking sheets. Sprinkle each puff with a pinch of the remaining grated cheese and a pinch of coarse salt. Bake until puffed and brown, about 20 minutes. Serve as soon as possible.

MELISSA These puffs are definitely at their peak when served straight from the oven, but they will still be avidly consumed at room temperature. I've even polished off leftovers the next morning for breakfast, and they still taste great, though the texture is a little limp. In fact, these are sturdier than you'd expect. If you somehow end up with leftovers, freeze them in Ziploc bags and then reheat directly from the freezer at 350°F. for 10 to 15 minutes.

CHEF These are a perfect vehicle for any creamy, flavorful filling, from minced sautéed mushrooms to smoked salmon mousse to a buttery sauté of escargots. To fill, slice off the cap of the puff, pipe or spoon in some filling, then replace the cap.

PETER HOFFMAN, Savoy, New York

Turkish Red Pepper and Walnut Dip

In 1990, when Savoy opened on the fringes of SoHo, Peter Hoffman was an urban pioneer in the sustainable and local agriculture movement, which at that time was really just picking up steam. The network of New York City farmers' markets soon found its footing and began its tremendous, borough-wide expansion. Now, every chef espouses this farmers' market rhetoric. But Peter is one of maybe a handful who I actually see there on a regular basis, trolling the stands for the season's first oniony ramps or the last tiny, fragrant strawberries. This recipe is based on *muhammara*, a Middle Eastern spread that he often uses as a building block for other dishes at the restaurant. But taken back to its roots, it makes a spicy, intense dip that's even easier to prepare if you use purchased roasted peppers (see Melissa's Tips) — though of course you can imagine where Peter gets his. Make this a day or so ahead and store it in the refrigerator to give the flavors a chance to come together. Just bring the dip to room temperature before serving. You can serve this dip with toasted pita wedges or other breads, or with raw or lightly cooked veggies. Or serve it warmed, as a sauce for plain chicken or fish. PREPARATION TIME: 30 MINUTES

MAKES 3 CUPS; SERVES 8

4 large red bell peppers

1 1/2 cups walnuts

1/2 cup dried bread crumbs (see sidebar)

1 small, dried hot red chile pepper, stemmed and seeded (see Melissa's Tips)

2 tablespoons pomegranate molasses (see Melissa's Tips)

1 1/2 tablespoons freshly squeezed lemon juice (from 3/4 lemon), plus additional to taste

1/2 teaspoon toasted and ground cumin (see Chef's Tips, page 57)

3/4 teaspoon coarse sea salt or kosher salt, or to taste

1/2 teaspoon sugar, or to taste

CHEF'S TIPS Take your time when **charring** the peppers. They should be black on all sides. It's easiest to peel the peppers while they are still warm. Use a paper towel to help remove the skin and seeds, but don't run them under water, which dilutes the flavor. Choose thick, meaty, dark **red peppers** for this recipe. They have the best flavor.

1. Over an open flame, or right below the heat element of the broiler, **char** the **bell peppers** well on all sides, about 15 minutes. Place them in a bowl, cover with a plate or plastic wrap, and let them steam until cool. When cool, remove the skin and seeds and set aside.

2. In a large skillet over medium-high heat, toast the walnuts, tossing, until fragrant and darkened, about 5 minutes. Transfer to a plate and let cool. (Alternatively, toast the nuts in a 350°F. oven until fragrant and golden around the edges, about 15 minutes, stirring once or twice.)

3. In a food processor, process the walnuts, **bread crumbs, chile pepper, pomegranate molasses,** lemon juice, and cumin until mixed. Add the roasted peppers and process until smooth. Season with salt, sugar, and additional lemon juice to taste.

HOMEMADE BREAD CRUMBS

Whenever you have an old loaf of plain artisanal bread, let it dry out thoroughly, then cut off the crusts and grind it to coarse crumbs in a food processor. If you want to make bread crumbs with fresher bread, cut away the crust, slice the loaf, place the slices on the oven rack, and dry at 325°F. until they are thoroughly brittle (this can take up to 45 minutes) before grinding them to crumbs. Dried bread crumbs will keep, stored in an airtight container in a cool, dry place, for a month or two. Sample them before using to make sure they don't taste stale.

MELISSA'S TIPS Peter would never do it, but you can use purchased roasted **red peppers** to prepare this dip—that takes the prep time down to about 3 minutes. Just make sure to seek out really high-quality ones, preferably from an Italian or specialty market. You can tell those that have been roasted by the dark brown smudges on the flesh. Skip the ones packed in jars in brine; their flavor is usually pretty dubious.

Stores that cater to Mexican cooks stock numerous **dried red chile peppers.** For this recipe, any small pepper will work, but they do vary in spiciness and flavor. Dried chiles that are wrinkled tend to offer more flavor and sweetness than the more pungent smooth-skinned ones. Chiles de árbol and New Mexico red chiles are both spicy, long, skinny red peppers (use a 1- to 2-inch segment for this recipe since they are longer than needed). In general, chiles get hotter as they ripen from green to red, and the spice is concentrated when they are dried. If you are not a fan of heat, don rubber gloves, slice the pepper open, and remove the potent seeds. The dried, seedless pepper will deliver a greater ratio of flavor to heat.

Thick and dark ruby-black, **pomegranate molasses** is a sweet-tart Middle Eastern syrup made from nothing but concentrated pomegranate juice. It is traditionally used in everything from soups to shish kebabs, as well as dips like this. Middle Eastern stores are the best source, or you can mail order it from Kalustyan's (800-352-3451; www.kalustyans.com). If you cannot get your hands on a bottle, balsamic vinegar also works in this recipe.

TOM COLICCHIO, Craft, New York

Mushroom Tarte Tatin

This clever appetizer is a takeoff on a classic apple tarte Tatin, but made savory with mushrooms and onions. The recipe was a collaboration between Tom Colicchio, the chef at Gramercy Tavern and Craft, and Claudia Fleming, his former pastry chef, who worked out the pastry part. I pared this recipe down by using frozen puff pastry and eliminating a delicious but time-consuming onion confit. But even so, it's a ridiculously impressive dish that's way easier than you—or your guests—would think. PREPARATION TIME: 50 MINUTES, PLUS 20 MINUTES BAKING

SERVES 4

3 to 5 tablespoons extra-virgin olive oil

4 large shallots, thinly sliced

Coarse sea salt or kosher salt and freshly
  ground black pepper

2 anchovy fillets (optional)

2 tablespoons fresh thyme leaves

1 tablespoon white wine vinegar

¾ pound mixed wild and cultivated mushrooms,
  brushed clean of grit, thickly sliced
  (about 4 cups)

1 garlic clove, minced

3 tablespoons sugar

½ teaspoon sherry vinegar

8 ounces prepared puff pastry, thawed if frozen
  (see Melissa's Tips, page 249)

1. In a skillet over medium-high heat, warm 1 tablespoon of the olive oil. Add the shallots and salt and pepper to taste and cook, stirring occasionally, until soft and brown on the edges, 5 to 6 minutes. Add the anchovies, if using, and 1 tablespoon of the thyme, and cook for 1 more minute, mashing the anchovies with a spoon. Transfer the mixture to a bowl, swirl the white wine vinegar in the pan for 30 seconds, then pour it over the shallot mixture. Set aside.

CHEF'S TIPS If you want to try some unusual, flavorful **wild mushroom** varieties in this recipe, look for them at farmers' markets or order them from my favorite purveyor, Marché aux Delices (888-547-5471; www.auxdelices.com). Buy mushrooms that feel heavy, moist (but not slimy), and flexible, rather than dried out and brittle. It's best not to wash mushrooms under running water, and a dry brush is all you need to clean most. But if you're contending with grit-

2. Add another 1 to 2 tablespoons of the oil to the pan and warm it over medium-high heat. Add just enough **mushrooms** to cover the bottom of the pan in a single layer. Add a pinch each of salt and pepper and cook, turning the mushrooms as they brown, about 2 minutes for the first side. Add half of the garlic and 1½ teaspoons of the thyme, and continue cooking until the mushrooms are tender and golden, about 2 minutes more. Transfer the mushrooms to a plate and wipe out the skillet. Add another tablespoon or two of oil and repeat with the remaining mushrooms, garlic, and thyme.

3. Preheat the oven to 425°F. In a small saucepan over medium heat, combine the sugar with 1 tablespoon water. Swirl the pan until the sugar has completely dissolved, then let the mixture boil, swirling occasionally, until the sugar caramelizes and turns nut brown, about 8 minutes (if the sugar starts to cling to the sides of the pan, dip a pastry brush in water and brush around the sides of the pan). Swirl the sherry vinegar into the caramel and remove from the heat.

4. Pour the caramel into four 4-ounce ramekins and let cool for 1 minute. Spoon the mushrooms into the dishes and top with the shallot mixture.

5. Roll out the puff pastry to ¼ inch thick. Cut the pastry into four circles slightly larger than the opening of the ramekins. Lay the pastry circles over the top of each ramekin, pressing the pastry onto the lip of the dish, and place on a baking sheet. Bake for about 20 minutes, until the pastry is puffed and golden. Cool for 1 to 2 minutes, then carefully invert each tart onto a plate. Serve warm or at room temperature.

filled crevices, give the mushrooms a swirl in a bowl of water, then blot them dry right away with a paper towel.

When **cooking mushrooms,** avoid overcrowding the pan, which causes the mushrooms to release their liquid and steam to a rubbery texture instead of caramelizing to a nice brown on the outside.

MELISSA'S TIP Wild mushrooms have so much flavor that a few interesting ones, mixed in with cultivated button and cremini mushrooms, will provide all the mushroomy flavor you need. Choose whatever looks the most plump and fragrant, which might include standards like shiitake and portobello, or some of the more unusual-looking fungi at the farmers' market like oyster, hen-of-the-woods, maitake, or even fresh morels and porcini when in season. These are expensive, but a little goes a long way.

MOHAN ISMAIL, Kalustyan's Café, New York

Chicken Samosas with Cilantro Sauce

Kalustyan's is a specialty food shop in Manhattan with an emphasis on South Asian and Middle Eastern ingredients. I used to live a block away and never took it for granted that I could get kaffir lime leaves and white cardamom pods, black sesame seeds and chickpea flour whenever the urge, or a recipe, called. Now that I live in Brooklyn, I need to plan ahead a little more or choose dishes that use more easily available ingredients. And that's the beauty of these samosas. Although they were created by Mohan Ismail, the chef at Kalustyan's Café (an offshoot of the store), you can buy most of the ingredients at your local supermarket. But the flavor—infused with the likes of coriander, ginger, and cumin—is no less compelling. PREPARATION TIME: 50 MINUTES, PLUS 20 MINUTES BAKING

MAKES 15 SAMOSAS; SERVES 6 TO 8

SAMOSAS

3 tablespoons extra-virgin olive oil

1 Spanish onion, chopped

3 garlic cloves, minced

¼ cup ground coriander

2 tablespoons ground cumin

1 tablespoon grated fresh gingerroot (see Chef's Tips)

Pinch of ground turmeric

1 large tomato, diced

1 pound ground chicken breast (see Chef's Tips)

2 tablespoons tamarind paste or concentrate, or to taste (see Melissa's Tips)

Coarse sea salt or kosher salt

1 teaspoon sugar, or more to taste

¼ teaspoon cayenne pepper, or more to taste

2 tablespoons chopped fresh cilantro

10 sheets filo dough, thawed if frozen (see Melissa's Tips)

6 tablespoons (¾ stick) unsalted butter, melted

CILANTRO YOGURT SAUCE

1 bunch of fresh cilantro, leaves only

2 cups plain yogurt, preferably whole-milk

2 tablespoons freshly squeezed lime juice (from 1 lime)

1 tablespoon toasted cumin seeds, ground (see Chef's Tips, page 57)

Coarse sea salt or kosher salt

CHEF'S TIPS To grate **fresh ginger,** use a plump, unshriveled root. Peel with a paring knife or the tip of a spoon, then grate it using a fine cheese grater, Microplane zester, or ceramic Asian ginger grater. Grate over a bowl to catch all the juice, and scrape the pulp from the back of the grater. You need about 1½ inches of gingerroot to get 1 tablespoon grated ginger.

1. Make the filling: In a skillet over medium-high heat, warm 2 tablespoons of the oil. Add the onion and sauté until translucent, about 3 minutes. Add the garlic, coriander, cumin, **ginger,** and turmeric and sauté until fragrant, about 1 minute. Add the diced tomato and cook for 5 to 6 minutes, until the tomato begins to break down. Push the mixture to one side of the pan and add the remaining tablespoon of oil to the clear side. Add the **ground chicken** in one layer on the oil and let it sear until brown, about 5 minutes. Stir and continue cooking until the chicken is no longer pink, about 2 minutes longer. Stir together the chicken and tomato mixture and cook for 3 more minutes, then stir in the **tamarind** paste and salt, sugar, and cayenne to taste. Remove from the heat. When the mixture has cooled, stir in the 2 tablespoons cilantro.

2. Preheat the oven to 375°F. Lay out 1 sheet of **filo** on a work surface (keeping the remaining sheets covered with plastic or a damp towel) and brush all over with melted butter. Lay a second sheet on top and brush with more butter. Cut the filo lengthwise into thirds. Place a heaping spoonful of chicken mixture onto the bottom right-hand corner of each rectangle, and fold each one up, diagonally, to form a little triangle; use a bit of melted butter to help seal the ends. Arrange the samosas on a baking sheet and repeat with the remaining filo and chicken. (You can freeze the unbaked samosas for up to 3 months. Just bake them while they are still frozen, adding 5 to 10 minutes to the baking time.) Bake until golden brown, about 20 minutes. Let cool slightly before serving.

3. While the samosas cool, make the sauce: Puree the cilantro leaves with half of the **yogurt** in a blender or food processor. Pour into a bowl and fold in the rest of the yogurt, the lime juice, cumin, and salt to taste. Serve with the samosas.

It's better not to use all white breast meat for the **ground chicken** or you risk dry samosas. You need a little of the fat from dark meat.

MELISSA'S TIPS Tamarind pods are long and brown and filled with a wonderfully tangy brown paste and a lot of big seeds. You can buy bricks of tamarind paste (sold with the seeds still in it), though you will have to soak chunks of it in a little hot water and then strain it through a fine sieve before using. Or you can buy jars of tamarind concentrate (Laxmi is a good brand), which is already strained for you. Since tamarind concentrates vary in potency, you may want to start with a tablespoon and add more to taste. Look for tamarind products in Indian and South American groceries, or order it from Kalustyan's (800-352-3451; www.kalustyans.com).

Mohan uses pan roll (aka spring roll) wrappers to make the samosas, and if you can find them and you'd prefer, you can substitute them for the **filo** dough. However, I actually prefer the filo version, which is a little lighter and flakier and, I think, much easier to handle. Even if the samosas do come out looking a little like your mother's favorite spinach triangle hors d'oeuvres from the 1980s, they certainly don't taste like them.

I could go on about the superiority of whole-milk **yogurt,** but suffice it to say I never use the lower-fat stuff, which has a chalky texture unless filled with additives. While you could use fat-free yogurt for the dipping sauce, the texture won't be nearly as velvety.

ZAK PELACCIO, 5 Ninth, New York

Fried Mortadella Sandwich with Ricotta and Capers

With Zak Pelaccio in the kitchen, you just never know what's going to end up on your plate. It might be a deconstructed calf's head with each part—tongue, brain, cheek—prepared differently. Or it might be a huge bowl of fresh peas, pea shoots, and pork belly; or something as simple as home-cured anchovies that you just can't stop eating. In this dish, he deep-fries mortadella, a soft Italian salami, until crisp, then sandwiches it with fresh ricotta cheese and sharp, briny capers. It's a combination I can't imagine any other chef coming up with, but I've learned not to be surprised by Zak, just delighted. In my version, I dispense with the deep-frying and pan-fry the mortadella slices instead. They may not be quite as crisp, but the result is pretty close, thanks to the panko bread crumbs Zak favors (see Melissa's Tips). And the cleanup is much easier. PREPARATION TIME: 30 MINUTES

MAKES 4 SANDWICHES; SERVES 12 AS AN HORS D'OEUVRE OR 8 AS AN APPETIZER

⅓ cup capers, drained

¼ cup good-quality extra-virgin olive oil

Pinch of crushed red pepper flakes

2 slices mortadella, each ⅓ inch thick, about 12 ounces (see Melissa's Tips)

¾ cup all-purpose flour

2 large eggs, lightly beaten

1½ cups panko or unseasoned bread crumbs (see Melissa's Tips)

⅓ cup olive oil, for frying

Freshly ground black pepper to taste

4 brioche hamburger buns or other rolls, or sliced ciabatta or baguette

1 cup (8 ounces) fresh ricotta (see Melissa's Tips, page 54)

CHEF'S TIP I use salted Sicilian capers to make the **caper paste.** If you want to substitute them for the regular brined kind, you'll need to soak them in several changes of cold water to get rid of a lot of the salt, then leave them in vinegar overnight in the refrigerator (where they'll last for several months). Drain before making the paste.

MELISSA'S TIPS Zak uses thick slices of **mortadella** for this recipe, which you can get by having it sliced to order at a deli. If you can only get precut mortadella in skinny slices, you can compensate by stacking several on top of each other so the pile is about ⅓ inch tall. Compress them slightly with your hands, and they will stick together for frying.

1. To make the **caper paste,** combine the capers, extra-virgin olive oil, and red pepper flakes in a blender or food processor. Puree until smooth. This mix will keep virtually indefinitely in the refrigerator.

2. Peel the thin rind from the **mortadella** slices and cut each slice into 6 wedges (like a pizza). Place the flour in one shallow bowl, the eggs in another, and the panko in a third. Dip the mortadella slices in the flour, then in the eggs, and finally in the **panko.**

3. In a skillet over medium-high heat, warm the ⅓ cup olive oil. Add the mortadella and fry until golden, 1 to 2 minutes per side. Transfer to a plate lined with paper towels to drain, and season with black pepper to taste.

4. Split each bun in half and spread both sides with caper paste. Place the fried mortadella on top and add a spoonful of the fresh ricotta. Cut the sandwiches into halves or quarters, and serve.

DAVID WONDRICH, MIXOLOGIST INTERRUPTED

Considering how unctuous and intense this sandwich is, it should come with its own digestivo.

SCOZZESE

Place 1 teaspoon liquid honey and 1 teaspoon hot water in the bottom of your shaker and stir until the honey has dissolved. Add:

1 1/2 ounces blended Scotch
1/2 ounce Hendrick's gin
1/2 ounce Campari
1/2 ounce fresh-squeezed lime juice

Fill the shaker with cracked ice, shake well, and strain into a chilled cocktail glass.

MELISSA Most **mortadellas** are approximately 8 inches in diameter, though the size can vary. If yours is a lot bigger, ask for just as many 1/3-inch-thick slices as will equal 12 ounces. Then just cut it into more wedges.

Panko are Japanese bread crumbs available in Asian markets and gourmet stores, or you can order them from the Oriental Pantry (978-264-4576; www.orientalpantry.com). They give fried foods a particularly crunchy, feathery texture. You can substitute regular bread crumbs—just make sure to buy the unseasoned kind.

Heirloom Pea Pancakes with Smoked Salmon and Crème Fraîche

At the sorely missed, 3-star JUdson Grill, where Bill Telepan was chef until it closed in 2004, he used to serve these luscious pancakes as an anchor to a seasonal spring vegetable plate, on which he would show-case all the newly harvested produce he could get, like needle-thin asparagus and plump morels. I liked the pea pancakes so much on their own, however, that I took his basic recipe and changed the presentation. Now I serve them as easier and prettier blini substitutes (they have a lovely pale green color) for a smoked salmon or caviar topping. They are always a huge hit at cocktail parties because they are some-what familiar from the smoked salmon, yet the pea is always unexpected. You can also serve them for brunch, with fried or poached eggs on top, and bacon or smoked salmon on the side. PREPARATION TIME: 30 MINUTES

MAKES ABOUT 14 PANCAKES; SERVES 4 TO 5

Coarse sea salt or kosher salt

4 ounces sugar snap peas, trimmed

1/2 cup green peas, preferably freshly shelled

2 tablespoons whole milk

1 tablespoon heavy cream

1 large egg, lightly beaten

1/4 cup all-purpose flour

1/2 teaspoon baking powder

1/2 teaspoon sugar

2 tablespoons unsalted butter

Freshly ground black pepper to taste

1 cup crème fraîche or sour cream

4 ounces smoked or cured salmon, sliced

Freshly snipped chives, for garnish

CHEF'S TIP During the brief spring sea-son when fresh **peas** are available, I shell lots of them, toss them in a bag, and freeze them. They'll last for about three or four months, though I usually go through them long before that.

MELISSA'S TIPS When bringing fresh **peas** back from the market, store them immediately in the refrigerator and try to use them within 24 hours. Or use frozen peas. Even Bill does when he can't get good fresh ones (he only uses peas he's frozen himself, but the recipe still works with those regular freezer-section boxes).

1. Fill a bowl with ice water. Bring a pot of water to a boil then lightly salt it. Blanch the sugar snap peas in the boiling water for 2 minutes. Use a slotted spoon to transfer the sugar snaps to the ice-water bath (keep the water at a boil). Once cool, use a slotted spoon to transfer the sugar snaps to a bowl.

2. Add more ice to the water bath. Repeat the blanching process for the shelled **peas,** blanching them for 3 minutes or until tender, and shocking them in the ice bath. Transfer the cooled peas to a small bowl and coarsely mash them with a fork.

3. In a blender or food processor, combine the sugar snap peas, milk, and cream, and puree until smooth. Transfer the mixture to a large mixing bowl and whisk in the egg. Add the flour, baking powder, sugar, and a pinch of salt, and whisk to combine. Fold the mashed peas into the batter.

4. Preheat the oven to 250°F. In a large ovenproof skillet over medium-high heat, melt ½ tablespoon of the butter. Drop tablespoons of batter into the pan. When the edges are lightly browned after 2 minutes, flip the pancakes, lower the heat as far as it will go, and cook until the pancakes are done in the center and the bottoms are browned, about another 2 minutes. Transfer the pancakes to a baking tray lined with paper towels and sprinkle with salt and pepper to taste. Keep the pancakes in the warm oven until all the batter has been used.

5. Serve topped with a dollop of crème fraîche, a slice of **salmon,** and a sprinkling of chives.

Smoked **salmon** is my favorite, but you can use other smoked fish here, such as trout or sturgeon, or even salmon roe or other caviar if you want to be fancy about it.

BOBBY FLAY, Bolo, New York

Spanish Tortilla

At Bolo, Bobby Flay serves this dense and creamy potato omelet with romesco sauce, which is delicious but an awful lot of work charring and peeling several kinds of chiles, etc. That's typical, though, since Bobby is known for his larger-than-life flavors. Being of more subtle temperament myself, not to mention wanting to save several steps and about 30 minutes' prep time, I like to serve the tortilla unadorned, like they do in Spain. With its roasted potatoes and caramelized onions, it has enough flavor on its own. And if you want a little zip, a few dribbles of Tabasco perk things right up. PREPARATION TIME: 1 HOUR AND 15 MINUTES, PLUS 45 MINUTES CHARRING AND BAKING

SERVES 4 TO 6

2 red bell peppers

3 tablespoons extra-virgin olive oil, plus additional for brushing

2 tablespoons unsalted butter

2 Spanish onions, thinly sliced

2 garlic cloves, finely chopped

Coarse sea salt or kosher salt and freshly ground black pepper

4 small new potatoes

12 large eggs, lightly beaten

2 tablespoons finely chopped fresh flat-leaf parsley, plus additional for garnish

Tabasco or other hot sauce, for serving (optional)

MELISSA'S TIPS For tips on roasting **red bell peppers** or substituting purchased roasted peppers, see pages 18 and 19.

1. Preheat the broiler. Brush the **bell peppers** with olive oil and place them on a baking sheet. Broil the peppers, turning them and watching carefully, until the skins are charred on all sides. Transfer the peppers to a paper bag, twist the top closed, and let steam for 5 minutes. Scrape the skins off the peppers, cut out their stems, and remove their seeds. Slice the flesh into thin strips.

2. Reduce the oven temperature to 400°F.

3. Heat the butter with 1 tablespoon of the oil in a medium sauté pan over medium heat. Add the onions and cook, stirring occasionally, until soft and golden, about 30 minutes. Add the garlic and cook for 2 more minutes. Season with salt and pepper.

4. Meanwhile, brush the potatoes with olive oil. Place them in a small baking dish and roast in the oven until just cooked through, about 25 minutes. When cool enough to handle, slice the potatoes into ¼-inch-thick slices.

5. Increase the oven temperature to 425°F. Add the roasted peppers, and roasted potato slices to the pan with the caramelized onions and cook for 1 minute. Pour in the **eggs** and season with salt and pepper. When the eggs begin to cook around the edges, use a rubber spatula to gently push them from the edge of the pan into the center. While the mixture is still loose, add the parsley. Continue to pull the eggs toward the center of the pan as they cook.

6. When the bottom of the **tortilla** is lightly golden brown and beginning to set, place the pan in the oven and bake until the tortilla is set and slightly puffed, 6 to 8 minutes. Invert the tortilla onto a large plate, cut it into wedges, and garnish with parsley. Serve with hot sauce, if desired.

CHEF'S TIP You don't want to overcook **eggs,** or they turn rubbery. Bake them until they are a shade less set than you like, then pull the pan out of the oven— the residual heat will finish the cooking in a minute or two.

MELISSA You can serve the **tortilla** hot from the oven or, as they do in Spain, at room temperature. Make it up to 4 hours ahead and loosely cover with foil until serving time.

MICHAEL CIMARUSTI, Providence, Los Angeles

Hand-Cut Tuna Tartare with Avocado and Red Radish

Tuna tartare isn't the kind of thing most people think to make at home. In the first place, working with raw tuna and serving it to guests may seem a little scary if there's any doubt about the freshness of the fish. In the second place, it's pretty easy to get on any menu around town, so why bother? But this recipe, by one of LA's most beloved seafood chefs, converted me. With the slices of red radish and avocado, it's absolutely gorgeous. And the balance of flavors and textures—at once creamy, crunchy, piquant from green peppercorns, and suave from the sweet fish—is perfect, which is rare in what can often be a woefully underseasoned dish. But the best part: it's absolutely foolproof once you find sashimi-quality tuna.

PREPARATION TIME: 30 MINUTES

SERVES 6

1 pound sashimi-quality bluefin tuna
   (free of sinew and connective tissue, see
   Melissa's Tips)

3 small, ripe Hass avocados

5 tablespoons freshly squeezed lemon juice, plus
   additional for the salad (about 2 lemons)

3 tablespoons finely diced red onion (from about
   ¼ medium onion)

2 bunches of fresh chives, finely chopped
   (¼ cup)

½ cup extra-virgin olive oil, plus additional for
   drizzling

Coarse sea salt or kosher salt and freshly
   ground white pepper (see Chef's Tip,
   page 57)

1½ tablespoons brined green peppercorns,
   plus their liquid

1½ teaspoons Dijon mustard

6 red radishes, thinly sliced (preferably with a
   mandoline) and reserved in ice water

2 cups mixed micro or baby greens

1 baguette, sliced and toasted, for serving

1. Cut the **tuna** into ¼-inch **dice** and place it in a large bowl. Place a sheet of plastic or parchment paper directly on top of the tuna to prevent oxidation, and refrigerate until needed (up to 12 hours).

2. Cube and scoop out the avocado flesh and place it in a mixing bowl. Fold in 3 tablespoons of the lemon juice, 2 tablespoons of the red onion, half the chives, 2 tablespoons of the olive oil, and salt and white pepper to taste. Set aside.

3. To make the **vinaigrette,** in a blender, combine the remaining 2 tablespoons of lemon juice with the green peppercorns and 1½ teaspoons of their liquid, the mustard, a pinch of salt, and a few turns of white pepper. Blend on low speed to pulverize the peppercorns, then turn the blender to a higher speed and begin to stream in the remaining 6 tablespoons of olive oil. The dressing should emulsify and become fairly thick. If it seems too thick, add a splash of water and readjust the seasoning. Chill well before proceeding.

4. To finish the dish, begin by drizzling a small amount of olive oil over the tuna. This will cut down on the friction that occurs while seasoning the tuna and will keep the fish from getting pasty or heavy as you add the rest of the ingredients. Add the remaining tablespoon of diced red onion and the remaining chives. Dress the tuna lightly with the vinaigrette and season with salt and white pepper. Toss gently until the fish is just coated. Adjust the seasoning and the amount of dressing to taste. Place the tartare over ice or in the fridge as you prepare the plates.

5. Drain the **radish** slices. Lay overlapping slices of radish in the center of each of 6 chilled salad plates. Mound about 2 tablespoons of the avocado salad in the center of the radishes, making a flat base. Next, spoon a heaping ¼ cup of the tartare atop the avocado. Place the **micro greens** in a bowl and season with a squeeze of lemon juice, a drizzle of olive oil, and salt and white pepper to taste. Place the micro greens on top of the tartare, drizzle the **vinaigrette** over the plate, and serve with toasted baguette slices.

CHEF'S TIPS Ask for sashimi-quality **tuna.** When selecting the tuna, first and foremost look for fat. The higher the fat content, the richer the flavor. Next look at the color, which should be a rich or medium red without brown spots.

MELISSA'S TIPS If you do end up with a sinewy piece of **tuna,** it won't affect the quality of the dish. But you will want to get in there and pick out at least some of the sinew and connective tissue so that the finished dish is not tough. (The amount of sinew depends on where the flesh was cut from the fish.) It's not a hard task, just time consuming.

CHEF When **dicing** the tuna, be sure to use the sharpest knife possible so as not to damage the muscle fiber of the fish, which will make the tartare mushy. Also be sure to use a stainless-steel knife. A carbon steel knife could react with the fish and affect its flavor.

MELISSA The ice water crisps the **radishes,** which then offer a nice contrast to the soft fish and avocado, so please don't skip this step.

If you can find pink and purple **radishes,** use those along with the standard red ones. They make a particularly pretty presentation.

Baby arugula or baby spinach make good substitutes for **micro greens.**

This recipe will yield extra green peppercorn **vinaigrette,** which is a great change of pace on green salads.

If you'd rather, skip the greens and radishes and just serve this with toast or crackers.

MELISSA KELLY, Primo, Rockland, Maine

Warm Grape-Leaf–Wrapped Goat Cheese with Olives and Grilled Sourdough

This is another dish that's just a fancier way to present what is essentially a molten heap of melted cheese, ensconced in an edible grape-leaf wrapper. Of course, the very talented (and beautiful) Melissa Kelly, formerly of Chez Panisse and An American Place, does one better by marinating the packets first in good olive oil and plenty of fresh herbs, which gives them an incredible depth of flavor. It also means you can prepare the cheese packets several days ahead and just grill or broil them at the last minute. She serves these with olives and grilled homemade flatbread, but any grilled or toasted bread slices, or crackers, will do. I also like to use this as a hot dip for cut-up vegetables, especially fennel and bell peppers. Just open the packets to expose the soft, warm cheese within. Bring the wraps to room temperature before cooking so that the cheese will warm evenly. These packets are an elegant starter or after-dinner cheese course at a dinner party, or they could be the main course for a cheese-lover's lunch. PREPARATION TIME: 15 MINUTES, PLUS OVERNIGHT MARINATING

SERVES 6

6 grape leaves in brine, rinsed

Three 4-ounce logs goat cheese (see Chef's Tips)

2 teaspoons chopped fresh thyme

2 teaspoons chopped fresh rosemary

2 teaspoons chopped fresh summer savory or oregano

2 teaspoons dried lavender (see Melissa's Tips)

1 teaspoon freshly ground black pepper, or to taste

Extra-virgin olive oil, to cover (about 1 cup)

Grilled sourdough bread or crackers, for serving

MELISSA'S TIPS When you open your jar of **grape leaves,** you'll find they're all rolled up together. It's easiest to just remove the entire batch and peel off the ones you need, rather than try to fish them out of the jar one at a time. (This sounds intuitive but wasn't for me, anyway.)

CHEF'S TIPS Fresh **goat cheese,** or chèvre, is a tangy cheese with a fair degree of saltiness and an almost-smooth texture. Some varieties are moist and creamy enough to spread like cream cheese, while others have a crumblier, dry, small-curd texture. For

1. Lay the **grape leaves** vein side up on a cutting board. Cut each log of **goat cheese** in half crosswise and use the palm of your hand to flatten each piece into a ½-inch-thick disk. Place a disk of goat cheese in the center of each grape leaf.

2. Divide the **herbs** and the pepper evenly among the 6 wraps. Wrap the sides of the grape leaves up over the top of the cheese to seal.

3. Place the packets in a small shallow dish, cover with olive oil, and marinate in the refrigerator overnight. The next day, drain off the **oil** and reserve for another use.

4. Preheat the grill or broiler. Grill or broil the **wraps** until they are heated through and soft in the center, about 1 minute per side.

DAVID WONDRICH, MIXOLOGIST INTERRUPTED

I resisted my natural impulse to go with something anisey. This has some sharpness and spice to point up the cheese's richness.

OLD BAY RIDGE

In an old-fashioned glass or small tumbler, muddle 1 sugar cube, 1 teaspoon water, and 2 dashes Angostura bitters until the sugar has dissolved. Add 1 ounce straight rye whiskey (e.g., Wild Turkey Rye or Old Overholt) and 1 ounce Linie Aquavit. Stir, add 3 or 4 ice cubes, stir again, and twist a largish swatch of thin-cut lemon peel over the top.

this recipe, look for a fairly creamy fresh goat cheese from France, or from an artisanal American farm, packaged in individual logs. The packages may be 4, 6, or 8 ounces each, and you want 2 ounces for each of the 6 servings, so do the math accordingly.

MELISSA If you don't want to bother with three kinds of fresh **herbs** (thyme, rosemary, and savory or oregano) just choose one and triple the quantity. You can also skip the lavender if you like.

Little purple lavender blossoms are used fresh and dried to give a sweet, floral, almost spicy flavor to recipes. Dried lavender is stronger than fresh and should be used sparingly so the results don't taste like a sachet. Look for dried lavender at stores that sell spices or tea, or order it from Pure Spice (866-532-1703; www.purespice.com), or use fresh instead, increasing quantities by about threefold.

CHEF Don't throw out the olive **oil** you use to marinate these in. If it seems cloudy, strain the oil through a coffee filter, then use it for salad dressing or cooking.

BRYCE WHITTLESEY, Wheatleigh, Lenox, Massachusetts

Foie Gras Terrine with Asian Pear Marmalade

As a chef, Bryce Whittlesey has a bit of a split personality. On the one hand, he's meticulously trained in the classic French repertoire, having worked with Michelin-starred chefs all over France, including Michel Rostang. But he also has a bit of a wild streak that manifests in fusion combinations like tuna coated in fennel pollen, served with shiso tempura and edamame. This dish is more moderate, a blending of the French tradition—that is, foie gras terrine served with a fruit condiment—and the eclectic, in the guise of Asian pear and star anise marmalade. Naturally, I use purchased foie gras terrine for this recipe, but it's also good with any pâté, cured meat product, or even cheese. PREPARATION TIME: 2 HOURS

MAKES 3 CUPS MARMALADE, ENOUGH FOR 6 SERVINGS

9 shallots (unpeeled)

½ cup dried currants

½ cup cider vinegar

¼ cup honey

3 Asian pears, quartered, cored, and cut into 1 by 1½-inch pieces

1 star anise

½ teaspoon coarse sea salt, plus more to taste

¼ teaspoon freshly ground black pepper, plus more to taste

One 9-ounce foie gras terrine (see Chef's Tips, page 42)

Freshly toasted bread, for serving

CHEF'S TIP Roasted shallots are so sweet and soft they make a great addition to salads, soups, and sauces, as well as this marmalade. You can also spread them on a sandwich. So make extra while you're at it.

MELISSA'S TIPS Asian **pears** are round tan or yellow fruits the size of a large apple (or larger). They are crisp, sweet, juicy, and very fragrant and can be eaten raw or cooked. Cooked, they retain their texture well, making them more interesting in this recipe than an apple or pear would be. Look for unbruised fruits at good produce stands, grocery stores, or Asian markets, and store them in the refrigerator (they will keep for up to 2 months).

1. Preheat the oven to 300°F. Place the whole shallots on the upper rack of the oven and place a rimmed baking sheet on the rack below to catch any drips. Roast the shallots until they are completely tender, 35 to 40 minutes. Set the **roasted shallots** aside to cool until needed.

2. Place the currants in a bowl and pour the vinegar over them. Set aside while you prepare the pears.

3. In a heavy saucepan over high heat, heat the honey until it bubbles. Cook until it is dark amber, about 4 minutes. Immediately add the **pears** and cook, stirring, until they are coated and caramelized, about 4 more minutes.

4. Strain the vinegar into the pears, reserving the currants. Bring the contents of the pan to a boil and cook until thick and syrupy, about 5 minutes. Add ½ cup of water, the **star anise,** and the salt and pepper. Bring the liquid to a simmer and cook gently until the pears are very tender, about 40 minutes.

5. Trim the ends from the roasted shallots and squeeze them out of their skins into the pear mixture. Stir in the currants and cook for another 2 or 3 minutes, mashing the shallots and pears a little with a wooden spoon to achieve a rough texture. Taste and add more salt and pepper if necessary. Let cool, then refrigerate in an airtight container for up to 2 weeks.

6. To serve, cut the foie gras terrine into 6 slices and arrange on plates. Garnish with spoonfuls of the marmalade and serve with warm toast.

MELISSA Grown in Asia, the starfish-like brown pods sold as **star anise** are dried fruits from a small tree. They have a distinct anise taste that is infused into dishes like red-cooked Chinese pork and are a component of Chinese five-spice powder. A little goes a long way, so one star anise is usually enough to spice a fruit jam or compote like this one. Star anise keeps for up to a year; smell it if you think it's lost its potency.

JAMIE SHANNON, Commander's Palace, New Orleans

Spicy Tasso Shrimp with Crystal Hot Sauce–Beurre Blanc

When Tory McPhail took over the helm at Commander's Palace, he kept the late Jamie Shannon's amazing shrimp dish on the menu. This recipe is spicier than you'd think, given its gentle-seeming creamy sauce. But don't let that fool you: the hot sauce heightens the fire quotient to slow burn—it gets more intense the more you eat. I've cut some steps from the original recipe, but didn't change the chile ratio. That's up to you—if you can't take the heat, that is (see Melissa's Tips). For a cool crunch, serve the shrimp with sliced pickled okra, which you can buy in jars at many groceries, or order online (see Chef's Tip). When I don't want to bother with pickled okra, I like to serve these shrimp with a crispy vegetable such as sliced radish or cucumber or Belgian endive leaves on the side. You can also serve them as a main course, over rice, though you might want to cut down on the hot sauce. PREPARATION TIME: 45 MINUTES

SERVES 8 AS AN APPETIZER OR 4 AS A MAIN COURSE

¾ cup all-purpose flour

2 teaspoons Creole seasoning (see Chef's Tip)

1½ pounds jumbo shrimp (about 35 shrimp), peeled and deveined

½ cup hot sauce, preferably Crystal brand (see Chef's Tip)

¼ cup heavy cream

6 garlic cloves, minced

2 tablespoons minced shallot (1 small)

6 tablespoons (¾ stick) unsalted butter, softened

Coarse sea salt or kosher salt

¼ cup extra-virgin olive oil

Freshly ground black pepper

3 ounces tasso, cut into 1¼-inch-long matchsticks (about 1 cup)

¾ cup prepared pepper jelly (see Chef's Tip)

MELISSA'S TIPS This recipe is mouth-searingly spicy; if you want to bring the heat down a notch, simply leave out the **Creole seasoning** and reduce the amount of hot sauce. This is crucial if you plan to serve this as a main course, since the heat builds with each mouthful.

1. In a shallow bowl, combine the flour with the **Creole seasoning.** Lightly dredge each shrimp. Set aside while you make the **beurre blanc.**

2. In a small saucepan over medium heat, combine the **hot sauce,** cream, garlic, and shallot, and bring to a simmer. Keep at a simmer, stirring frequently, until the mixture is reduced by half, about 5 minutes. Take the pan off the heat and slowly whisk in the softened butter a bit at a time (briefly place the pan back over very low heat if the butter is not incorporating). Pass the sauce through a fine-mesh sieve, add salt to taste, and cover to keep warm while you cook the shrimp.

3. In a large skillet over medium-high heat, warm the oil. Add enough of the shrimp to fit in one layer without crowding the pan and fry until golden, about 1 to 2 minutes on each side. Use a slotted spoon to transfer the shrimp to plates lined with paper towels, season with salt and pepper to taste, and let drain briefly. Place the shrimp in a large bowl and toss with the beurre blanc. Repeat with the remaining shrimp. Add the **tasso** to the pan and cook until heated through, about 2 minutes. Add to the bowl with the shrimp.

4. Place a spoonful of pepper jelly on each of 8 appetizer plates and arrange several shrimp and pieces of tasso next to the jelly. Serve immediately.

DAVID WONDRICH, MIXOLOGIST INTERRUPTED

For this, it'll need to be refreshing, but not wimpy, and it'll have to have New Orleans all over it.

CARONDELET FIZZ

Put 1 teaspoon superfine sugar in your shaker, add the juice of half a medium lemon, and stir briefly until the sugar has dissolved. Add:

2 ounces VSOP cognac
½ teaspoon Herbsaint (New Orleans' absinthe substitute) or Pernod
2 dashes Peychaud's bitters (www.sazerac.com) or Angostura bitters

Fill the shaker with cracked ice, shake vigorously, and strain into a chilled highball glass (no larger than 10 to 12 ounces). Fill with chilled seltzer or club soda.

Beurre blanc is an emulsion of butter and liquid that should, ideally, be satiny smooth. Like all emulsions, it is prone to breaking if you let it boil, which means the sauce can take on a curdled appearance. If your sauce does break, don't worry; the curdling won't affect the flavor. And since you'll be tossing the shrimp into the sauce anyway, no one will really notice one way or the other.

CHEF'S TIP Crystal Hot Sauce is a brand made locally in New Orleans. It has a balanced spiciness and more flavor than many other brands. Of course, feel free to substitute your favorite hot sauce instead. A good source for Southern products like Crystal Hot Sauce, pickled okra, pepper jelly, and Creole seasoning (a blend of red pepper, garlic powder, and other spices) is the Louisiana General Store (504-525-2665; www.nosoc.com).

MELISSA Tasso is a Cajun-spiced, smoky ham. You can order it from www.cajungrocer.com (888-272-9347). Don't stress over the size and shape of the tasso pieces; as long as they aren't too distractingly large, they don't have to be perfect matchsticks.

LYNN MCNEELY, Barbuto, New York

Grilled Calamari with Greens and Aioli

Lynn McNeely, the brilliant executive chef at Barbuto, got the idea for this stellar recipe after a trip to Spain, where he ate crispy pan-fried squid with a garlicky mayonnaise called *allioli* as often as he could. His version is a little more refined, served over greens to cut the richness, and with croutons to add crunch. My version is easier. PREPARATION TIME: 45 MINUTES

SERVES 6 TO 8

2 garlic cloves, minced

½ teaspoon coarse sea salt or kosher salt, plus more to taste

¼ teaspoon finely grated lemon zest

1 large egg yolk

3 tablespoons fresh lemon juice, plus additional to taste

1 cup extra-virgin olive oil

Freshly ground black pepper

1½ cups cubed Italian bread, such as ciabatta

2 pounds calamari, cleaned, bodies cut into ¾-inch pieces, tentacles left whole (see Sidebar, page 87)

½ cup white wine

1 quart mixed torn radicchio and arugula leaves (about 4 ounces)

CHEF'S TIPS You can make the **aioli** 5 days ahead and store it in the refrigerator.

MELISSA'S TIPS Catalonian allioli, which is what Lynn based this dish on, was traditionally prepared without eggs. But now chefs tend to add some egg, which makes a more reliably smooth sauce. The result is what French chefs call *aïoli*—a thick, garlicky mayonnaise that's perfect with seafood. Here, it is added to the cooked calamari and warmed with the juices to become a creamy, flavorful sauce. Because *aioli,* like homemade mayonnaise, is made with egg yolk, you have to warm it very gently once you add it to the calamari pan so the heat doesn't scramble the egg. If the sauce begins to curdle, pull the pan off the burner and stir!

1. In a food processor or blender, combine the garlic, ½ teaspoon salt, and lemon zest and blend. Add the egg yolk and juice of 1 lemon and blend well. With the motor running, very slowly drizzle in ¾ cup of the olive oil. The **aioli** will become moderately thick. Taste and season with salt and pepper and additional lemon juice, if desired.

2. Preheat the oven to 325°F. Toss the ciabatta cubes in 2 tablespoons of the oil, sprinkle with salt and pepper to taste, and spread out on a baking sheet. Toast the cubes until golden, about 8 minutes. Let cool.

3. In a very large skillet over medium heat, warm the remaining 2 tablespoons of olive oil. Add the calamari and fry in a **single layer,** without tossing, until the calamari are golden on the bottom, 3 to 4 minutes. When nicely colored, add the white wine, reduce the heat to low, and vigorously stir in ¾ cup of the aioli so that it becomes a smooth sauce. Keep the heat very low (to avoid scrambling the egg yolk in the aioli).

4. Place the greens in a large shallow serving dish and add the ciabatta croutons. Pour the calamari and aioli mixture over the top, season with salt and pepper and the juice of the remaining ½ lemon. Let the dish sit for a minute or two to lightly wilt the greens before serving.

You can buy good-quality French **aioli** at specialty food markets. If you do, preparing this dish takes about 10 minutes and absolutely no brain power — just mix everything together and don't overcook it.

CHEF If you can't fit all the calamari in **one layer** in your pan (which is essential for browning), cook it in batches, then heap it all back into the pan before adding the wine and aioli.

TOM VALENTI, Ouest, New York

Oyster Pan Roast with Chives and Curried Crouton

Pan roasts are, by nature, some of the easiest things to make—seafood such as oysters or scallops are quickly cooked in a mix of cream and seasonings. Tom Valenti takes this basic formula and embellishes it with curry oil, roasted tomato, and sautéed black trumpet mushrooms. In my interrupted version, I split the difference between the classic and Tom's elevated version by keeping the easily made, super-flavorful curry oil and skipping the rest of his garnishes. The result has a nutty, spicy, unique flavor that's achieved in the five minutes it takes to make the oil. PREPARATION TIME: 45 MINUTES

SERVES 4

1 Idaho potato, peeled and cut into ½-inch dice (about 1½ cups)

1 garlic clove, crushed

1 teaspoon coarse sea salt or kosher salt, plus additional to taste

¼ teaspoon freshly ground black pepper, plus additional to taste

4 slices white bread

1½ tablespoons curry oil (see Sidebar)

6 ounces bacon, finely diced (about 1½ cups)

½ cup dry white wine

12 shucked oysters, reserved in their own juice (see Tips)

⅔ cup whole milk

⅔ cup heavy cream

1 tablespoon unsalted butter

Freshly squeezed juice of ½ lemon, plus additional to taste

2 tablespoons minced chives

MELISSA'S TIPS Brushing toast with curry oil adds a wonderful dimension to the recipe, but curry oil needs to be made a day in advance. If you prefer, rub the bread with a halved garlic clove, brush it with oil, and toast it, then proceed with the recipe.

CHEF'S TIP I recommend buying big **oysters** such as Bluepoint or Wellfleet for this recipe. When buying fresh oysters, choose heavy-feeling ones and have your fishmonger shuck them for you, saving the strained liquor from the shells if possible.

1. Place the potato in a skillet with ¾ cup water, the garlic, salt, and pepper. Bring to a simmer over medium heat and cook for 5 to 7 minutes, until the potato is tender. Drain and spread the potato cubes out on a plate to cool.

2. Use a cookie cutter or the rim of a small bowl to cut the bread slices into 3-inch rounds. Toast the rounds, then brush them with **curry oil** and reserve.

3. In another skillet over low heat, cook the bacon until it starts to crisp, about 5 minutes. Use a slotted spoon to transfer the cooked bacon to a plate lined with paper towels.

4. Pour off the fat from the bacon pan, then add the white wine. Strain the liquor from the shucked **oysters** into the pan and scrape up the browned bits from the bottom of the pan.

Raise the heat to high, add the milk and cream, and bring to a boil. Swirl in the butter and season with salt and pepper to taste.

5. Strain the sauce into a small saucepan. Add the juice of ½ lemon, squeezing in additional juice if desired. Add the bacon and potatoes and simmer the mixture for 2 minutes. Add the oysters, swirling them in the sauce until just warmed through, 1 minute.

6. Place a curried toast round in the center of each of 4 bowls. Use a slotted spoon to transfer 3 oysters onto each crouton. Spoon all of the creamy broth around the oysters and serve at once, sprinkled with minced chives.

CURRY OIL

To make curry oil, place 3 tablespoons of curry powder in a bowl and stir in 3 tablespoons warm water to make a paste. Mix in 1⅓ cups neutral oil such as grapeseed or canola and let steep at room temperature overnight. Pour the oil that rises to the top into a jar (leaving behind the settled curry powder paste) and keep on hand for drizzling over veggies, seafood, pasta, rice, toast, or anything you can think of.

MELISSA Oysters bought and shucked the day you're cooking them are ideal here, but this recipe is too yummy to put off if you can't coordinate that. Instead, you can buy freshly shucked oyster meat in jars, packed in the clear juices from their shells (called oyster liquor), at good fish markets (these will have a "use-by" date). Or purchase frozen shucked oysters and let them thaw in the fridge before making the pan roast.

You can substitute shrimp or scallops for the oysters. Just cook them for about 2 minutes in the broth and substitute a little more wine for the oyster liquor.

LAURENT TOURONDEL, BLT Steak, New York

Foie Gras BLT

This is the sandwich that launched a thousand ships—or at least a thousand mentions in the press. Laurent Tourondel took a plain BLT and re-created it to fit his French haute-cuisine profile, meaning he added foie gras. Of course, he makes his own foie gras for this recipe (need you ask?), and of course, I don't (ditto). Purchased terrine is a fine substitute. It certainly makes for the best darn rendition of this diner classic I've ever had. If you're into pressed sandwiches, by all means press this one using a panini press or "clamshell" electric grill (e.g., a George Foreman grill). PREPARATION TIME: 45 MINUTES

SERVES 6

3 large tomatoes, each thickly sliced into 4 slices

24 slices (about 1½ pounds) bacon, preferably applewood-smoked

12 slices *filone* or other crusty bread

¼ cup extra-virgin olive oil

¼ cup mayonnaise

½ cup (½ ounce) baby arugula leaves

One 9-ounce terrine of foie gras, cut into 6 slices (see Chef's Tips)

12 romaine lettuce leaves (use crisp inner leaves)

CHEF'S TIPS Roasting the **tomatoes** intensifies their flavor and makes the sandwich less mushy.

MELISSA'S TIP *Filone* is an Italian **bread** with a crackly, golden crust. A thick baguette is a good substitute.

CHEF Foie gras comes from ducks or geese that have been fattened especially for the purpose of enlarging their livers. Using prepared terrine instead of starting with a raw lobe of duck or goose liver is a great time-saver, since the terrine is made by first cleaning the foie gras, which is an involved process, then marinating the foie gras overnight, pressing it, cooking it very slowly and gently, skimming its fat, then letting it rest, weighted, in the fridge. You can buy it from specialty markets and via mail order from D'Artagnan (800-327-8246; www.dartagnan.com).

1. Preheat the oven to 325°F. Lay the **tomato** slices in a single layer on a baking sheet and roast until golden around the edges, about 20 minutes.

2. In a skillet over medium-low heat, cook the bacon until crispy, about 7 minutes. Use tongs to transfer the bacon to a paper plate lined with paper towels.

3. Preheat a grill, grill pan, or heavy skillet. Brush one side of each slice of **bread** with olive oil and spread mayonnaise on the other side. Layer the arugula, roasted tomato, **foie gras,** lettuce, and bacon on the mayonnaise side, and top with the other slice of bread, again placing the mayonnaise side next to the sandwich filling (so both outer surfaces are coated with olive oil).

4. Place the **sandwiches** on the grill or in a skillet and cook for 2 minutes per side. Serve hot.

JASON DENTON, 'ino, New York

Truffled Egg Toast

Basically, this dish is a combination of two nursery foods—grilled cheese and toad in a hole—made fit for grown-ups with the addition of truffle oil. Technically, it's too simple for this book, since the ingredients and techniques didn't really need interrupting. But it belongs here nonetheless because it's the best of its kind—that is, kid comfort food made over for adults. PREPARATION TIME: 20 MINUTES

SERVES 4

4 slices white bread (each 1½ inches thick)

8 large egg yolks (see Chef's Tips, page 258)

Coarse sea salt or kosher salt and freshly ground black pepper

6 ounces Fontina, grated (about 1½ cups, packed)

½ teaspoon white truffle oil, or to taste

CHEF'S TIP Use a Pullman loaf or pain de mie, or any other hearty, unsliced white bread loaf.

MELISSA'S TIPS For a quick snack, you can cook these in the toaster oven, toasting the bread first, then popping them in again after adding the egg and cheese.

You can substitute any semifirm **cheese** for the Fontina: Cheddar, Gruyère, Comté, and even something more pungent like Taleggio or Morbier will also work well.

If you hate—or don't have—**truffle oil,** skip it. Though any pretense of this being sophisticated will be completely gone.

1. Preheat the oven to 450°F. Arrange the bread slices on a baking sheet and toast in the oven for 2 minutes.

2. Remove the toast from the oven and scrape out a ¾-inch-deep depression in the center of each (scoop down about halfway through the slice). Slide 2 egg yolks into each hole and sprinkle salt and pepper on top. Sprinkle 6 tablespoons of **cheese** over the entire slice, drizzle with ⅛ teaspoon **truffle oil,** and return to the oven to melt the cheese, 3½ to 4 more minutes. Serve while still hot and runny.

Salads and Soups

Arugula–Mint Salad with
Apricots and Cumin
SUZANNE GOIN, Lucques

Fennel and Prosciutto Salad with
Persimmon Vinaigrette
MELISSA KELLY, Primo

Fava Bean Salad with Pecorino Toscano
and Fresh Oregano
MARCO CANORA, Hearth

Shaved Asparagus Salad with Pecans,
Baby Greens, and Lemons
RICHARD REDDINGTON, formerly of
Auberge du Soleil

Asparagus and Potato Salad with
Tarragon–Riesling Vinaigrette
DAVID BOULEY, Danube

Heirloom Tomato and Watermelon
Salad with Sheep's-Milk Ricotta
DAN BARBER, Blue Hill

Parsley and Pancetta Salad
MARK LADNER, Lupa

Goan Avocado Salad
FLOYD CARDOZ, Tabla

Cornbread Panzanella
FRANK STITT, Highlands Bar and Grill

Braised Heirloom Bean Salad
with Tomatoes, Onions, and Herbs
CESARE CASELLA, Beppe

White Gazpacho with Crab,
Green Grapes, and Almonds
RICK MOONEN, formerly of Restaurant rm

Red Gazpacho with
Tomato–Olive Oil Sorbet
JOËL ANTUNES, Joël

Yellow Pepper and Almond Soup
PETER BERLEY, formerly of Angelica Kitchen

Curried Sweet Corn and Coconut Soup
with Caramelized Mango
NORMAN VAN AKEN, Norman's

Vidalia Onion Chowder with Shrimp,
Smoked Bacon, and Spicy Aioli
BEN BARKER, Magnolia Grill

Pumpkin Soup with Caramelized
Onions, Sage, and Gruyère Croutons
ALFRED PORTALE, Gotham Bar and Grill

SUZANNE GOIN, Lucques, Los Angeles

Arugula–Mint Salad with Apricots and Cumin

Los Angeles's sprawling distances, the stop-and-start nausea-producing traffic, and my native New Yorker's general terror of driving means I'm usually somewhat stressed by the time I get to dinner when I'm there. That's one reason why I love Lucques. It's the kind of sophisticated yet understated place that immediately calms me. And the daydreams of Suzanne Goin's braised pork cheeks with mustard gremolata, rabbit with wide noodles and Tuscan black cabbage, or seared albacore with tapenade spur me on, as I snail over Interstate 10 and along those surface streets until I reach her heirloom-garlic–scented door. This recipe is typical Suzanne in that it's both supremely creative and comfortingly familiar at the same time.

PREPARATION TIME: 30 MINUTES

SERVES 6 TO 8

DRESSING

6 tablespoons sherry vinegar

2 tablespoons red wine vinegar

1 large shallot, diced

1/2 teaspoon ground cumin

1/2 teaspoon coarse sea salt or kosher salt

2 very ripe apricots, pitted

2 cups extra-virgin olive oil

SALAD

8 cups arugula (about 8 ounces), washed and dried

1 bunch of fresh mint, leaves torn off

8 small or 4 large ripe yet firm apricots, cut into thin wedges

1 small shallot, thinly sliced (about 1/4 cup)

1/2 cup sliced or slivered almonds, toasted and coarsely chopped (see Sidebar, page 51)

Coarse sea salt or kosher salt and freshly ground black pepper to taste

CHEF'S TIPS Letting the shallot **rest** for 10 minutes in the vinegar–salt mixture helps the flavor mellow and pickles it slightly, so it's not quite as strong and oniony as eating regular shallot.

MELISSA'S TIP You need two very ripe **apricots** for this dressing and some slightly firmer ones to cut up on the salad. When possible, choose smaller, funnier-looking apricots from a farmers' market over the big, scentless grocery-store beauties.

CHEF Extra dressing will keep in the fridge for up to 5 days.

1. For the dressing, combine both vinegars, the shallot, cumin, and salt in a bowl and let **rest** for 10 minutes. Meanwhile, puree the **apricots** with a mortar and pestle (or by mashing them in a bowl with a wooden spoon or pulsing in a food processor). Whisk the apricot puree into the shallot mixture, then gradually whisk in the olive oil.

2. For the salad, toss all the ingredients with just enough dressing to coat—you will have **extra dressing.** Serve immediately.

MELISSA KELLY, Primo, Portland, Maine

Fennel and Prosciutto Salad with Persimmon Vinaigrette

I remember Melissa Kelly from my days at An American Place, Larry Forgione's famous Manhattan restaurant, when I was in college. I worked the coatroom; she cooked on the line, and she was always so nice to me, passing me little bits of food when I visited the kitchen—a spoonful of Larry's amazing spoonbread or a morsel of his cedar-planked salmon. Working at An American Place was my first job at an upscale restaurant, and even from the dining room I learned a lot about what goes on in the kitchen.

Now, of course, Melissa is the chef at Primo in Portland, Maine, where she serves seasonal food that's simple, ingredient driven, and extremely clever in its combinations. Perfect for inclusion in this book.

This is the quintessential autumn/winter salad that's different and elegant enough to be dinner party fare, especially if you are serving something heavy as a main course and need a vegetable-based starter that's not as ho-hum as a regular green salad. PREPARATION TIME: 20 MINUTES

SERVES 8

½ pound thinly sliced prosciutto

¼ cup plus 3 tablespoons extra-virgin olive oil

Coarse sea salt or kosher salt and freshly ground black pepper

1 very ripe persimmon, peeled, seeded, and coarsely chopped, with its juice

1 small shallot, minced

3 tablespoons white wine vinegar

2 ripe Anjou pears, peeled, cored, and thinly sliced

1 large fennel bulb, trimmed, cored, and thinly sliced

½ pound frisée or curly chickory, washed, dried, and torn into pieces

TIPS FROM TWO MELISSAS Duck **prosciutto,** or smoked duck breast, is an alternative to the pork.

With their vivid orange skins and pretty green caps, **persimmons** are stunning. Once ripe, their super-sweet, juicy pulp can be eaten from the skin with a spoon. You can use either Hachiya (also called Japanese) or Fuyu persimmons in this recipe. Hachiya are taller, with a fat acorn shape, and they can be eaten only when their flesh is custard-soft. Hachiya can take up to a few weeks at room temperature to ripen, so avoid buying rock-hard ones. Fuyu is a smaller, squat, tomato-shaped variety that can be eaten when crisp as well as when ripe (they also ripen more quickly).

1. Arrange the **prosciutto** around the edge of a platter and drizzle it with 1 tablespoon of the olive oil. Season with salt and pepper.

2. In a large bowl, combine the **persimmon,** shallot, and vinegar. Whisk in the remaining ¼ cup plus 2 tablespoons of olive oil and season with salt and pepper. Add the pears, fennel, and **frisée,** and toss well.

3. Mound the salad in the middle of the platter and serve.

MARCO CANORA, Hearth, New York

Fava Bean Salad with Pecorino Toscano and Fresh Oregano

The first time I ever made fava beans, I was in college. A friend who had lived in Israel talked me into buying them from a Middle Eastern specialty shop and said she would help me prepare them. I didn't realize it was her first time making them too, and neither of us quite understood the pod-to-bean ratio. So after shucking and peeling what seemed like a mountain of pods, we were left with just a coffee mug full of beans—hardly enough to feed the five people we were going to have for dinner that night. Instead, she and I just ate them raw, with a little salt and olive oil. It was the perfect something-to-nibble-on-while-making-dinner snack.

This recipe, from Marco Canora of the beloved Hearth restaurant in the East Village, is really just one step beyond that naked presentation. He does blanch the beans, which tames their starchy texture and makes them slippery and tender. But he dresses them simply, in good olive oil and fresh oregano. The fresh Pecorino cheese, however, which would have been way beyond my college knowledge, makes a savory, salty addition. This salad can be made with other fresh shell beans as well, such as cranberry or lima beans, or with fresh or frozen edamame. It will have a very different personality depending on what bean you use, and most beans should be blanched for longer than favas (cranberry beans may take up to 6 minutes to become tender). But the vinaigrette and cheese in this recipe are equally delicious with all of them.

PREPARATION TIME: 35 MINUTES

SERVES 4 TO 6

Coarse sea salt or kosher salt

2 pounds fava beans, shelled (2 cups) (see Melissa's Tips)

¼ cup thinly sliced red onion (¼ medium onion)

1 tablespoon chopped fresh flat-leaf parsley

1 tablespoon chopped fresh oregano

⅛ teaspoon crushed red pepper flakes

½ cup extra-virgin olive oil

1 tablespoon white wine

½ tablespoon white wine vinegar

Freshly ground black pepper

½ cup (3 ounces) fresh Pecorino cheese, cut into ¼-inch dice (use a fresh, soft Pecorino—ask your cheese store for the youngest they have)

MELISSA'S TIPS Fava beans—also known as broad beans, or *ful*—are available fresh in the spring, in long, puffy, flattish green pods. Snap an end of a pod and run your finger down it to pop out the flat, lima-like beans into a bowl. Many Mediterranean cooks use the favas as is, which is fine when you have super-fresh, young, early spring

1. Bring a large pot of salted water to a rolling boil and fill a bowl with water and ice. Add the **beans** to the boiling water and blanch until tender, about 2 minutes. Immediately drain and transfer to the ice bath to stop the cooking, then drain again. Use a paring knife to slit the skin of each bean, and squeeze the bean out into a large serving bowl.

2. Toss the beans with the onion, parsley, oregano, red pepper flakes, and oil. Let marinate for 15 minutes to an hour.

3. Right before serving, toss the salad with the white wine and vinegar and plenty of salt and pepper. (The acid in the white wine and vinegar will turn the beans a dull, gray-green color. So for aesthetics, it's important to leave those two ingredients out until the very last moment.) Mix in the cheese and serve.

favas. But as the crop matures, they are far more tender and delicate tasting once you remove the tough pale green jacket from each bean, exposing the soft, brighter green bean within. To do this, blanch the shelled beans in boiling water for a couple minutes, chill them down before they overcook and get mealy, then use a paring knife to slit the jackets and squeeze out the beans. Out of season, frozen favas are available in bags in the freezer section. Blanch for a minute or so more, then proceed with the peeling. This is the easiest option.

DAVID WONDRICH, MIXOLOGIST INTERRUPTED

What could this possibly call for but a Marsala Cobbler?

CALZOLAIO, OR MARSALA COBBLER

Put 1 teaspoon superfine sugar, 2 half-wheels of blood orange (or other orange), and 1 half-wheel of lemon in the bottom of your shaker. Press the fruit lightly with a muddler, then add:

1½ ounce dry Marsala
1½ ounce sweet Marsala

Fill halfway with cracked ice, shake vigorously, and pour unstrained into a tall glass. Garnish with a half-wheel of blood orange and *frutti di bosco* in season. Add a straw.

RICHARD REDDINGTON, formerly of Auberge du Soleil, Rutherford, California

Shaved Asparagus Salad with Pecans, Baby Greens, and Lemons

I met Richard Reddington while he was the chef at the regal Auberge du Soleil in Napa Valley, where he made this unusual raw asparagus salad with violet-tinged asparagus and candied lemon zest. I've skipped the candied zest and substituted regular green asparagus, though if you come across the purple kind at a farmers' market, by all means use it. It makes a gorgeous lavender, pale green, and alabaster-hued tangle on the plate. PREPARATION TIME: 20 MINUTES

SERVES 4

1 large bunch of asparagus (about 1 pound), trimmed

¼ cup freshly squeezed lemon juice (from 2 lemons)

¼ teaspoon minced garlic (1 small clove)

1 tablespoon shredded fresh basil leaves

1 tablespoon chopped fresh mint leaves

Grated zest of ½ lemon

Coarse sea salt or kosher salt and freshly ground black pepper

6 tablespoons extra-virgin olive oil

8 cups loosely packed baby greens (about 8 ounces), washed and dried

⅓ cup chopped toasted pecans (see Sidebar)

CHEF'S TIP Don't use pencil-thin **asparagus** for this recipe; since the aim is to slice them lengthwise into ribbons, you want to make sure they are wide enough not to end up looking like bits of string.

MELISSA'S TIPS Tarragon is a nice substitute for the **mint,** and pine nuts can stand in for **pecans.**

Grate the **zest** from half the lemon before you cut and juice it (it's easier to zest a whole lemon).

1. Using a mandoline, or holding each stalk of **asparagus** flat on a board and running a vegetable peeler along it, slice the asparagus lengthwise into thin, broad ribbons.

2. In a bowl, toss the asparagus with half of the lemon juice, then let marinate at room temperature for 5 minutes.

3. Make the dressing: In a bowl, whisk together the remaining lemon juice, the garlic, basil, **mint,** and **zest,** and season liberally with salt and pepper. Whisking constantly, drizzle in 5 tablespoons of the olive oil.

4. Season the asparagus with salt and pepper, then drizzle with the remaining olive oil and toss to coat.

5. Place the greens in a bowl and toss with enough of the dressing to lightly coat, then taste and add salt and pepper, if desired.

6. To serve, divide the asparagus among 4 salad plates. Mound some of the dressed greens on top of the asparagus and sprinkle with the **pecans.** Serve immediately.

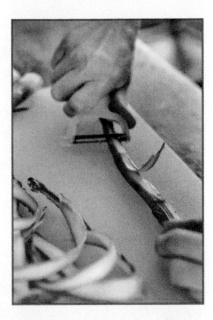

TOASTING NUTS

Toasting shelled nuts gives them a richer, nuttier flavor and more crunch. You can use either the oven or a skillet. The oven is easier since you don't have to hover over them, but if it's in use for something else, the skillet option is handy to know about.

To toast nuts in the oven, preheat the oven to 325°F. and spread the nuts in a single layer on a rimmed baking sheet. Toast, tossing and mixing every 5 minutes or so, until the nuts are fragrant and slightly darker, about 8 to 12 minutes, depending on the size of the nut.

To toast nuts in a skillet, stir them constantly over medium-low heat until they are fragrant and slightly darker, 3 to 6 minutes.

Once the nuts have been toasted, transfer them to a plate and let cool completely. They can be kept in an airtight container in a cool, dry place for several months.

MELISSA If you don't have a mandoline and your vegetable peeler is a decade old and blunt as a chopstick, it's time to invest in a new one before attempting this recipe. Otherwise it's an exercise in frustration and jagged, sloppy, thick slices instead of gossamer ribbons.

DAVID BOULEY, Danube, New York

Asparagus and Potato Salad with Tarragon–Riesling Vinaigrette

David Bouley has known me for five years, but I've known him for over twelve. The first time I met him, I was undercover for my thesis in graduate school. I snuck into his kitchen thinking I'd get a firsthand glimpse of the star-chef-abuse-in-the-kitchen I'd heard so much about. With the help of a friend, I donned chef's whites and stole in the back entrance, then took a place in the prep kitchen, where, among the interns and other transient kitchen workers, no one looked at me twice. But if I was hoping to witness fireworks and tantrums, I was in the wrong place. David was all quiet concentration, absorbed in the task at hand and not focused on the turmoil of the kitchen at large. This was also my experience ten years later, when we wrote his cookbook *East of Paris*. David's brilliance is both internal and roaming, and my job as coauthor was to focus him. It was one of the hardest books I ever wrote, trying to follow his far-ranging associations and thoughts. A question about asparagus would lead to stories about his childhood, his travels in Europe, and then the time he went on a motorcycle camping trip through the desert with Lyle Lovett and Julia Roberts. He may have even cooked asparagus out there under the stars with the stars. With David, it was hard to tell.

David makes this salad with fresh white asparagus, which is extremely expensive when you can even get it. If you'd like to substitute it here for the green, go ahead. I actually prefer the fresher, grassier flavor of the green. **PREPARATION TIME: 35 MINUTES**

SERVES 6

Coarse sea salt or kosher salt

2 large bunches of thin asparagus (about 2 pounds), tough ends trimmed

1 pound Austrian crescent or Yukon Gold potatoes, scrubbed

1 teaspoon whole coriander seeds

¼ cup fresh tarragon leaves

¼ cup fresh flat-leaf parsley (leaves only)

2 tablespoons coarsely chopped fresh chives

¼ cup Riesling or other white wine

1½ tablespoons champagne vinegar, plus additional to taste

1 teaspoon Dijon mustard

9 tablespoons extra-virgin olive oil

Freshly ground black pepper

CHEF'S TIP If you can find Austrian crescent **potatoes** (farmers' markets often have them), they are my first choice for this recipe. They have a creamy texture and buttery flavor that work really well with the tart dressing. But Yukon Gold, which are pretty widely available, work almost as well.

1. Bring a large pot of salted water to a rolling boil and fill a bowl with water and ice. Add the asparagus to the boiling water and blanch until crisp-tender, about 2 minutes. Use tongs to transfer the asparagus to the ice bath to stop the cooking, keeping the pot at a boil. When the asparagus are cool, transfer them to a dish towel and blot them dry. Put the asparagus in a bowl and sprinkle them with salt.

2. Cook the **potatoes** in the boiling asparagus water until tender, about 20 minutes, then drain.

3. Meanwhile, prepare the vinaigrette: Lightly pound the coriander seeds with a mortar and pestle to crack them, then transfer to a blender or food processor. Add the tarragon, parsley, and chives, and pulse to chop the herbs. Add the **Riesling,** vinegar, mustard, and $1/2$ teaspoon salt and process until very smooth, about 5 minutes. With the motor running, gradually drizzle in the olive oil until emulsified. Season the dressing with pepper and additional salt, if desired.

4. While the potatoes are still warm, slice them and place them in a bowl. Toss them with about $1/4$ cup of the dressing and season with salt and pepper and extra vinegar, if desired.

5. To serve, divide the asparagus among 6 plates and drizzle each serving with about 2 teaspoons of dressing. Mound some of the potatoes on top of each plate, drizzle with additional dressing, and serve.

MELISSA'S TIP David likes to use **Riesling** in this recipe because of its spicy, citrus character, and because it fits with the Austro-German profile of his restaurant, Danube. But any white wine will work.

DAN BARBER, Blue Hill, New York

Heirloom Tomato and Watermelon Salad with Sheep's-Milk Ricotta

As much as I adore Dan Barber for his intellectual and personal complexity—he's the kind of guy who listens to tapes on Rudolf Steiner (the Austrian founder of biodynamics) while commuting to Blue Hill at Stone Barns, his other restaurant in Westchester County, New York—I love him just as much for the innate simplicity of his food. This salad is a perfect example. The centerpiece is a multihued combination of heirloom tomatoes, which he salts and lets sit just long enough for the tomatoes to give off their sweet, earthy juices—an interruption, actually, of David Bouley's famed tomato water, but without having to hang tomatoes in cheesecloth over a bowl overnight. Then Dan embellishes the tomatoes with watermelon to play up their fruitiness, and he adds herbs for fragrance and fresh ricotta cheese and olive oil for richness. Sometimes at Blue Hill, when he's feeling baroque, he might also include various swags such as tomato gelée or balsamic emulsion. But even he agrees they are not essential. The soul of this dish is right here.

PREPARATION TIME: 40 MINUTES

SERVES 6

3 large heirloom tomatoes (the more colors the better), cut into ¾-inch cubes

1 cup cherry tomatoes, halved

1 cup cubed seedless watermelon (or remove the seeds)

Coarse sea salt or kosher salt and freshly ground black pepper

1 cup fresh ricotta cheese, preferably sheep's-milk (see Melissa's Tips)

3 tablespoons extra-virgin olive oil

3 tablespoons chopped mixed fresh herbs such as basil, lemon thyme, marjoram, mint, or chives

CHEF'S TIPS If you don't grow fifty different kinds of **tomatoes** like I do (or even *any* kinds of tomatoes), try to buy yours at a farmers' market for this recipe. They have the most flavor.

MELISSA'S TIPS You can substitute other cheeses for the fresh **ricotta,** including a mild feta or fresh mozzarella.

If you don't have really good fruity **olive oil,** splurge and buy some for this recipe.

CHEF The longer this salad sits before serving, the more juice the tomatoes give off, so **serve** it with a spoon to catch every drop.

1. Divide the heirloom and cherry **tomatoes** and the watermelon among 6 plates. Sprinkle with salt and pepper and let rest for 10 to 20 minutes, until the tomatoes and watermelon begin to give off some of their liquid.

2. Dot the tomatoes with spoonfuls of the **ricotta** cheese, drizzle with the **olive oil,** and sprinkle with the herbs. **Serve** immediately.

MARK LADNER, Lupa, New York

Parsley and Pancetta Salad

I love piquant salads in which herbs stand in for lettuces. In this case, parsley leaves are the only green, while the crisp white parsley root adds a mellower parsley flavor and a crunchy texture. Pancetta and cheese are decadent and necessary garnishes. At Lupa this salad is part of the antipasti selection, but I think it's interesting enough to stand on its own or served as a side dish with roasted meats or fish.
PREPARATION TIME: 20 MINUTES

SERVES 4

6 ounces pancetta, cut into ¼-inch dice

4 cups fresh flat-leaf parsley (leaves only)

2 large or 3 medium parsley roots, peeled and grated (about 2 cups)

2 cups coarsely grated Parmesan cheese (about 6 ounces)

¼ cup extra-virgin olive oil

3 tablespoons freshly squeezed lemon juice (from 1½ lemons)

Coarse sea salt or kosher salt and freshly ground black pepper

MELISSA'S TIP Parsley root is a fall and winter root vegetable that looks like a parsley-sprouting beige carrot and tastes like a cross between carrot, celery, and parsley. Its leaves can be used as you would any other parsley, and the root is terrific grated into salads, roasted with olive oil in a hot oven, or added to soups and stews. Look for it at a farmers' market or specialty store. If you can't find it, you can make an equally excellent, if slightly different, salad by substituting celeriac.

CHEF'S TIPS The **Parmesan** should be grated into coarse strands, like you'd get from a box grater. Or you can shave it using a vegetable peeler. But don't use a fine cheese grater, or the cheese will get lost in the greens.

1. In a large skillet, cook the pancetta over medium heat until crisp, about 5 minutes. Drain on a plate lined with paper towels.

2. In a large serving bowl, combine the parsley leaves, **parsley roots, Parmesan,** and pancetta. In another bowl, whisk together the olive oil, lemon juice, and salt and pepper to taste. Just before serving, pour a little of the **dressing** on the salad, toss, and add more dressing to taste. This salad is not meant to be drenched in dressing, which would kill the flavor of the pancetta. Dress it lightly and toss well to make sure all the parsley is coated, only adding more dressing after you've tasted it. Serve immediately.

FLOYD CARDOZ, Tabla, New York

Goan Avocado Salad

Avocados are not hugely popular in India, but their buttery flesh is a perfect vehicle for Floyd Cardoz's bright, spicy combination of lime, onion, tomato, cilantro, and spices. Floyd serves it with homemade flatbreads straight out of the tandoor; I like it on a bed of greens as a first course. Or you can mash the avocado a little with a fork and serve it with spiced pappadums (lentil wafers sold in Indian groceries and available at Kalustyan's: 800-352-3451; www.kalustyans.com) or tortilla chips, like an Indian-spiced guacamole. PREPARATION TIME: 15 MINUTES

SERVES 4

4 ripe yet firm avocados, peeled, halved, pitted, and cut into ½-inch cubes

Grated zest and juice of 1 lime

3 plum tomatoes, cored and diced

½ cup finely minced red onion (about ½ onion)

4 sprigs of fresh cilantro, leaves removed and sliced into fine ribbons

1 teaspoon ground cumin

½ teaspoon ground coriander

Coarse sea salt or kosher salt and freshly ground black pepper

Cayenne pepper to taste

2 tablespoons extra-virgin olive oil

CHEF'S TIPS It's easiest to **zest the lime** before halving and juicing it.

I like to toast and grind my own spices. To do this, toss each spice separately in a dry skillet over medium heat until fragrant, about 2 minutes. Immediately transfer to a plate to cool, then grind fine with a mortar and pestle or in a clean electric coffee grinder. Freshly ground spices can be stored in airtight containers for up to 6 months, though some spices lose their fragrance sooner; sniff to be sure.

MELISSA'S TIP This salad is best eaten on the day it's made, though leftovers are terrific in sandwiches.

In a large bowl, combine the cubed avocados with the **lime zest** and juice. Add the tomatoes, onion, and cilantro. Mix well, taking care not to smash the avocado and the tomatoes. Next add the cumin and coriander, and salt, pepper, and cayenne to taste. Drizzle in the olive oil, toss again, then cover with plastic and refrigerate for at least 2 hours. Adjust the seasonings just before serving.

FRANK STITT, Highlands Bar and Grill, Birmingham, Alabama

Cornbread Panzanella

In Italy, *panzanella* is a recipe designed to use up the leftovers from the larder—stale bread, olive oil, and tomatoes. Frank Stitt, one of the South's most eminent chefs, substitutes cornbread, the Southern equivalent of crusty Italian bread, and adds cucumbers for a little bit of crunch and roasted peppers because, well, why not? He serves it as a side dish, but add leftover steak, cubes of soft cheese like mozzarella, roast chicken, or shrimp, and you could call it a light lunch. PREPARATION TIME: 1 HOUR

SERVES 8

CORNBREAD

2 cups yellow cornmeal

1/2 cup all-purpose flour

1 teaspoon baking powder

1 teaspoon baking soda

3/4 teaspoon fine sea salt

3/4 cup whole milk

3/4 cup buttermilk

7 tablespoons unsalted butter, melted

1 large egg, lightly beaten

SALAD

1 red bell pepper

1 yellow bell pepper

3 tablespoons red wine vinegar

2 tablespoons sherry vinegar

Coarse sea salt or kosher salt and freshly ground black pepper

3/4 cup extra-virgin olive oil

6 ripe tomatoes, halved, seeded, and cut into 1-inch chunks (about 4 cups)

1 small red onion, quartered lengthwise and thinly sliced crosswise

1/2 cup kalamata olives, pitted and halved

2 Kirby cucumbers, halved lengthwise and cut into 1/4-inch-thick slices

1/2 cup fresh basil leaves

1/2 cup fresh mint leaves

1/2 cup fresh flat-leaf parsley leaves

CHEF'S TIPS You can make the **cornbread** a day or two in advance and keep it wrapped in foil in the refrigerator. The vegetables can be prepared several hours ahead; just toss everything together right before serving.

1. To make the **cornbread,** preheat the oven to 450°F. and place a 9-inch cast-iron pan on the middle rack. In a large bowl, combine the cornmeal, flour, baking powder, baking soda, and salt. Use a wooden spoon to stir in the milks a little at a time. The batter will be quite loose.

2. Add the butter to the pan and return to the oven for about 3 minutes. Remove the skillet and pour all but 1 tablespoon of the hot butter into the cornmeal mixture. Stir to combine, then stir in the egg. Pour the mixture into the hot pan and immediately return the pan to the oven. Bake for 20 to 25 minutes, until golden brown. Remove from the oven and turn the bread out onto a wire rack to cool.

3. To make the salad, **roast** the red and yellow **bell peppers** directly on the burner of a gas stove over high heat, turning occasionally with tongs, until the skins are blackened, 10 to 12 minutes. Alternatively, place the peppers on the broiler rack and broil, turning, until charred. Transfer the peppers to a bowl and cover with a plate or plastic wrap. Set aside for 20 minutes. When the peppers have cooled, remove the skins, stems, and seeds, and cut the peppers into 1-inch squares.

4. Meanwhile, reduce the oven temperature to 400°F. Slice the cornbread into ¾-inch cubes and arrange them in a single layer on a baking sheet. Toast in the oven until the edges are lightly browned, about 10 minutes. Let cool.

5. In a large bowl, combine the red wine and sherry vinegars, and salt and pepper. Slowly whisk in the oil in a steady stream. Add the tomatoes, onion, and olives, tossing to coat. Let marinate for 10 to 15 minutes. Add the roasted peppers, **cucumbers,** basil, mint, and parsley, and toss well. Add the cornbread and toss to moisten evenly. Adjust the seasonings to taste and serve immediately.

MELISSA'S TIPS This is a truly great **cornbread** recipe, and in fact it took all my willpower not to eat the whole batch before I made the panzanella. But this salad is also an ideal way to use up leftover cornbread, if you happen to have any lying around. Or, of course, substitute purchased cornbread. You will need 10 cups.

If you don't feel like **roasting the peppers,** go ahead and leave them out. The salad doesn't suffer that much for their absence and is much quicker to prepare.

CHEF For more tips on **roasted bell pepper,** see page 18.

MELISSA If you can't get Kirby **cucumbers** (the small kind often used for pickles), just use one regular cucumber, though you'll have to peel and seed it first.

CESARE CASELLA, Beppe, New York

Braised Heirloom Bean Salad with Tomatoes, Onions, and Herbs

With an herb garden of fresh oregano, thyme, and sage sprouting from his chef's whites like a leafy pocket square, Cesare Casella is not only fanatical about fresh ingredients, he's downright dramatic. The drama seeps into his cooking, too, such as in the number of bean varieties he uses in this vibrant salad. I cut his original seven, however, down to a more manageable one, though you can increase that, if you please (see Melissa's Tips). But whatever you do, don't skimp on the fresh herbs, though you needn't wear them. Unless you want to. PREPARATION TIME: 20 MINUTES, PLUS OVERNIGHT SOAKING, 2 HOURS COOKING, AND 30 MINUTES MARINATING

SERVES 10 TO 12

1½ pounds dried beans, of one or several varieties (see Sidebar), picked through to remove any little stones

3 garlic cloves

1 sprig of fresh sage

1 sprig of fresh thyme

1 sprig of fresh rosemary

Coarse sea salt or kosher salt and freshly ground black pepper

1 large or 2 small red onions, sliced very thin

1 cup red wine vinegar

3 ripe tomatoes, diced

3 celery stalks, cut into ¼-inch dice

1 bunch of fresh flat-leaf parsley (leaves only), chopped

½ cup extra-virgin olive oil, plus additional to taste

CHEF'S TIPS When soaking **beans** in the summer months, keep them in the refrigerator overnight. Too much heat will cause the beans to release too much protein, which turns the water frothy and shortens the shelf life of the beans after they're cooked.

Adding the **salt** at the end of the cooking prevents the beans from bursting.

1. A minimum of one day before making the salad, place the **beans** in a large pot or bowl, fill with cold water, and let soak overnight or for at least 8 hours. If using different kinds of beans, soak them separately.

2. Drain the water and rinse the beans. Place them in a large pot (or several medium pots if using more than one variety), and cover with a lot of cold water. Add the garlic and fresh herbs. Cook over medium heat until the beans are tender—this may take anywhere from 30 minutes to 2 hours, depending on your beans. Once cooked, season with **salt** and pepper to taste, and let the beans cool in their cooking liquid. Refrigerate if not using immediately.

3. While the beans are cooling, in a bowl, toss the sliced **onions** in the vinegar and let marinate at room temperature for at least 30 minutes and up to 2 hours.

4. In a large bowl, toss the cooked beans with the onions and their soaking vinegar. Add the tomatoes, celery, parsley, **olive oil,** and salt and pepper. Either serve at once while the beans are still a little warm, or store in the refrigerator for up to 2 days, and reheat gently. Just before serving, season generously with salt, pepper, and extra-virgin olive oil.

MELISSA'S TIP Pickling the **onions** in vinegar before adding them to the salad softens their flavor, but you can skip that step if you are in a hurry. Or leave out the onions altogether.

CHEF Don't be afraid to use a lot of good-quality extra-virgin **olive oil** in this salad.

SEVEN BEANS

The seven varieties of beans Cesare uses to make this salad at Beppe are zolfini, spagna, diavolo, cannellini, Sorano, borlotti, and angelo. You could use any one of these or any other dried bean of your choice. Although this recipe calls for only one type, I think it's best to use more if you can. I recommend using three types, ½ pound of each, though you will have to soak and cook each separately. Just divide the garlic and herbs among three pots (you'll need more herbs; use one sprig per pot) and cook the beans until each kind is tender—the cooking times will vary depending upon the type of bean you use and its age. As dried beans age, they continue to dry out and will even shrivel. Fresher dried beans will cook more quickly and evenly, so buy your beans from a store that does a brisk business. Italian and Middle Eastern stores are good sources of interesting dried beans, or you can order more esoteric varieties from Cesare's company, Republic of Beans (212-982-8274), or from Heritage Foods (212-980-6603; heritagefoodsusa.com).

RICK MOONEN, formerly of Restaurant rm, New York

White Gazpacho with Crab, Green Grapes, and Almonds

Ajo blanco means "white garlic," but it's also the name for white gazpacho, a traditional cold Spanish soup from Andalusia, made by blending almonds, garlic, stale bread, and olive oil. Grapes are a traditional garnish, their crisp sweetness providing a refreshing contrast to the smooth, savory soup. Rick Moonen, seafood genius that he is, adds crabmeat-stuffed avocado dumplings and a roster of lovely summery garnishes like perfumed almond oil and little purple chive blossoms. Of course, I deconstructed the dumplings and made the garnishes optional in my version. Even served unadorned, this soup makes a seductive and elegant starter for a summer meal. PREPARATION TIME: 45 MINUTES, PLUS 6 HOURS CHILLING

SERVES 6

¾ cup blanched almonds

1 garlic clove

½ teaspoon coarse sea salt or kosher salt, plus additional to taste

4 slices day-old white bread, crusts removed

6 tablespoons extra-virgin olive oil

2 tablespoons white wine vinegar, plus additional to taste

1½ tablespoons sherry vinegar, plus additional to taste

2 ripe avocados

Freshly squeezed juice of 1 lemon

Freshly ground black pepper

4 ounces jumbo lump crabmeat

1 teaspoon finely chopped fresh chives

1 teaspoon finely chopped fresh tarragon (optional)

1 teaspoon finely chopped fresh flat-leaf parsley

1½ cups seedless green grapes, halved

Chive flowers, for garnish (optional)

2 tablespoons toasted almond oil (optional)

CHEF'S TIP Most **crabmeat** sold is from cooked blue crabs and has been pasteurized. It will be great in this recipe—buy meat labeled *jumbo lump* or *backfin,* the best grade consisting of the largest pieces. Or if you can get it from a good fishmonger, fresh unpasteurized crabmeat that has just been picked is even more delicious. Of course, you can steam your own blue crabs and pick out the meat, using about 1 pound of crab to yield the 4 ounces of meat needed for this recipe—but buying the meat picked saves a lot of time!

1. In a food processor, puree the almonds, garlic, and ½ teaspoon salt to a fine consistency.

2. In a bowl, soak the bread in 1 cup of cold water until it's thoroughly soggy, about 3 minutes or longer, depending on how hard your bread was to begin with.

3. Add the water and bread to the almond mixture and blend. With the motor running, pour in the oil and another cup of cold water in a slow, steady stream. Add the white wine and sherry vinegars and blend on high speed for 2 minutes. Add 1 more cup of cold water and blend for 2 more minutes (you will have used 3 cups, total). Transfer the mixture to a bowl and add salt and vinegar to taste. Chill the mixture for 6 hours, then pass through a fine-mesh sieve and season again with salt and vinegar to taste.

4. Halve the avocados, remove the pits, scoop out the flesh with a large spoon, and cut it into ½-inch cubes. Toss with half of the lemon juice and add salt and pepper to taste.

5. Mix the **crabmeat** with the chopped herbs, the remaining lemon juice, and additional salt and pepper, if needed.

6. To serve, divide the halved grapes, avocado cubes, and crab mixture among 6 chilled bowls. Pour in the soup, garnish with **chive flowers,** and drizzle with toasted **almond oil,** if desired.

MELISSA'S TIPS Flowering chive is easy to grow and is available in the summer at farmers' markets. The purple blossoms look a little like small thistle flowers and have a delicate chive taste, but here they are mostly used for visual effect. If you have them, float a few blossoms atop each bowl; if you don't, it won't really change the dish.

Almond oil is an optional garnish for this soup. It's a fragrant nut oil that is nice on salads, can be used for cooking (it can withstand high cooking temperatures), and is also very good for your skin—in fact, it's a favored massage oil. Really, no household should be without the stuff. Look in gourmet shops for French almond oil, which has more flavor than the stuff available at natural food stores.

JOËL ANTUNES, Joël, Atlanta

Red Gazpacho with Tomato–Olive Oil Sorbet

If Rick Moonen's take on white gazpacho (page 62) is all about subtlety in its flavors, textures, and pale, pretty colors, Joël Antunes's is the polar opposite. Although equally refined, his edgy, scarlet soup, imbued with good olive oil and racy sherry vinegar, is more about intensity than delicacy. The sweetness of the tomato sorbet is integral to the composition of the dish, so don't be tempted to leave it out. If you don't have an ice-cream maker, follow my tip for making granita, below. **PREPARATION TIME: 45 MINUTES, PLUS 12 HOURS CHILLING AND FREEZING**

SERVES 8

GAZPACHO

2½ pounds ripe tomatoes (about 5 large), thickly sliced and seeded

1 large red bell pepper, split in half, seeds and white membranes removed

¾ pound cucumbers, peeled and seeded (2 cucumbers)

½ cup fresh basil leaves

½ cup extra-virgin olive oil, plus additional for serving

¼ cup sherry vinegar, plus additional to taste

¾ teaspoon coarse sea salt or kosher salt, plus additional for serving and to taste

⅛ teaspoon Tabasco, or to taste

SORBET

2 cups tomato juice (see Melissa's Tips)

½ cup extra-virgin olive oil

¼ cup sugar

2 tablespoons sherry vinegar

1 small celery stalk

2 fresh basil leaves

CHEF'S TIP When making the **gazpacho,** bear in mind that you want the flavor to be on the tart side to balance out the sweetness of the tomato–olive oil sorbet. If the soup–sorbet combination tastes cloying, drizzle it with a little vinegar along with the oil and salt.

MELISSA'S TIPS Make sure you purchase plain old tomato juice without any added ingredients, like MSG or corn syrup or unknown "spices."

If you don't have an **ice-cream maker,** you can turn the sorbet into a granita. Pour the liquid into a shallow, preferably metal, container and freeze it, stirring every 30 minutes until it resembles slush. Stir again before serving.

1. Prepare the **gazpacho:** In a blender or food processor, working in two or three batches, puree all the ingredients with 4 cups of water (make sure there's enough water for each batch). Transfer the pureed soup to a large container, stir well, cover, and refrigerate for 12 hours.

2. Prepare the sorbet: In a blender or food processor, puree all the ingredients. Pass the mixture through a fine-mesh strainer. Transfer the puree to an **ice-cream machine** and freeze according to the manufacturer's instructions. Place the sorbet in a container and store in the freezer until ready to use.

3. To serve, spoon the chilled gazpacho into soup bowls, place a scoop of tomato sorbet on top, drizzle with olive oil, and sprinkle with salt.

PETER BERLEY, formerly of Angelica Kitchen, New York

Yellow Pepper and Almond Soup

I loved the irony of working on *The Modern Vegetarian Kitchen* with Peter Berley, the former chef at Manhattan's vegan Angelica Kitchen. He hadn't touched meat for decades, but by the time we started testing recipes, he was eating beef, pork, and poultry, albeit organic kinds. So we sat in his kitchen, writing about tofu scramble and snacking on artisanal salami. Peter's passion for vegetarian recipes was very much in evidence, though, in dishes like this nutty Spanish yellow-pepper soup, traditionally made with chicken broth. PREPARATION TIME: 1 HOUR

SERVES 6

2 tablespoons unsalted butter

1 tablespoon extra-virgin olive oil

2 cups sliced blanched almonds

Coarse sea salt or kosher salt

2 medium red onions, sliced (about 3 cups)

2 tablespoons minced garlic (about 2 large cloves)

2 bay leaves

2 sprigs of fresh thyme

1 teaspoon saffron threads

1/2 teaspoon crushed red pepper flakes

4 yellow bell peppers, seeded, stemmed, and chopped (about 6 cups)

4 small carrots, chopped (about 1 cup)

4 cups vegetable broth, low-sodium if canned

Sour cream, for garnish

Chopped fresh flat-leaf parsley, for garnish

CHEF'S TIP Sautéing and then pureeing nuts as a thickener is a great technique that can be applied to other soups as well. It's a wonderful way to up the nutritional value of a soup, making it more hearty and substantial.

MELISSA'S TIP To make this unvegetarian, you can use chicken **broth,** which gives the soup a more intense flavor. Both versions are excellent.

1. In a large pot over medium heat, warm the butter and oil. Add the almonds and **sauté** until browned, about 3 minutes. Use a slotted spoon to transfer the almonds to a plate, draining the fat back into the pot. Sprinkle the almonds with salt and let cool.

2. Add the onions to the pot with a pinch of salt and stir well. Cover, reduce the heat to low, and cook for 15 minutes, or until soft.

3. Add the garlic, bay leaves, thyme, saffron, and red pepper flakes, stir, and cook for 3 minutes. Add the yellow peppers, carrots, and vegetable **broth,** and bring to a boil.

4. Cover the pot, reduce the heat to low, and cook for 20 minutes, or until the vegetables are completely soft.

5. In a food processor, puree 1 cup of the toasted almonds, adding a little broth from the soup to create a smooth paste (reserve the remaining almonds for serving). When the vegetables are tender, remove the bay leaves, use a slotted spoon to transfer all the solids to the food processor and puree until smooth. Return the puree to the broth in the pot, stir well, and season with salt.

6. To serve, ladle soup into bowls and top each serving with a dollop of sour cream, a sprinkling of the reserved almonds, and chopped parsley.

NORMAN VAN AKEN, Norman's, Coral Gables, Florida

Curried Sweet Corn and Coconut Soup with Caramelized Mango

Here's a confession: I've never met Norman Van Aken, one of the fathers of "New World" cuisine. Nor have I ever been to his restaurant. But I love his menus, and the dishes I've seen of his in magazines, newspapers, and his two cookbooks. He uses ingredients in combinations that I just wouldn't think of. For example, how many recipes for corn soup are there? Thousands, if not more. So why is this one unique? It's definitely not the curry. Curried cream soups remind me of the 1980s. Nor is it the use of fresh rather than frozen corn; that's an improvement over the standard recipe, but not anything more than you'd expect from an ingredient-driven chef. Van Aken's genius becomes apparent in the clever little touches he employs to add layers of flavor to his recipe, such as using coconut milk and apple juice as part of the liquid. How brilliant to put those two together, along with buttery sweet corn, a good jolt of tongue-stinging curry powder, and a garnish of caramelized mango. The whole recipe is easy, and you can find the ingredients anywhere. My only changes were to streamline it and cut out a few cheffy steps (he strains it three times and uses about a dozen more pans than I do here). Trust me — it is very special. **PREPARATION TIME: 2 HOURS**

SERVES 4 TO 6

2 tablespoons unsalted butter

4 cups fresh white corn kernels (from about 6 ears)

2 large leeks, white parts only, thinly sliced (about 1 cup)

2 tablespoons curry powder

1½ cups unfiltered apple juice or apple cider

¼ teaspoon coriander seeds

5 black peppercorns

6 stems of fresh cilantro (leaves chopped and reserved for garnish)

3 cups chicken broth (low-sodium if canned)

1½ cups heavy cream

1 cup unsweetened coconut milk

Coarse sea salt or kosher salt and freshly ground black pepper

1 ripe but firm mango, thinly sliced (optional)

¼ cup sugar (optional)

Sour cream, for garnish

MELISSA'S TIPS Norman would never use frozen **corn.** And I wouldn't say that if you do, the soup will taste just as delicious. But a good brand of frozen corn will make a better soup than fresh, out-of-season, starchy corn. If you substitute, just don't tell Norman.

1. In a medium pot over medium heat, melt the butter. Add the **corn** and leeks and cook until soft (not browned), about 5 minutes. Add the **curry powder** and cook, stirring, for 1 minute. Add the **apple juice,** bring to a simmer, and allow to reduce by three quarters, about 10 minutes. Set aside.

2. If you have **cheesecloth,** make a bouquet garni by placing the coriander, peppercorns, and cilantro stems in a 6-inch square and tying it closed with kitchen string. Place the bouquet garni in a large saucepan. (Alternatively, just add the spices to the pot.) Pour in the chicken broth, bring to a boil, and simmer uncovered for 20 minutes.

3. Add $\frac{1}{2}$ cup of the cream to the saucepan, bring to a simmer, and reduce the mixture by half, about 20 more minutes.

4. Take the pot off the heat, add the coconut milk, and set aside for at least 30 minutes to meld the flavors (you can also make this ahead and refrigerate it for a day). Remove and discard the bouquet garni and add the liquid to the pan with the corn. (Or if you didn't use cheesecloth, strain the mixture directly into the pan with the corn, discarding the coriander, peppercorns, and cilantro stems.)

5. Using an immersion blender or stand blender and working in batches, if necessary, puree the soup until smooth. Stir in the remaining cup of cream. If you want to, you can strain the soup through a sieve into a medium bowl (it's also good, though less smooth, as is). Season to taste with salt and pepper. Chill thoroughly if it's not already cold.

6. Meanwhile, prepare the caramelized **mangos** if using. Preheat the broiler. Spread half the sugar in a thin layer on a rimmed baking sheet. Lay the mango slices in a single layer on the sugar and sprinkle the remaining sugar over them to lightly and evenly coat. Broil until the sugar melts and the slices are caramelized, 8 to 10 minutes. Let cool on a wire rack.

7. Serve the soup with dollops of sour cream and the mango slices, if desired, and garnished with the chopped cilantro leaves.

CHEF'S TIPS If you use a hot **curry powder** in place of a sweet curry powder, you will end up with a fairly intense level of heat.

If you don't have fresh, fragrant **curry powder** (you can tell by smelling it), buy some for this recipe. It makes a tremendous difference. (You can get it at Kalustyan's: 800-352-3451; www.kalustyans.com).

Look for unfiltered **apple juice** or apple cider. Or, for the best flavor, purchase just-squeezed apple juice from a juice bar and use it within a day or so. It will turn brown, but that doesn't matter here.

MELISSA If you don't have any **cheesecloth,** or don't want to bother with it, but still want to save a step by not having to add the spices to the pot and strain them out afterward, try putting them in a tea ball.

While **mangos** work really well with the coconut milk, they can be a pain to cut into nice, thin slices. Feel free to substitute other fruit such as thinly sliced tart apples (good old Granny Smiths are perfect here) or even papaya. Or skip the fruit garnish and serve the soup with just the sour cream and cilantro. If your guests don't know it was supposed to be there, they'll never miss it.

BEN BARKER, Magnolia Grill, Durham, North Carolina

Vidalia Onion Chowder with Shrimp, Smoked Bacon, and Spicy Aioli

If you're thinking bland, creamy chowder, think again: this one has a lot more going on. It's smoky from the bacon renderings and sweet from the Vidalia onions, with nice spice from red pepper flakes and a healthy jolt of hot sauce. Cooking the shrimp and potatoes separately then combining everything in the soup bowls keeps the flavors clean and intense. When I asked Ben Barker about including the chowder in this book, he interrupted this recipe himself, substituting prepared mayo for the usual egg-and-oil emulsion in the aioli. And don't just use his peppery aioli here; it's also terrific as a spread on sandwiches or even as a dip for veggies or grilled bread. PREPARATION TIME: 1½ HOURS

SERVES 8

CHOWDER

¼ pound bacon, preferably applewood-smoked, cut crosswise into ½-inch-thick strips

2 tablespoons unsalted butter

4 large Vidalia onions, chopped (about 8 cups)

1 bay leaf

2 tablespoons minced garlic (5 cloves)

2 tablespoons all-purpose flour

¼ teaspoon crushed red pepper flakes, or to taste

2½ cups chicken broth, low-sodium if canned

¾ cup white wine

2 large red potatoes, cut into 1-inch cubes (about 1½ cups)

1 cup crème fraîche or half-and-half

Grated zest of ½ lemon

Cider vinegar, to taste

Texas Pete hot sauce or Tabasco sauce, to taste

Coarse sea salt or kosher salt and freshly ground black pepper

¾ pound large shrimp, peeled, deveined, split in half lengthwise, and quartered

AIOLI

¼ cup mayonnaise

1½ teaspoons Texas Pete hot sauce or Tabasco sauce

½ teaspoon freshly squeezed lemon juice

Pinch of salt

FOR SERVING

2 tablespoons fresh thyme leaves

2 tablespoons snipped fresh chives

CHEF'S TIPS Texas Pete **hot sauce** is actually made in North Carolina and apparently is used for Buffalo wings. Its balanced heat and interesting flavor make it perfect in this recipe, though you can substitute your favorite brand.

1. In a large pot over low heat, cook the bacon until crisp, about 5 minutes. Transfer the bacon to a plate lined with paper towels to cool, reserving half of the rendered fat in the pot. (Set the remaining fat aside to use later.) Raise the heat to medium, add the butter, and heat until the butter foams. Add the onions and bay leaf and cook, stirring frequently, until the onions are softened and lightly caramelized, about 25 minutes.

2. Add the garlic, flour, and red pepper flakes, and cook, stirring constantly, for 2 minutes. Stir in the broth and wine, bring to a simmer, add the potatoes, and cook, stirring occasionally, for 15 minutes.

3. Whisk the crème fraîche or half-and-half and the lemon zest into the soup and season to taste with cider vinegar, **hot sauce,** and salt and pepper. Remove the bay leaf.

4. In a skillet over medium-high heat, heat the reserved bacon fat until shimmering. Add the shrimp and cook, stirring, until pink, about 1½ minutes.

5. In a small bowl, combine all of the aioli ingredients, season to taste, and set aside.

6. To serve, divide the shrimp and thyme among 8 warm soup bowls. Ladle the hot soup over them. Sprinkle with bacon and chives. Dollop a spoonful of aioli in the center of each bowl and serve immediately.

MELISSA'S TIPS If you are set on finding it, look for Texas Pete **hot sauce** in stores or online, wherever a variety of hot sauces are sold, or head right to the source: *www.texaspete.com.*

This soup should be lush and thick, with a creamy texture; to fix a soup that is too thin, let it simmer and reduce. If the soup is too thick, add some more broth or crème fraîche.

CHEF The chowder can be prepared ahead through step 2 and stored in the refrigerator for up to 24 hours. To finish, simply reheat and resume where you left off.

ALFRED PORTALE, Gotham Bar and Grill, New York

Pumpkin Soup with Caramelized Onions, Sage, and Gruyère Croutons

For all of Alfred Portale's spectacular culinary tricks (a former jewelry designer, he was the inventor of arranging food vertically on the plate), when you strip it down, most of his repertoire is firmly rooted in familiar French, Italian, and American classics—but with his personal twists. This recipe combines the crisp-edged, molten cheese topping of a French onion potage with a creamy, sage-flavored American pumpkin soup underneath. It's such a winning dish that even Alfred doesn't try and chefify it with vertical croutons and the like. **PREPARATION TIME: 1 1/2 HOURS**

SERVES 4 TO 6

1 small pumpkin or medium butternut squash (about 3 pounds), peeled, seeded, and cut into 1/2-inch cubes (about 7 cups)

3 tablespoons unsalted butter

Coarse sea salt or kosher salt and freshly ground black pepper

2 medium onions, peeled and thinly sliced (about 3 cups)

1 thinly sliced celery stalk (about 1/2 cup)

2 garlic cloves, minced

6 fresh sage leaves, sliced into thin ribbons (see Chef's Tips, page 97)

4 1/2 cups chicken broth, low-sodium if canned

1 bay leaf

12 slices baguette, cut 1/4 inch thick and lightly toasted

2 cups grated Gruyère cheese (about 1/2 pound), or substitute a combination of Gruyère and Parmesan, if desired

MELISSA'S TIPS A vegetable peeler is all you need to peel a butternut squash. A pumpkin takes a paring knife.

CHEF'S TIPS This recipe is delicious with any dense, orange-fleshed winter squash—the main consideration is what looks best in market and how much time you have to prepare the squash, since those with harder, ridged peels like kabocha or hubbard may take a little longer to peel and roast than a butternut.

1. Preheat the oven to 450°F. Place the pumpkin on a rimmed baking sheet, dot with 1 tablespoon of the butter, and season well with salt and pepper. Roast, tossing a few times, until the pumpkin pieces are caramelized and beginning to soften, 15 to 20 minutes.

2. Meanwhile, in a heavy pot, melt the remaining 2 tablespoons of butter over medium heat. Add the onions and cook slowly, stirring occasionally, until they are soft, sweet, and evenly golden, about 25 minutes.

3. Season the onions with salt and pepper. Add the celery, garlic, and sage and cook for another 2 minutes. Add the pumpkin, **broth,** and bay leaf and bring to a boil. Reduce the heat, cover, and let simmer for 15 minutes. Taste and adjust the seasoning if necessary. Remove the bay leaf. Cool and store in the refrigerator for up to 5 days, if desired. Reheat before continuing with the rest of the recipe.

4. To serve, preheat the broiler. Ladle soup into ovenproof crocks and place them on a baking sheet (you may need to broil the bowls two at a time so they are exposed to equal and direct heat). Float 2 toasts on each bowl of soup and top each with ⅓ to ½ cup of the grated cheese. Broil until browned and bubbly, about 3 minutes. Serve immediately.

MELISSA For a vegetarian soup, substitute vegetable **broth** for the chicken broth.

This soup can be refrigerated for up to 5 days or frozen for up to a month, then reheated and topped with the toast and cheese just before serving.

Pasta, Risotto, and Pizza

Fresh Handkerchief Pasta with
Zucchini Puree, Mint, and Eggs
MICHAEL ROMANO, Union Square Cafe

Egg Fettuccine with Beets,
Parmesan, and Poppy Seeds
ANNA KLINGER, Al Di La

Gnudi with Brown Butter and Sage
APRIL BLOOMFIELD, The Spotted Pig

Prune-Stuffed Gnocchi with
Foie Gras–Vin Santo Glaze
BARBARA LYNCH, No. 9 Park

Mint Postcards with Spicy Lamb
Sausage and Minted Pea Puree
MARIO BATALI, Babbo Ristorante e Enoteca

Spicy Linguine with
Sautéed Baby Squid and Chorizo
ERIC RIPERT, Le Bernardin

Cavatelli with Braised Duck and
Prosciutto Ragout, Sheep's-Milk Ricotta,
and Baby Arugula
GERRY HAYDEN, formerly of Amuse

Spaghetti with Preserved Tuna, Lemon
Zest, Hot Pepper, Capers, and Olives
JUDY RODGERS, Zuni Cafe

Pear and Pecorino Ravioli
FORTUNATO NICOTRA, Felidia

Kabocha Squash Risotto with Radicchio
and Parmesan
SUZANNE GOIN, Lucques

Mushroom Risotto with
Truffle Tea Foam
MARCUS SAMUELSSON, Aquavit

Morel Pizza with Fontina,
Asparagus, and Country Ham
PATRICK O'CONNELL, Inn at Little Washington

Green Garlic Pesto, Ricotta,
and Mozzarella Pizza
ANDREW FEINBERG, Franny's

Basic Pizza Dough

MICHAEL ROMANO, Union Square Cafe, New York

Fresh Handkerchief Pasta with Zucchini Puree, Mint, and Eggs

At the long-lived Union Square Cafe, Michael Romano makes his own pasta, of course. In fact, most of the chefs in this book do. It's exactly the kind of thing I love to interrupt, since you can so easily buy high-quality fresh pasta—or macaroni, as the guy at the pasta shop says. In Michael's kitchen, the pasta is rolled thin and divided into squares to resemble handkerchiefs (hence the name). I cut up fresh lasagna noodles instead. They are a little thicker, so the dish is heartier than Michael's delicate original, but no less addictive. **PREPARATION TIME: 30 MINUTES**

SERVES 6

ZUCCHINI PUREE

Coarse sea salt or kosher salt

¼ cup extra-virgin olive oil

6 garlic cloves, thinly sliced

14 to 18 very small zucchini (3 pounds), quartered lengthwise and thinly sliced

1 tablespoon chopped fresh mint

2 medium tomatoes, seeded and diced (about 2 cups)

2 cubes or 2 teaspoons chicken bouillon base

¼ teaspoon freshly ground black pepper, plus additional to taste

PASTA AND EGGS

1 pound fresh lasagna noodles, cut into 4- or 5-inch squares

Freshly squeezed juice of 1 lemon

Coarse sea salt or kosher salt and freshly ground black pepper

2 tablespoons unsalted butter

6 large eggs

1 tablespoon extra-virgin olive oil

6 tablespoons grated Parmesan cheese, preferably Parmigiano-Reggiano

2 tablespoons chopped fresh mint leaves

CHEF'S TIPS I like to use tender, small **zucchini.** They have the best flavor.

MELISSA'S TIPS If you can't find very small **zucchini** (not miniature, about 5 inches long), you can use larger ones. Michael may not approve, but it really won't kill the dish.

CHEF On its own, this zucchini **puree** is a great accompaniment for chicken or fish. Or try it as a topping for crostini.

1. Put a large pot of salted water on to boil.

2. Make the puree: In a large skillet over low heat, warm the ¼ cup oil. Add the garlic and sauté until softened but not browned, 2 minutes. Raise the heat to high and add the **zucchini,** mint, tomatoes, chicken bouillon, 1 teaspoon of salt, and the pepper. Cook, stirring occasionally, until the zucchini is al dente, 5 to 6 minutes. Let cool slightly.

3. Transfer half the mixture to a food processor and pulse until it is the texture of porridge. Return the **puree** to the pan and warm through, stirring constantly, over medium heat.

CHEF For an unusual brunch dish, spoon the **puree** onto warm plates and top with poached or fried eggs. Serve with toasted garlic bread.

Adjust the seasonings and keep warm, or reheat before serving.

4. Make the pasta and eggs: Add the lasagna noodles to the boiling water and cook until al dente, about 3 minutes. Scoop out a cup of pasta water and reserve (to thin the sauce), then drain the noodles. In a bowl, toss the noodles with the zucchini sauce and lemon juice, and thin with the reserved pasta water as needed. Season with salt and pepper and keep warm.

5. In a medium saucepan with a lid, melt the butter over medium heat. Gently add the **eggs,** taking care not to crack the yolks, and season with salt and pepper. Cover and cook until the whites are just set and the yolks are as cooked as you like them but still at least slightly runny, 2 to 4 minutes.

6. Serve the noodles and zucchini sauce in warmed pasta bowls. Top each bowl with an egg and garnish with a drizzle of olive oil and a scattering of Parmesan cheese and mint.

MELISSA One of my favorite ways to cook an **egg** is to braise it in butter, which creates the silky texture of a poached egg but with far less trouble. Plus, the little bit of added butter accentuates the richness of the yolk. A trick to cooking just one or two eggs this way is to use the smallest pot you can find, which will give the eggs a more attractive, compact, round shape rather than a sprawling, fried-egg shape. Make sure to use organic free-range eggs.

You could serve the pasta without the eggs. I'd miss them, but I am unduly fond of eggs. If you aren't, save a step and lighten the dish by skipping them.

ANNA KLINGER, Al Di La, Brooklyn, New York

Egg Fettuccine with Beets, Parmesan, and Poppy Seeds

Finally, I'm lucky enough to live in a place with one of those small, homey restaurants to which people from all different neighborhoods flock. Al Di La, along with Franny's, are two of my favorite restaurants in the city, and they both happen to be located within walking distance of my house in Brooklyn. This means I don't often make this earthy and intense dish, since I can get Anna's original version faster than the pasta water can come to a boil (on nights when there's no line at the restaurant, that is). But chances are you live far afield from Park Slope, so I've adapted the recipe here. Anna's original calls for making beet ravioli (called *casunziei*), but I think this simplified version, which keeps all the delectable flavors of the original, is nearly as good. And way more convenient. **PREPARATION TIME: 35 MINUTES**

SERVES 6

Coarse sea salt or kosher salt

10 baby or small beets (about 1½ pounds without greens), scrubbed and trimmed

¼ cup poppy seeds

6 tablespoons (¾ stick) unsalted butter

Freshly ground black pepper

1 pound fresh (or dried) fettuccine

⅔ cup grated Parmesan cheese, preferably Parmigiano-Reggiano

Balsamic vinegar, for garnish (optional)

¼ cup minced chervil or chives, for garnish (optional)

CHEF'S TIP Small **beets** with the greens still attached will have the sweetest flavor.

MELISSA'S TIPS Poppy seeds can go rancid, so if yours seem a little funky, buy fresh ones from a store that does a brisk business in them. Store them in the freezer and replace a few times a year. (You can order poppy seeds from Kalustyan's: 800-352-3451; *www.kalustyans.com*).

Any good, sharp **cheese** that will stand up to the sweetness of the beets and the richness of the butter will work well here, so feel free to substitute an aged Pecorino Romano or even a ricotta salata or an aged goat cheese that is hard enough to grate.

1. Bring a large pot of salted water to a boil. Grate the **beets** in a food processor fitted with the grating disk. (Alternatively, grate by hand.)

2. In a heavy saucepan over high heat, toast the **poppy seeds** until they smell slightly nutty, 1 to 2 minutes. Transfer to a bowl.

3. Reduce the heat and melt 5 tablespoons of the butter in the saucepan. Stir in the shredded beets and sauté for 2 minutes. Season with salt and pepper, then reduce the heat to low, cover the pan, and cook for another 8 to 10 minutes, until the beets are tender.

4. Meanwhile, cook the pasta in the boiling water until it is al dente (2 to 4 minutes for fresh pasta, 7 to 10 for dried). Drain and transfer to a large serving bowl. Toss the hot pasta with the remaining tablespoon of butter, the grated **cheese,** and salt and pepper to taste. When the beets are tender, toss them with the pasta. Sprinkle with the poppy seeds and adjust the seasoning, adding a teaspoon or two of balsamic vinegar, if desired. Garnish with chervil or chives, if using, and serve immediately.

APRIL BLOOMFIELD, The Spotted Pig, New York

Gnudi with Brown Butter and Sage

I'm not one to order the same dish every time I go to a restaurant—nor am I one to go back to a place very often, since there's always somewhere new to try. But my three exceptions are the *casunziei* at Al Di La (see page 78), the spicy tripe at Babbo, and these gnudi from The Spotted Pig. Although neither difficult nor time-consuming, the recipe is a bit persnickety, and you need to follow directions to the letter. But the reward will be a plate of ethereal little ricotta dumplings submerged in a savory sage—butter sauce so compelling you'll probably need a spoon to get every last drop. Do not expect leftovers, no matter how many you make; someone will eat them all, most likely you. PREPARATION TIME: 40 MINUTES PLUS OVERNIGHT CHILLING

SERVES 4

1 pound fresh sheep's-milk ricotta

⅓ cup (about 1 ounce) plus 1 tablespoon freshly grated Parmesan cheese, preferably Parmigiano-Reggiano, plus additional for serving

Coarse sea salt or kosher salt and freshly ground black pepper

1½ cups semolina flour

6 tablespoons (¾ stick) unsalted butter

10 small sage leaves, washed and patted dry

CHEF'S TIPS Start this dish a day in advance, since the gnudi need to rest in the refrigerator overnight.

Use very fresh, very soft sheep's-milk **ricotta** for this, not the drier, crumbly kind.

MELISSA'S TIPS If you can't find sheep's-milk **ricotta,** use fresh cow's-milk ricotta and blend in about a tablespoon of fresh lemon juice to give it a little tang.

Buy fresh **semolina** flour for this recipe, since you'll need about 8 ounces total and it does go rancid fairly quickly in the pantry.

1. In a bowl, mix the **ricotta** and ⅓ cup of the Parmesan together well. Taste and season with salt and pepper. Pour about a ½-inch layer of **semolina** into a shallow baking pan. Using a pastry bag, a Ziploc with a corner cut off, or a spoon, pipe or drop the cheese mixture into tablespoon-size blobs onto the semolina in the pan. Pour more semolina over the gnudi to cover. Refrigerate the pan, **uncovered,** overnight.

2. In a small skillet over medium heat, melt 2 tablespoons of the butter. Add the **sage leaves** and fry until crisp, about 2 minutes. Use a slotted spoon to transfer the leaves to a plate lined with paper towels. Reserve the sage-flavored butter separately.

3. Bring a large pot of salted water to a rolling **boil.** Gently drop the chilled gnudi into the water and cook until heated through, about 3 minutes. Use a slotted spoon to carefully transfer the whole gnudi (and gnudi bits) to a colander. Reserve ¼ cup of the cooking water.

4. In another small skillet over medium-high heat, add the remaining 4 tablespoons butter and 2 tablespoons of the gnudi water and cook, stirring, until the butter is melted. **Turn off the heat** and stir in 1 tablespoon of Parmesan cheese. Very gently toss the gnudi with this sauce, adding a little more reserved cooking water if needed to coat. Divide the gnudi among four plates.

5. Warm up the sage butter and drizzle it on top of the gnudi. Top with the crispy sage leaves, black pepper, and more Parmesan, and serve immediately.

CHEF Don't cover the gnudi while they sit in the fridge overnight. They need to dry and firm up before you can cook them.

MELISSA Drying off the **sage leaves** before frying makes them extra crisp. Use paper towels or a clean dishcloth.

These gnudi tend to fall apart in the **boiling** water, and while they won't be as pretty, you can still serve the crumbled bits along with the lucky ones that made it through intact. The sage butter hides all sins.

CHEF Make sure you **turn the heat off** under the butter sauce before adding the Parmesan; otherwise, it will clump.

BARBARA LYNCH, No. 9 Park, Boston

Prune-Stuffed Gnocchi with Foie Gras–Vin Santo Glaze

This is a signature dish at No. 9 Park, one of Boston's favorite restaurants, and according to Barbara Lynch, the inspiration came from a sweet prune gnocchi recipe given to her by one of her cooks from Bergamo, Italy. She added a superluxe foie gras and vin santo sauce to turn a homey dish into a restaurant-worthy one. Barbara uses a raw lobe of foie gras, which is not only expensive but also a little messy and not appropriate for the squeamish (part of the preparation involves picking out bloody veins). Instead, I use a prepared foie gras terrine. PREPARATION TIME: 1 HOUR, PLUS 3 TO 24 HOURS MARINATING AND 20 MINUTES CHILLING

SERVES 6

20 pitted prunes

2 cups vin santo or Madeira (see Chef's Tips)

Coarse sea salt or kosher salt

1 ½ pounds Idaho or Yukon Gold potatoes (2 to 3 large potatoes)

2 cups all-purpose flour, or as needed

1 large egg

⅛ teaspoon grated nutmeg

Freshly ground black pepper

4 ounces goose or duck foie gras terrine or pâté, at room temperature

1 shallot, diced

15 sprigs of fresh thyme

12 black peppercorns

¼ cup heavy cream

Good-quality balsamic vinegar, for drizzling (see Melissa's Tip)

Freshly snipped chives, for garnish

1. Macerate the prunes in the **wine** for at least 3 and up to 24 hours, covered, at room temperature.

2. Bring a pot of salted water to a boil and cook the potatoes in their skins until very soft, about 25 minutes. Drain. When they are cool enough to handle, peel off the skins and rice or mash the potatoes. Place them in a large bowl and refrigerate until cool.

3. Stir 1 cup of the flour, the egg, and the nutmeg into the potatoes, and mix until just combined. Season with salt and pepper. Add enough of the remaining flour to make a delicate but slightly sticky dough. Transfer half of the dough to a floured work surface and roll it into a sheet about ⅛ inch thick. Use a 2 ½-inch round cookie cutter to cut out rounds of dough. Repeat rolling and cutting with the remaining dough; you will have about 36 circles.

4. Drain the prunes, reserving the wine. Halve the prunes lengthwise. Place a prune half on each dough circle, then fold the rounds into half-moons, pressing to seal the edges. Lay the finished **gnocchi** in a floured pan and freeze or refrigerate for 20 minutes before cooking to firm them. (They can also be frozen, then transferred to a plastic bag and kept in the freezer for several days.)

5. About 20 to 30 minutes before you're ready to eat, bring a large pot of salted water to a boil. Push the foie gras through a fine sieve. Pour the reserved wine from the prunes into a small saucepan and add the shallot, thyme, and peppercorns. Bring the liquid to a boil over high heat and simmer until the mixture is reduced to a thick glaze (you'll end up with about ¼ cup of liquid). Add the cream and simmer until it reduces slightly, 3 to 5 minutes. Lower the heat and stir in a little of the foie gras at a time, whisking vigorously and adding more as it is incorporated into the sauce. When all the foie gras has been incorporated, strain the sauce, discarding the herbs. Keep the strained sauce warm but not hot or it will break (curdle). If the sauce does break, whisk in a little hot water and it will emulsify again.

6. Just before adding the gnocchi to the pot of boiling water, reduce the heat a little to bring the liquid down to a gentle boil, and drop a few gnocchi at a time into the water. Do not overcrowd the pot or the gnocchi will fall apart while cooking. The gnocchi are done when they rise to the top, about 2 minutes. Use a slotted spoon to transfer the gnocchi to a warm serving bowl and keep warm until they are all cooked. Spoon sauce over the gnocchi, drizzle with **balsamic vinegar,** garnish with snipped chives, and serve.

CHEF'S TIPS Vin santo is a deep golden, sweet Italian **wine.** It is made from semidried grapes and is usually fragrant and nutty, making it well suited to dried fruit and desserts, and wonderful with foie gras. Madeira, from the Portuguese island of the same name, is a fortified wine like port or sherry. Slow aging in wood gives it a caramelized flavor that also works well in this recipe. Use whichever you can find, or have.

The **gnocchi** can be prepared and frozen for a few days before serving.

MELISSA'S TIP For me, **balsamic vinegar** is only worth using if you use a high-quality aged one, produced in the area around Modena and Reggio-Emilia. Otherwise, you're just using a sugary liquid colored with caramel and spiked with vinegar, which has none of the complexity of the good stuff. Better to leave it out altogether.

MARIO BATALI, Babbo Ristorante e Enoteca, New York

Mint Postcards with Spicy Lamb Sausage and Minted Pea Puree

At Babbo, Mario Batali's original dish, called mint love letters, involves stuffing homemade pasta ravioli with a sweet minted pea puree. My shortcut version takes the puree out of the pasta and dollops it on top instead. You get the same ingenious flavor combination, but the whole dish is ready in under an hour—less time than you'd likely spend trying to get through to the deservedly popular Babbo for a reservation.

PREPARATION TIME: 1 HOUR

SERVES 4 TO 6

1 box (10 ounces) frozen peas, or 2 cups fresh shelled peas

1 cup fresh mint leaves, plus additional chopped mint for garnish

1 cup (about 3 ounces) freshly grated Parmesan cheese, preferably Parmigiano-Reggiano

⅓ cup heavy cream

1 tablespoon extra-virgin olive oil

1½ pounds merguez (spicy lamb sausage), sliced ½ inch thick

3 garlic cloves, minced

1 can (28 ounces) plum tomatoes, preferably San Marzano

1 bay leaf

Coarse sea salt or kosher salt and freshly ground black pepper

1 pound fresh pappardelle or tagliatelle pasta

1⅓ cups (about ¼ pound) freshly grated Pecorino Romano cheese

MELISSA'S TIPS Frozen **peas** are generally more reliably sweet and tasty than most fresh peas, which, by the time we get them, are usually days old and starchy. Of course, fresh peas from the farmers' market, bought the day you plan to use them, are the best of all if you can get them—just cook them a minute or so longer than the frozen.

You can prepare the pea puree and tomato–merguez sauce in advance, then warm them up as you cook the pasta.

1. In a small saucepan over medium heat, cook the **peas** with ¼ cup of water until they are just tender, about 2 minutes.

2. Using a slotted spoon, transfer the peas to a blender along with the mint, **Parmesan,** and cream (reserve the pea cooking water). Blend until smooth. If the puree seems too thick (it should drop from the spoon easily), blend in a little of the pea cooking water.

3. Meanwhile, in a skillet over medium-high heat, warm the oil. Add the **merguez** and sauté until brown, about 5 minutes. Use a slotted spoon to transfer the sausage to a plate lined with paper towels. Toss the garlic into the pan and sauté until fragrant, about 1 minute. Add the **tomatoes** and bay leaf and simmer, mashing the tomatoes a bit to break them up, for 20 minutes. Return the sausage to the pan and simmer until the mixture is a thick sauce, about 20 minutes longer. Season with salt and pepper.

4. While the sauce is simmering, bring a large pot of salted water to a boil. Add the pasta and cook until just al dente, about 3 minutes. Drain, add to the tomato sauce, and toss well. Remove the bay leaf. Divide the pasta among 4 to 6 plates. Dollop the pea sauce over the top of each serving, garnish with the Pecorino and mint, and serve immediately.

CHEF'S TIPS When I say **Parmesan** cheese I mean Parmigiano-Reggiano, the crumbly, nutty-tasting grating cheese produced and aged in a defined region of northern Italy that includes the counties of Parma and Reggio-Emilia. The big 80-pound wheels of this cheese are aged for at least 12 months, though I recommend one that has been aged for twice that long. Parmigiano-Reggiano is ranked in six grades, so buying a top grade from a good cheese store will make a big difference. True, your pasta will be excellent with any good Parmesan cheese. But taste a piece of top-quality Reggiano Parmesan and you'll see what I mean.

Merguez is a spicy lamb sausage from North Africa, flavored with garlic and the peppery mix called harissa, along with black pepper and fennel seeds.

Though there are plenty of good-quality canned **tomatoes** on the market, the crème de la crème are San Marzano, an intense tomato with a perfect balance of sweetness and acidity. They are available canned, imported from Italy. But so are a lot of impostors. Look for San Marzanos with the letters DOP on the can, which indicates that they were grown and packed near Mount Vesuvius according to traditional methods.

ERIC RIPERT, Le Bernardin, New York

Spicy Linguine with Sautéed Baby Squid and Chorizo

This dish is as much about the squid as it is about the pasta, and for that reason I vacillated between placing it here and in the seafood chapter. But since small portions make a perfect pasta course for a blow-out meal, the pendulum swung here. The idea of combining squid, chorizo, and pasta came from Eric Ripert's gorgeous book, *A Return to Cooking*. His recipe uses cuttlefish, a harder-to-find relative of squid, and is naturally a lot more complex than my adaptation. But the essential flavors of briny seafood, earthy pork, and paprika are happily much the same. PREPARATION TIME: 30 MINUTES

SERVES 4 AS A MAIN COURSE, 8 AS A SMALL PASTA COURSE OR APPETIZER

Coarse sea salt or kosher salt

½ pound linguine

4 tablespoons extra-virgin olive oil

1¼ cups (about 4 ounces) thinly sliced chorizo (see Melissa's Tip, page 138)

3 garlic cloves

¼ teaspoon hot paprika (see Melissa's Tip)

1 pound squid, cut into rings (see Sidebar)

Freshly ground black pepper to taste

2 tablespoons freshly squeezed lemon juice (from 1 lemon)

2 tablespoons chopped fresh flat-leaf parsley, for garnish

1 tablespoon chopped fresh chives, for garnish

MELISSA'S TIP Hungary is the source of the freshest, sweetest ground **paprika,** a vermillion powder made from dried peppers and available in hot and sweet varieties. It's worth seeking out paprika from one of two Hungarian towns, either Szeged or Kalosca. It is most often sold in tins; buy it from a shop with a high turnover to ensure fresh-ness, or order it from Penzeys Spices (800-741-7787; www.penzeys.com), and store it in a cool place (or in the fridge). To get the most flavor from paprika, you need to gently let it "bloom" in warm oil—it should darken slightly, but watch carefully to keep it from getting brown and burnt since it can turn bitter.

1. Bring a large pot of salted water to a boil. Add the pasta and cook until just al dente. Drain and toss with 1 tablespoon of the oil to prevent sticking.

2. In a large skillet over low heat, warm the remaining 3 tablespoons of oil. Add the chorizo and cook it slowly until it has rendered its fat and begun to get crisp on the edges, about 6 minutes. Add the garlic and **paprika** along with a pinch of salt and sauté for 1 minute, taking care not to burn the garlic. Add the **squid** and cook for 2 more minutes, tossing well. Add the cooked linguine and toss to coat. Season generously with salt and pepper.

3. Just before serving, add the lemon juice, toss, and garnish with the fresh parsley and chives.

SQUID AND CALAMARI

Squid and calamari should smell fresh and saline and look gray on the outside. You can have your fishmonger clean the squid for you, or spend a few minutes doing it yourself. To clean squid, cut off the tentacles just below the eyes, pull out the hard beak, and rinse the tentacles well to remove any grit. Run the back of a large knife along the squid's body, scraping the innards out the open end. Pull or scrape off the remaining gray membrane from the bodies. Rinse well and slice the bodies and tentacles into rings.

Most squid you buy at the fishmonger's has already been frozen and thawed, so I usually get it still frozen and only thaw as much as I need at one time. It defrosts in a few minutes under cool running water.

GERRY HAYDEN, formerly of Amuse, New York

Cavatelli with Braised Duck and Prosciutto Ragout, Sheep's-Milk Ricotta, and Baby Arugula

Even before he married my dear friend Claudia Fleming (the pastry chef whose recipes appear on pages 224 and 257), I was a huge fan of Gerry Hayden. No matter what the venue, from the chichi Aureole on the Upper East Side to the trendy Allison at the Beach in the Hamptons, Gerry's food is always down to earth, yet with a creative twist. In this recipe he uses duck in place of pork for a Bolognese sauce, which gives it a heady, gamy flavor. The only tricky part is finding ground duck, which you can get at a good butcher but not the supermarket. It's worth seeking out. **PREPARATION TIME: 3 HOURS**

SERVES 6

2 tablespoons extra-virgin olive oil

1 large onion, chopped

2 carrots, chopped

2 celery stalks, chopped

5 garlic cloves, minced

Coarse sea salt or kosher salt

1 bottle (750 ml) dry white wine

½ pound pancetta, diced small

½ pound prosciutto, chopped

Freshly ground black pepper

2 pounds ground duck meat (not too lean, see Chef's Tip)

1 quart whole milk

1 can (15 ounces) plum tomatoes

1 tablespoon fresh thyme leaves

1 tablespoon chopped fresh rosemary

1 bay leaf

1 pound fresh cavatelli

4 cups baby arugula

2 cups fresh sheep's-milk ricotta

Grated Parmesan cheese, for serving

CHEF'S TIP Make sure to get the **duck** ground with some of its fat, or it will be too lean for this recipe. I usually use the meat from duck legs, which I don't trim, and that meat-to-fat ratio is perfect. If your butcher wants to use duck breast instead, have him (or her) trim off some but not all of the fat before grinding.

1. In a large, heavy pot over medium heat, warm the oil. Add the onion, carrots, celery, garlic, and a large pinch of salt, and cook, stirring occasionally, until the vegetables are soft and brown, about 20 minutes. If they begin to stick and burn, add a little of the white wine, or a few tablespoons of water, to the pan.

2. In a separate pan over high heat, cook the pancetta and prosciutto until they begin to brown, about 8 minutes. Season with salt and pepper, then use a slotted spoon to transfer the

RECIPE CONTINUES

MELISSA'S TIPS For a more traditional Bolognese, just substitute ground pork or beef or a combination of the two for the **duck.** Or try a pork-less Bolognese: Use duck prosciutto and turkey bacon (you'll need some more olive oil to cook the turkey bacon).

meat to a plate lined with paper towels. Drain off and reserve the fat from the pan. Return the pan to high heat, add the **duck,** and brown well, stirring, for about 8 minutes. If the meat gets too dry, add some of the reserved fat from the pancetta and prosciutto. Return the pancetta and prosciutto to the pan and cook a little more until everything is nice and brown, about 15 minutes.

3. Use a slotted spoon to transfer the meat to the vegetable mixture. Pour the remaining grease out of the meat pan, then pour in about $\frac{1}{4}$ cup of the wine and stir over medium heat, scraping up the bits from the bottom of the pan. Pour the wine from the pan into the meat and vegetables. Add the milk and cook the mixture for about 1 hour, until it reduces and the milk coats the meat. Add the remaining wine, the tomatoes, thyme, rosemary, and bay leaf. Reduce the heat to low and simmer for 1 more hour. Remove the bay leaf.

Bagged baby **arugula** is a great convenience for this recipe (and for those last-minute salads). If you can't find arugula, baby spinach is a fine substitute.

4. Bring a large pot of salted water to a boil. Add the pasta and cook until al dente, about 5 minutes. Drain. In a serving bowl, toss the pasta with the sauce, **arugula,** and ricotta. Serve immediately, garnished with the Parmesan.

JUDY RODGERS, Zuni Cafe, San Francisco

Spaghetti with Preserved Tuna, Lemon Zest, Hot Pepper, Capers, and Olives

Everything Judy Rodgers cooks at Zuni Cafe is impeccable, and so it is with her cookbook, *The Zuni Cafe Cookbook.* In this straightforward but incredibly savory recipe, she combines preserved tuna (i.e., high-quality canned tuna) with hot pepper, capers, olives, and lemon. While preserving the tuna yourself may seem like unnecessary chefiness (and isn't required here), it's actually pretty easy, and the leftovers are excellent in salads, especially with tomatoes in summer. Give it a try. **PREPARATION TIME:** 1 HOUR

SERVES 4 TO 5

¾ cup extra-virgin olive oil

½ tablespoon freshly grated lemon zest

½ teaspoon crushed red pepper flakes, or to taste

½ teaspoon freshly ground black pepper, plus additional to taste

⅛ teaspoon fennel seeds

1 garlic clove, slivered

1 bay leaf

1 tablespoon chopped picholine or other green olives

1 tablespoon capers, drained

10 ounces preserved tuna (recipe follows)

1 tablespoon chopped preserved lemon or limequat, optional (see Melissa's Tips)

1 pound dried spaghetti

¼ cup shredded fresh basil leaves (see Chef's Tips, page 97)

2 tablespoons freshly squeezed lemon juice (from 1 lemon)

Coarse sea salt or kosher salt

MELISSA'S TIPS Judy's original recipe calls for either **olives or capers,** but I like using both. If you prefer, you can omit one and just use the other — simply double the quantity to 2 tablespoons.

The optional **preserved lemon or limequat** in the pasta is what it sounds like: lemon or limequat (a small, yellow-green cross between a lime and a kumquat) preserved in water and salt for about a month. Preserved lemons are a staple in Moroccan kitchens and add a salty-sour citrus flavor. Look for them in specialty food shops, or order them from Kalustyan's (800-352-3451; www.kalustyans.com).

1. In a large skillet over medium heat, warm the oil. Add the lemon zest, red pepper flakes, ½ teaspoon black pepper, fennel seeds, garlic, and bay leaf. Reduce the heat to low and let the flavors infuse for 15 minutes. Stir in the **olives and capers.**

2. Remove the **tuna** from its oil (do not discard the oil) and add the tuna to the skillet. Break the tuna chunks up into smaller pieces with a wooden spoon. Add about 6 tablespoons of the preserving oil and the **preserved lemon or limequat,** if using. Raise the heat to medium-low and warm through.

RECIPE CONTINUES

3. To prepare the pasta, bring a large pot of salted water to a boil. Drop in the pasta, stir once, and cook until al dente. Drain the pasta and add it to the warm tuna mixture. Remove the bay leaf. Add the **basil,** lemon juice, and more of the preserving oil to taste, and adjust the salt and pepper.

Preserved Tuna

PREPARATION TIME: 2¾ TO 3¾ HOURS

¾ to 1 pound fresh tuna

Coarse sea salt or kosher salt

1 tablespoon freshly grated lemon zest

2 bay leaves

1 teaspoon crushed red pepper flakes

¼ teaspoon freshly ground black pepper

2 garlic cloves, slivered

¼ teaspoon fennel seeds

¾ to 1 cup extra-virgin olive oil

1. Cut the tuna into walnut-size chunks and sprinkle evenly with salt. Cover and refrigerate until very cold, 2 to 3 hours.

2. Pat the tuna dry. Pack the chunks into a 2-quart saucepan, distributing the lemon zest, bay leaves, red pepper flakes, black pepper, garlic, and fennel seeds among the pieces. Add olive oil to barely cover. Set over the lowest possible heat and bring to a mere simmer. Don't let the oil boil. Cook uncovered, stirring and turning a few times, for about 30 minutes. The tuna will become hard, but will soften eventually. Leave it to cool in the oil, stirring once or twice, before using.

FORTUNATO NICOTRA, Felidia, New York

Pear and Pecorino Ravioli

In Italian this dish is mellifluously called *cacio pepe e pere*. On the plate, that translates into slightly sweet pear ravioli with melting cheese centers and a buttery, peppery sauce. The recipe is nearly what you'll get at Felidia except that there, Fortunato makes his own pasta. I use wonton wrappers, which, while not a perfect substitute for lovingly prepared homemade dough, are nonetheless a darn good one. PREPARATION TIME: 45 MINUTES

SERVES 6

Coarse sea salt or kosher salt

2 Bartlett pears, peeled, cored, and grated

2 cups (about ½ pound) coarsely grated fresh Pecorino Romano

½ cup (about 2 ounces) plus 1 tablespoon grated aged Pecorino Romano

1½ tablespoons mascarpone

1 package (340 g) wonton wrappers, thawed if frozen

6 tablespoons (¾ stick) unsalted butter

Freshly ground black pepper

CHEF'S TIPS Pecorino is an Italian category of sheep's-milk cheeses made with ewe's milk, formed into curds, and salted and pressed. Fresh Pecorino is aged for between 3 weeks and 2 months and is moister and milder and good for melting; aged Pecorino is aged for up to a year and is drier, crumblier, and more intense. Beyond the salty sheep flavor they share, aged and fresh Pecorino are not similar enough to be used interchangeably. Here they are combined to showcase both aspects of the cheese.

MELISSA'S TIPS Mascarpone, a dense, creamy Italian cheese that's just this side of butter, is the kind of voluptuous dairy product that makes me go weak in the knees. Although you need only a little bit here, leftovers are terrific spread on toast, or tossed with hot pasta and Parmesan cheese.

1. Put a large pot of salted water on to boil.

2. In a bowl, mix together the pears, 2 cups of the fresh **Pecorino** Romano, the aged Pecorino Romano, and the **mascarpone.**

3. Lay out a wonton wrapper on a work surface and place a spoonful of filling in the center. Imagine a line running diagonally through the wrapper and moisten the edges of one of the triangular halves with a bit of water. Fold the wrapper in half diagonally and press down and pinch the edges to seal. Repeat with the remaining wrappers and filling.

4. In a large skillet over medium heat, melt the butter with 1 cup of water.

5. When the large pot of water has reached a rolling **boil,** carefully drop in the ravioli and simmer until the pasta is cooked through, 3 to 4 minutes. Drain and transfer the ravioli to the skillet with the melted butter. If the butter or the ravioli are not piping hot, reheat over a low flame for a minute or so. Transfer the ravioli to a serving platter, garnish with the remaining tablespoon of aged Pecorino and several twists of black pepper, and serve.

CHEF The ravioli can be made up to 1 month in advance and frozen. Freeze them until very firm on a baking tray, then store in the freezer in Ziploc bags or a plastic container. There's no need to defrost before boiling.

MELISSA When **boiling** the ravioli, don't add them all at once if you think it will crowd the pot. Cook them in batches, using a slotted spoon to transfer them to the pan with the butter as they cook.

SUZANNE GOIN, Lucques, Los Angeles

Kabocha Squash Risotto with Radicchio and Parmesan

This is not your average winter-squash risotto. Suzanne achieves an incredibly deep, potent squash flavor by roasting the squash before adding it to the rice. The árbol chile adds a nice kick, and the radicchio a slight bitterness, both of which help keep the dish from falling into the so-rich-and-starchy-I'm-bored-before-I-finish category. I nipped and tucked her recipe slightly, combining steps for a more streamlined technique. You'll relish every bite. **PREPARATION TIME: 45 MINUTES**

SERVES 6

10 ounces peeled kabocha squash, cut into ¹/₂-inch cubes (2 cups cubes)

3 tablespoons extra-virgin olive oil

1 tablespoon plus ¹/₂ teaspoon fresh thyme leaves

Coarse sea salt or kosher salt and freshly ground black pepper

3 cups chicken or vegetable broth, low-sodium if canned

2 tablespoons unsalted butter

1 cup diced onion (1 medium onion)

1 chile de árbol, crumbled with your hands

2 cups Arborio rice

¹/₄ cup white wine

1¹/₂ cups thinly sliced radicchio (¹/₂ medium head)

¹/₄ cup (about 1 ounce) freshly grated Parmesan cheese, preferably Parmigiano-Reggiano

¹/₄ cup chopped fresh flat-leaf parsley

MELISSA'S TIPS Kabocha **squash** has dense, dry, sweet orange flesh that's a little more intense than butternut or acorn. It's a very hard squash, so take care when cutting and peeling it; it may, in fact, feel like you are trying to cut a rock. A firm hand and a sharp knife will prevail, however. One trick is to microwave the squash for a few minutes before cutting it. That will soften the flesh enough to take the knife. Then I usually halve the squash, scoop out the seeds, and cut the flesh into half-moon-shaped slices that I can peel with a paring knife. If you prefer to substitute butternut or acorn squash, they will also be delicious, and they're easier to deal with.

1. Preheat the oven to 425°F. and place a rack on the top shelf.

2. Toss together the **squash,** 2 tablespoons of the oil, ¹/₂ teaspoon of the thyme, ³/₄ teaspoon of salt, and a healthy pinch of black pepper. Spread the squash out in a single layer on a baking sheet (either nonstick or lined with a nonstick liner, if possible) and roast, stirring once or twice, for about 20 minutes or until tender.

3. In a large saucepan, bring the broth and 3 cups of water to a boil. Turn off the heat and set aside.

4. In a large skillet over high heat, add the remaining tablespoon of oil and the butter. When the butter foams, add the onion, **chile,** the remaining tablespoon of thyme, and ¹/₂ teaspoon salt. Sauté until the onion is translucent and sizzling, about 5 minutes. Stir in ¹/₄ cup of the roasted squash, the

Arborio rice, and 1½ teaspoons salt. Sauté for 2 minutes, until the rice is well coated in oil and starting to toast.

5. Add the white wine and stir, scraping the bottom of the pan and stirring as it evaporates. Add ½ cup of the hot broth mixture, stirring constantly. Quickly add another ½ cup of broth and continue to stir and add broth ½ cup at a time as the liquid is absorbed; you probably won't use up all the broth. The **risotto** will take about 15 minutes to cook from the time the wine is added. When the rice is just al dente, add the remaining roasted squash. Stir well to combine and let the risotto come back to a bubble. Continue adding broth as needed.

6. Turn off the heat and quickly stir in the radicchio, Parmesan, and parsley. At this point you can add a little more broth if the rice seems dry. It will absorb more liquid than you might think, although you don't want it to be soupy. Adjust the seasonings to taste, and spoon the risotto into a large serving platter or bowl.

Chile de árbol is a long, fairly hot, dried red chile that's sold in bags in stores that cater to Mexican cooks. You can use any similar **dried red chile,** or just substitute ¼ teaspoon (or more, to taste) crushed red pepper flakes.

CHEF'S TIPS As you cook the **risotto,** adjust the heat up and down to ensure that the mixture is constantly bubbling and quickly absorbing the liquid.

To cut herbs or other leafy vegetables into ribbons (chiffonade, in chef-speak), stack the leaves and roll them into a cigar, then thinly slice the cigar crosswise so the leaves unfurl into strands. If your radicchio is a tight head rather than the loose-leaved kind (this will depend on the variety, and both kinds are fine here), you can just halve it, take out the core, and then thinly slice it. The slices will fall apart into ribbons.

MARCUS SAMUELSSON, Aquavit, New York

Mushroom Risotto with Truffle Tea Foam

I adore Marcus Samuelsson's cooking, in part because he has a culinary vision unlike any other chef out there. I've never left Aquavit thinking, "Been there, done that," because it's always different, both from what he himself has done before, and from what everyone else in town is doing. A good example is his signature foie gras. While most other restaurants in New York City were making seared slabs of foie gras garnished with fruit, Marcus fashioned the liver into a so-called "ganache"—his decadent, oozing version of a terrine. Similarly, while most chefs simply drizzle truffle oil onto mushroom risotto with indiscriminate abandon, Marcus adds his to a green-tea foam, which accents the truffle's earthiness while adding an herbal dimension of its own. It makes a spectacular risotto that no one at your table will have ever seen before. PREPARATION TIME: 1 HOUR

SERVES 8

8 ounces wild or exotic mushrooms, stems removed and reserved, caps roughly chopped (about 2 cups)

1¼ cups chicken broth, low-sodium if canned

3 tablespoons green tea leaves (or the contents of 3 green tea bags)

2 tablespoons unsalted butter

1 teaspoon black (or white) truffle oil (see Melissa's Tips)

2 quarts mushroom or vegetable broth, low-sodium if canned (see Melissa's Tips)

3 tablespoons extra-virgin olive oil

6 shallots, chopped

4 cups Arborio rice

1 cup white wine

Coarse sea salt or kosher salt and freshly ground black pepper

2 tablespoons finely chopped fresh chives

2 tablespoons finely chopped fresh flat-leaf parsley

2 teaspoons fresh thyme leaves

CHEF'S TIPS You can use any wild **mushrooms** in season for this risotto. Some favorites are chanterelles, black trumpets, and morels. Cultivated exotic mushrooms, such as cremini, oyster, and portobello, are easier to find and can be substituted.

MELISSA'S TIPS You can use vegetable **broth** in this recipe, and the risotto will be utterly delicious. But if you want to really go for an intense mushroom flavor, you can easily transform vegetable broth into mushroom broth. All you have to do is simmer about 8 ounces of

1. Prepare the liquid for the foam: In a small saucepan over high heat, combine the **mushroom** stems (not the caps) with the chicken broth and bring to a boil. Keep at a high simmer for 15 minutes, then turn off the heat and strain out the solids. Add the **tea** leaves to the hot broth and steep for 5 minutes. Strain again and stir in the butter and **truffle oil.** Set aside until just before serving.

2. Make the risotto: In a pot, bring the mushroom or vegetable **broth** to a simmer. Turn off the heat, covering the pot to keep the broth very hot.

3. In a large skillet over medium-low heat, warm 1 tablespoon of the olive oil. Add the shallots and sauté until translucent, about 5 minutes. Raise the heat to medium-high, add the rice, and toast for 1 minute. Add the wine and stir, scraping the bottom of the pan and stirring as it evaporates. Add ½ cup of the hot broth mixture, stirring constantly. Quickly add another ½ cup of broth and continue to stir. Add broth ½ cup at a time as the liquid is absorbed; you won't necessarily use up all the broth. Cook until the risotto is al dente, about 15 minutes from the time the wine is added. Season with salt and pepper.

4. In another skillet over medium heat, warm the remaining 2 tablespoons of olive oil. Add the chopped mushroom caps, chives, parsley, and thyme, and sauté for 5 minutes. Season with additional salt and pepper and stir into the finished risotto.

5. Once the risotto is finished, reheat the reserved mushroom and tea mixture, then use an immersion or regular blender to create a foamy texture, like a cappuccino. Season with salt and pepper. Serve the risotto with a dollop of this foam on top.

mushrooms (cremini and shiitake, alone or in combination, are excellent, but white buttons are fine too) with the vegetable broth for about 25 minutes, then strain.

CHEF Green tea is grown in China and Japan, and the leaves are harvested three or four times a year; the first flush, or harvest, in the spring yields the best-quality tea leaves. The leaves are then steamed and dried, but not fermented as they are for black tea. In this recipe, any variety of green tea is fine.

MELISSA Truffle oil is made by infusing either black or white truffles in flavorless oil—or by adding a nasty chemical that approximates the smell of truffles. In the 1990s, the oil was brutally overused by chefs, since it is an economical way to add an ineluctable perfume to otherwise mundane dishes. But if you splurge for the pure stuff (go to a reputable shop and make sure the oil lists truffles as an ingredient) and use it in moderation, truffle oil can add a lusty, compelling note when buying fresh truffles isn't an option (that is, most of the time unless you're shopping on someone else's dime). Buy small bottles, store them in a cool, dark place, and use them before they begin to fade or go rancid.

CHEF The easiest way to time the cooking of this dish is to make the mushroom–tea infusion first, then the risotto, and then reheat the infusion and proceed with the foam.

PATRICK O'CONNELL, Inn at Little Washington, Washington, Virginia

Morel Pizza with Fontina, Asparagus, and Country Ham

Patrick O'Connell's Inn at Little Washington is probably as close to a European inn as you can get in the States, which means you are pampered and cosseted and fed rarefied and elegant cuisine, and all you have to do is make your way from the dining room to your bedroom before passing out in a happy, well-fed slumber. So much better than driving home. Most of Patrick's dishes are on the fussy side, except for this addictive pizza, a signature dish. It's gooier and earthier than Franny's pesto pizza (see page 102), perfect for a winter meal, while the lighter pesto pizza is ideal for summer. **PREPARATION TIME:** 1 ½ HOURS

MAKES 1 LARGE PIZZA; SERVES 4 TO 6

CARAMELIZED SHALLOTS

¼ cup (½ stick) unsalted butter

3 cups sliced shallots (about 14)

Coarse sea salt or kosher salt and freshly ground black pepper

PIZZA

Coarse sea salt or kosher salt

5 asparagus spears, cut on the bias into ¼-inch slices

4 tablespoons extra-virgin olive oil

½ pound fresh morel mushrooms, halved (about 6 cups)

1 garlic clove, finely chopped

1 small shallot, finely chopped

Freshly ground black pepper

½ recipe Basic Pizza Dough (page 104)

Flour, for rolling out the dough

Cornmeal, for dusting the baking sheet

1 cup (about 4 ounces) grated Parmesan cheese

¾ cup (about 3 ounces) grated Fontina cheese

2 very thin slices (about ½ ounce) well-trimmed country ham, cut into strips

CHEF'S TIPS The **caramelized shallots** can be made up to a week ahead.

MELISSA'S TIPS You can use half olive oil and half **butter** for the shallots if you'd rather use less butter.

You need a very hot surface to slide your pizza onto. If you don't have a **pizza stone** you can preheat a heavy baking sheet (or stack two baking pans on top of each other).

1. Caramelize the shallots: In a medium saucepan over medium-high heat, melt the **butter.** Add the shallots and a generous pinch of salt and pepper. Reduce the heat to low and cook, stirring occasionally, for 30 minutes, or until golden brown. Season with more salt and pepper and cool to room temperature.

2. Place a **pizza stone** or heavy baking sheet in the oven and preheat to 450°F.

3. Bring a pot of salted water to a boil and fill a bowl with water and ice. Blanch the asparagus in the boiling water for

1 minute. Drain and immediately transfer them to the ice bath. When cold, drain, pat dry, and set aside.

4. In a large skillet over high heat, warm 2 tablespoons of the olive oil. Add the **mushrooms** and sauté until slightly wilted, about 2 to 4 minutes. Add the garlic and **shallot** and sauté for 1 minute more. Season with salt and pepper and set aside.

CHEF Pizza is not a precise affair—you can substitute onions for the **shallots,** and other **mushrooms** for the morels.

5. To **assemble** the pizza, roll out the **dough** on a floured surface to ⅛ inch thick (any shape is fine). Dust a flat cookie sheet with cornmeal and place the dough on it. Spread the caramelized shallots onto the dough, leaving a ½-inch border. Sprinkle on ½ cup of the Parmesan, followed by the wilted mushrooms and the Fontina. Using a spatula, carefully slide the pizza onto the preheated pizza stone or pan and bake until the crust is crisp and golden, about 15 minutes.

MELISSA Assemble the pizza on a flat cookie sheet or the back of a rimmed baking pan so it will easily slide off onto the hot pizza stone. If you have a pizza peel, use that of course!

Yes, you can substitute purchased pizza **dough,** but you knew that already.

6. Sprinkle the blanched asparagus slices onto the pizza and drizzle them with the remaining 2 tablespoons of olive oil. Return the pizza to the oven to cook until the asparagus is heated through and tender, about 2 minutes more.

7. Remove the pizza from the oven and sprinkle with the **ham** strips and remaining ½ cup of Parmesan. Serve immediately.

CHEF Prosciutto or jamón Serrano can be substituted for the country **ham.**

ANDREW FEINBERG, Franny's, Brooklyn, New York

Green Garlic Pesto, Ricotta, and Mozzarella Pizza

Even if it weren't only a block from my house, and the owners were not as dedicated to seasonal, locally produced food and the environment as they are, Franny's would still be one of my favorite restaurants in the city, simply because the food is exactly what I'm always in the mood for. Andrew Feinberg, the chef and owner (along with his wife, Francine Stephens), made it his goal to perfect pizza. And as far as I'm concerned he has—crackling crust, the right ratio of toppings, and all homemade. Unless you have a fancy brick pizza oven, you probably won't get the same charred, bubbling crust at home (I certainly don't). But don't let that stop you from making this recipe, which is as close to pizza heaven as you can get in a home kitchen. And the extra pesto you'll end up with is sublime on everything from toast to eggs to pasta.

PREPARATION TIME: 1 1/2 HOURS

MAKES 1 LARGE PIZZA; SERVES 4 TO 6

2/3 cup extra-virgin olive oil

1 head of garlic, cloves separated and peeled, or
    1/4 pound green garlic scapes, sliced 1/4 inch
    thick

1 1/4 cups fresh flat-leaf parsley leaves

1 cup fresh mint leaves

1 cup fresh basil leaves

1/2 cup pine nuts

1/2 cup grated Pecorino Romano cheese (about
    2 ounces)

4 anchovy fillets, regular or salt-cured (see
    Chef's Tips)

Coarse sea salt or kosher salt and freshly
    ground black pepper

1/2 recipe Basic Pizza Dough (page 104)

Flour, for rolling out the dough

Cornmeal, for dusting the baking sheet

1/4 pound fresh ricotta (about 1/2 cup)

1/4 pound fresh mozzarella, thinly sliced

MELISSA'S TIPS Green garlic **scapes** are curly shoots (actually, the buds of the garlic plant, which are removed so that the bulbs continue to grow) that look a little like fat, crazy chives and have a fresh garlicky bite that mellows when heated. Look for them at farmers' markets in the spring.

CHEF'S TIPS I use salt-cured **anchovies,** which need to be cleaned. Rinse them well under running cold water. Buy filleted anchovies to save time.

1. In a skillet over medium-high heat, warm 2 tablespoons of the olive oil. Add the garlic cloves or **scapes** and cook until pale golden around the edges, about 5 minutes. Let cool.

2. In a food processor, puree the parsley, mint, basil, pine nuts, Pecorino, and **anchovies** to a paste. Transfer the mixture to a bowl. Using a slotted spoon, add the garlic and its oil to the food processor and pulse until the texture is a very chunky puree. Combine the garlic with the herb mixture and stir in the remaining olive oil. Season with salt and plenty of black pepper.

3. Place a pizza stone or heavy-duty **baking sheet** in the oven and preheat to 450°F.

4. To assemble the pizza, roll out the dough on a floured surface to ⅛ inch thick (any shape is fine). Dust a flat cookie sheet with cornmeal and place the dough on it. Spread a thin layer of pesto onto the dough, leaving a ½-inch border. Top with dollops of **ricotta** and slices of **mozzarella.** Using a spatula, carefully slide the pizza onto the hot stone and bake until the crust is crisp and golden, about 15 minutes. Serve immediately.

MELISSA See the morel pizza recipe, page 100, for pizza **baking** tips

CHEF If you can find it, use sheep's-milk **ricotta,** which has more flavor than cow's-milk cheese. Fresh **mozzarella** is essential here.

MELISSA This unusually delicious pesto (made with parsley, mint, basil, and anchovies) is terrific on pasta and crostini. In fact, for an abbreviated version of this pizza with some of the same flavors, spread a thin layer of pesto on grilled or toasted country bread, then top with fresh ricotta and black pepper. Sliced tomatoes wouldn't be out of place, either.

Basic Pizza Dough

PREPARATION TIME: 15 MINUTES PLUS 1 HOUR RISING AND 10 MINUTES RESTING

MAKES ENOUGH DOUGH FOR 2 LARGE PIZZAS

1 package (2¼ teaspoons) active dry yeast

4¼ cups all-purpose flour, plus additional for kneading

2 tablespoons extra-virgin olive oil

1 tablespoon salt

MELISSA'S TIP If two pizzas aren't on the menu, you can **freeze** half the dough. After dividing it into balls, wrap well in plastic and freeze for up to 3 months. Put it in the refrigerator in the morning to thaw in time for pizza for dinner.

1. In a large mixing bowl, dissolve the yeast in 1½ cups warm water. Whisk in 2¼ cups of the flour and the olive oil. Cover with a damp cloth and set aside to rise in a warm, draft-free place until doubled, about 1 hour, or 4 to 6 hours in the refrigerator.

2. Stir in the remaining 2 cups of flour and the salt. Turn the dough out onto a floured surface and knead for 5 minutes, or until the dough is smooth and elastic. Let the dough rest for 10 minutes before rolling it out. Divide the dough into 2 balls, and either use immediately or **freeze.**

PIZZA DOUGH POINTERS

Although you don't need to do this, at Franny's in Brooklyn, New York (and many other fabulous pizza palaces), Andrew Feinberg lets the dough rise overnight in the fridge. The slower rise results in a more flavorful dough with a slightly better texture. All you have to do to adapt this recipe is to use half the amount of yeast called for, and let the dough rise in the refrigerator for at least 12 hours (longer is okay, too, up to 24 hours). If the dough starts creeping out of its bowl, just press it down to compact it.

Make sure the dough comes to room temperature before you begin stretching it. Cold dough won't stretch out nicely. This may take up to 4 hours if you keep the dough in one large piece in the bowl and the room is chilly (it will take less time in a warm room). If you plan to make the broiled pizzas, the dough will come to room temperature as the oven preheats (see below).

BROILED PIZZA

The pizza making technique in the preceding pages is foolproof, consistent, and will yield addictive and delicious pies, but I couldn't let the chapter close without mentioning another option: broiled pizza.

Andrew Feinberg and I developed this home-kitchen technique when I was writing an article about his clam pizza for *The New York Times*. The story called for him to make the pizza in his apartment kitchen, something he'd never done before (and why would he when his restaurant was only 3 blocks away?). Knowing that he'd never get a home oven hot enough to produce the charred, super crackly crusts he could get in his brick oven at Franny's, our thoughts turned to the hottest part of the stove: the broiler. Riffing on the idea of grilled pizza, we came up with this slightly fussy but very effective method. Follow the directions carefully. You can adapt any pizza recipe for the broiler.

1. Instead of making one pie, you should make three or four small ones so they are easier to handle. Divide the dough into 3 or 4 balls, flatten them into disks, and cover with a clean towel. Let them rest in a cool or at least not-too-warm place while you preheat the oven (the aim is to bring them to room temperature).

2. To make the pizzas, place a pizza stone (or 4 quarry tiles in a square) on the oven rack, either directly under the broiler if the broiler is in the top of your oven, or in the middle of the oven if the broiler unit is separate. Preheat the oven to 550° F (or as high as it will go) for 45 minutes to 1 hour.

3. Flour a pizza peel or rimless cookie sheet, then stretch one of the dough balls into a 12-inch round and lay it on the peel. Top the pizza as desired. Continue to assemble the remaining pizzas while you bake.

4. As they are ready, slide the assembled pies one by one onto the heated stone and bake until the crust is browned on the bottom (use tongs to check), about 4 minutes. Turn the broiler to high and broil the pizza until the top is nicely browned, 30 seconds to 1 minute. If your broiler unit is under the oven, use tongs to transfer the pizza to a cookie sheet and then side it under the broiler.

Fish and Seafood

Basque-Style Striped Bass with
Piperade and Seared Lemon
BILL YOSSES, Joseph's

Parmesan- and Herb-Crusted
Red Snapper with Tomato–Anchovy
Compote
DIDIER VIROT, Aix

Seared Swordfish with Stewed
Sicilian-Style Broccoli Rabe
DAVID PASTERNACK, Esca

Jumbo Lump Crab Cakes with
Lemon Anchovy Tartar Sauce
TODD GRAY, Equinox

Roasted Cod with Brandade Potatoes
CHRISTIAN DELOUVRIER, formerly of
Lespinasse

Miso Black Cod with Roe
ANITA LO, Anissa

Halibut with Pickled Shiitake
Mushrooms and Red Pepper Oil
WYLIE DUFRESNE, WD-50

Five-Spice–Crusted Tuna with
Roasted Carrots and Rutabaga Puree
CHARLIE TROTTER, Charlie Trotter

Slow-Cooked Salmon with Chive Oil
and Apple–Rosemary Puree
DAVID BOULEY, Danube

Fennel-Baked Salmon with
Summer Tomatoes
CORY SCHREIBER, Wildwood

Pastrami-Stuffed Trout with
Green Cabbage, Pickled Blueberries,
and Walnuts
CORNELIUS GALLAGHER, Oceana

Vanilla-Poached Shrimp with
Rhubarb and Pea Tendrils
TERRANCE BRENNAN, Picholine

Sea Scallops "Grenobloise" with
Lemon, Caperberries, and Croutons
KERRY HEFFERNAN, Eleven Madison Park

Crispy Soft-Shell Crab with
Pickled Watermelon, Arugula, and
Feta Salad
MICHELLE BERNSTEIN, formerly of Azul

BILL YOSSES, Joseph's, New York

Basque-Style Striped Bass with Piperade and Seared Lemon

Although most people know Bill Yosses as a pastry chef extraordinaire (after learning his craft in Paris, he spent nearly a decade at Bouley), he's also a genius on the savory side of the kitchen. Like his desserts, his main dishes are seasonally driven and based on clean, simple flavors. In this recipe, he sears lemon-covered fillets of striped bass until the lemons are crisp and brown, becoming like tart potato chips; then he steams the fillets on a bed of orange-zest-and-anchovy–spiked tomatoes and peppers. It's an easy and absolutely stunning way to cook fish that's even better if you can find multicolored heirloom tomatoes.
PREPARATION TIME: 45 MINUTES PLUS 2 HOURS ROASTING

SERVES 4

6 tomatoes, preferably heirloom (the more colors the better), cored, seeded, and coarsely chopped

1 red bell pepper, trimmed, seeded, and coarsely chopped

½ cup plus 1 tablespoon extra-virgin olive oil

3 white anchovies (see Melissa's Tips), coarsely chopped

Freshly grated zest of 1 orange

1 tablespoon drained capers

2 garlic cloves, minced

1 large sprig of fresh thyme

1 large sprig of fresh oregano

Coarse sea salt or kosher salt and freshly ground black pepper

4 striped bass fillets (8 ounces each)

2 lemons, ends trimmed, sliced paper-thin (you will need 16 nice lemon slices)

Chopped fresh basil or flat-leaf parsley, for garnish

MELISSA'S TIPS White **anchovies** marinated in vinegar, called *boquerones* in Spain, are sweeter and milder than the more common salt-cured anchovies. Look for them at specialty food stores or substitute 2 regular anchovies.

CHEF'S TIPS This recipe stars a roasted tomato **sauce** that is very simple to put together, though it does spend 2 hours in the oven. If the timing is more convenient, you can make the sauce up to a day in advance and then reheat it in the pan before adding the fish.

1. Preheat the oven to 275°F. In a 9 by 13-inch baking pan or similar-size gratin dish, toss together the tomatoes, red pepper, ½ cup of the oil, the **anchovies,** orange zest, capers, garlic, thyme, and oregano. Bake for 2 hours. The mixture should break down and look like a chunky **sauce.** If it seems too watery, continue to bake for up to another 30 minutes. Season to taste with salt and pepper.

2. Season the **fish** with a large pinch of salt and pepper. In a medium skillet over medium-high heat, warm the remaining tablespoon of olive oil. Layer 4 of the **lemon slices** on the bottom of the pan so they overlap by about ½ inch (or interlock them, see Melissa's Tips). Cook them until they just begin to turn golden, about 2 minutes. Gently place a fillet, flesh side down, on top of the slices. Cook for about 2 minutes, or until the fish begins to brown but before the lemons burn. Using a spatula, flip the fish so the lemons stay on top of the flesh. If the lemons come off, just rearrange them back on the fish. After the skin side is seared, about 2 minutes, slide the fish onto a plate and repeat with the remaining lemon slices and fillets.

3. Raise the oven temperature to 400°F. Carefully place the fish, lemon side up, on top of the tomatoes and cover the baking dish with foil (use an oven mitt for this; the baking dish will be hot). Bake the fish until the fillets are opaque and cooked to taste, 8 to 10 minutes. Serve the fish garnished with the basil or parsley.

You can use any white-fleshed, firm **fish** in place of the striped bass, such as dorade, halibut, or cod.

MELISSA A mandoline or Japanese Benriner is the perfect tool for quickly and thinly **slicing lemon** rounds, though you can also do this with a good knife. Once sliced, remove the seeds. In this recipe it helps to interlock the lemon slices by cutting along the radius of each slice and then fitting them into one another so that they stay joined when you flip the fish.

DIDIER VIROT, Aix, New York

Parmesan- and Herb-Crusted Red Snapper with Tomato–Anchovy Compote

Aix is a rare thing in the New York City restaurant scene: a truly excellent Upper West Side restaurant. Chef Didier Virot, who worked his way through many of France's 3-star restaurants before ending up in NYC, never lets his cuisine settle into neighborhood-favorite complacency. He is always challenging himself and his cooks to expand their repertoire and try something new. In the inspiration for this dish, he takes rouget, a sweet little red fish from the Mediterranean, and pairs it with correspondingly warm and sunny flavors like tomatoes, olives, and herbs. A crunchy bread-crumb and Parmesan crust provides just the right textural contrast to the tender fish. Because rouget is hard to find in the United States, I substitute red snapper. But if you happen to come across rouget, buy it immediately and use it here. It makes an already marvelous dish that much more interesting. PREPARATION TIME: 30 MINUTES, PLUS 2 HOURS MARINATING

SERVES 6

5 plum tomatoes, cored, each sliced into 8 wedges

½ cup pitted olives, sliced, a combination of green and black works well, or choose one

2 anchovy fillets

2 tablespoons sugar

Pinch of cayenne pepper, plus additional if desired

Coarse sea salt or kosher salt and freshly ground black pepper

12 tablespoons (1½ sticks) unsalted butter, melted

¾ cup panko (see Melissa's Tips, page 25)

6 tablespoons (about 1 ounce) grated Parmesan cheese

¼ teaspoon ground turmeric

5 tablespoons chopped fresh tarragon, plus additional for garnish

5 tablespoons chopped fresh chives, plus additional for garnish

6 red snapper fillets (6 ounces each)

MELISSA'S TIP If you do find rouget, you'll have to reduce the cooking time by a few minutes since the fillets are much smaller than snapper fillets. You'll still want about 6 ounces per person, but this will probably be two fillets, not one.

1. In a large bowl, toss together the tomatoes, olives, anchovies, sugar, cayenne, and salt and pepper to taste. Set aside to marinate for about 2 hours.

2. Put the marinated tomatoes in a saucepan over medium heat and cook until they have softened and begun to melt, about 5 minutes. Use a slotted spoon to transfer the solids to a bowl; discard the liquid.

3. Preheat the broiler. Meanwhile, prepare the crust for the fish: In a bowl, combine the butter, panko, Parmesan, and turmeric. Season with salt and a pinch of cayenne, if desired, then stir in the chopped tarragon and chives.

4. Place the fillets skin side down in a baking dish. Season them with salt and pepper, then coat the tops of the fillets with the bread-crumb mixture. Broil for 8 to 10 minutes, checking on them after about 6 minutes to make sure the bread crumbs are not burning (if they are, either lower the oven rack further from the heat, or finish the fish in a 400°F. oven).

5. Serve the fish on top of the tomatoes, garnished with chopped herbs.

CHEF'S TIP The general rule of thumb for fish is to cook 10 minutes per inch of thickness, but this isn't reliable enough to be your only guide. The main thing is to avoid overcooking (if the flesh begins to flake, it's overcooked!). As soon as the flesh turns from its raw appearance to a pearly opaqueness (make a little slit with a paring knife to check), the fish should come out of the oven.

DAVID PASTERNACK, Esca, New York

Seared Swordfish with Stewed Sicilian-Style Broccoli Rabe

I first met Dave Pasternack when I was in graduate school writing my thesis on chefs. Even back then, before Dave's cooking style crystallized into the Italian-accented, seafood-centric cuisine he's currently famous for at Esca, his greatest love was always the fish. An avid fisherman himself, he spent most of our interviews explaining the difference in texture and flavor of different aquatic species, whether they were on the menu or not. This recipe is a good example of Dave's style. It focuses on the meaty flavor of the swordfish itself, heightened only by a garlicky broccoli rabe. It was simple enough that rather than interrupting it, I merely adjusted it to home-cook–friendly proportions. PREPARATION TIME: 30 MINUTES

SERVES 4

6 tablespoons extra-virgin olive oil

6 large garlic cloves, peeled and lightly smashed with the back of a knife

1 teaspoon crushed red pepper flakes, or to taste

Coarse sea salt or kosher salt and freshly ground black pepper

2 bunches of broccoli rabe (about 2 pounds), leaves removed; thicker stems peeled, cut into 1-inch lengths, and kept separate

1/2 cup dry white wine

1/3 cup pitted black olives, such as kalamata

Freshly squeezed juice of 1 lemon

4 swordfish steaks (8 ounces each, 1 inch thick)

MELISSA'S TIP If the **broccoli rabe** is particularly bitter (taste a leaf to see), add sweet white wine instead of dry, or use the dry wine but add 1 teaspoon of honey.

CHEF'S TIP Swordfish is flavorful and firm, making it ideal for high-heat cooking methods like grilling and searing. For this recipe, you could substitute 1-inch-thick tuna or mahimahi steaks — just make sure your fish is firm and tight-fleshed, with no fishy odor.

1. In a large skillet over medium heat, warm 1 tablespoon of the oil. Add the garlic, red pepper flakes, a large pinch of salt, and a few grinds of black pepper. Cook until fragrant, about 1 1/2 minutes. Add the thicker **broccoli rabe** stems and wine, cover, and cook until half-tender, 5 to 6 minutes.

2. Add the rest of the broccoli rabe and cook, covered, for 6 more minutes, until very tender. Uncover the pan, add the olives, and cook for a few more minutes to evaporate the remaining liquid. Stir in the lemon juice, and season with salt and pepper. Drizzle with another tablespoon of olive oil and set aside to keep warm, or heat gently just before serving.

3. Heat a large skillet over medium-high heat for 2 minutes. Season the **swordfish** with salt and pepper. Drizzle each with 1/2 tablespoon of olive oil per side (4 tablespoons total). Place the fish in the hot skillet and cook for 4 to 6 minutes on each side. Serve immediately, with the broccoli rabe.

Hand-Cut Tuna Tartare with Avocado and Red Radish (PAGE 30)

Shaved Asparagus Salad with Pecans, Baby Greens, and Lemons **(PAGE 50)**

Heirloom Tomato and Watermelon Salad with Sheep's-Milk Ricotta **(PAGE 54)**

Kabocha Squash Risotto
with Radicchio and Parmesan
(PAGE 96)

Mint Postcards with
Spicy Lamb Sausage and
Minted Pea Puree **(PAGE 84)**

Spicy Linguine with Sautéed
Baby Squid and Chorizo
(PAGE 86)

Basque-Style Striped Bass
with Piperade and Seared Lemon
(PAGE 108)

Vanilla-Poached Shrimp with Rhubarb and Pea Tendrils **(PAGE 128)**

Seared Swordfish with Stewed Sicilian-Style Broccoli Rabe **(PAGE 112)**

Crispy Soft-Shell Crab with
Pickled Watermelon, Arugula,
and Feta Salad **(PAGE 132)**

Miso Black Cod with Roe

(PAGE 116)

Seared Duck Breast with Port Wine, Red Plums,
Cucumber, and Scallions (PAGE 148)

Grilled Quail with Tomato, Cucumber, and Farro Salad **(PAGE 152)**

Braised Basque Chicken with Tomatoes and Paprika **(PAGE 138)**

Flatiron Steak Rendang with Spiced Coconut Sauce

(PAGE 159)

Rack of Lamb with a
Cumin and Salt Crust, Lemon,
and Cilantro **(PAGE 173)**

Tagine of Lamb Shanks
with Prunes, Ginger, and
Toasted Almonds **(PAGE 168)**

Spring Vegetables
in an Iron Pot (PAGE 206)

Roasted Pork Chops with
Peaches and Basil (PAGE 184)

Cinnamon Plum Tart
(PAGE 232)

Rosemary Polenta Pound Cake and
Olive Oil Whipped Cream (PAGE 227)

Warm Chocolate Cakes with
Coffee Ice Cream and Cashew Brittle

(PAGE 229)

TODD GRAY, Equinox, Washington, D.C.

Jumbo Lump Crab Cakes with Lemon Anchovy Tartar Sauce

Crab cakes may not seem like they need interrupting, but then again they're also generally bland and dull and usually need something to spice them up. James Beard Award–winning chef Todd Gray's recipe, though simple, is one of those perfectly balanced dishes that also happens to be straightforward and easy. And, frankly, these are the best damn crab cakes I've ever had (no bread or cracker crumbs, please, but Old Bay seasoning and grainy mustard). So I've included it here because it's an archetype. You won't be disappointed. PREPARATION TIME: 30 MINUTES

SERVES 8

TARTAR SAUCE

½ cup mayonnaise

⅓ cup chopped gherkins or cornichons (see Melissa's Tips)

2 chopped anchovies

1 tablespoon chopped capers

2 teaspoons freshly squeezed lemon juice (from ⅓ lemon)

2 teaspoons chopped fresh flat-leaf parsley

2 teaspoons minced shallot (¼ shallot)

Coarse sea salt or kosher salt and freshly ground black pepper

CRAB CAKES

1 pound lump or backfin crabmeat, picked over (see Chef's Tip, page 62)

3 tablespoons mayonnaise

3 tablespoons whole-grain mustard

½ teaspoon Old Bay seasoning (see Melissa's Tips)

Coarse sea salt or kosher salt and freshly ground black pepper

1 tablespoon chopped fresh chives

1 tablespoon extra-virgin olive oil

Lemon wedges, for serving

MELISSA'S TIPS The gherkin is a knobby, diminutive cucumber that, when pickled, is tart, sometimes slightly sweetened, and very crisp. *Cornichon* is the French word, and either is fine here — though the American brands tend to be sweeter while the French are purely sour.

Old Bay is a seafood-friendly blend of spices that includes celery salt, paprika, bay leaves, black and red pepper, ginger, mace, cardamom, and cinnamon. Look for it in the spice aisle of grocery stores or at the fish market.

1. For the tartar sauce, combine all the ingredients and chill until ready to serve.

2. For the crab cakes, fold together all the ingredients except the olive oil and lemon wedges. Gently form 8 patty-shaped cakes. (You can prepare these crab cakes up to 8 hours ahead. Layer the formed cakes between wax paper and refrigerate until ready to fry and serve.)

3. In a nonstick sauté pan over medium heat, warm the olive oil. Fry the cakes until golden brown on both sides and warmed through, about 3 minutes on the first side and 2 to 3 on the second. Serve with lemon wedges and tartar sauce.

CHRISTIAN DELOUVRIER, formerly of Lespinasse, New York

Roasted Cod with Brandade Potatoes

Remember the foam craze, when chefs went wild for pouring various liquids into whipped-cream containers and squeezing out the mousselike result? A fad? Definitely. But unlike other fads such as solid soups and tobacco-flavored desserts, it's not one without merits. Modifying the form of an ingredient can alter its flavor, or at least the experience in the mouth. Transforming something earthbound, heavy, and rustic — such as brandade made with salt cod and potatoes — into an ethereal foam not only changes our perception of what brandade tastes like (in this case, from somewhat fishy and rather salty to airy, milky, and refreshingly saline), it also changes its context. Regular brandade is bistro fare — casual, hearty, and satisfying. Brandade foam is haute cuisine — elegant, refined, and fleeting.

In this recipe, created by Christian Delouvrier while at the late, lamented Lespinasse, both brandade and brandade foam are used to set off a fillet of perfectly cooked, pearly cod. I tweaked the recipe by changing the foam into a foamy sauce. It's easier to make. I also skip the garnish of very thinly sliced black truffles laid over the top of the fish. It doesn't need it, though of course if you have extra truffles lying around, feel free to indulge. PREPARATION TIME: 2 HOURS AND 15 MINUTES, PLUS OVERNIGHT SOAKING

SERVES 4

3 ounces skinless, center-cut salt cod

4 tablespoons (½ stick) unsalted butter, cubed

2 cups whole milk

2 medium Idaho potatoes

6 tablespoons plus 2 teaspoons extra-virgin olive oil

2 garlic cloves, minced

Coarse sea salt or kosher salt

4 skinless cod fillets, 1 inch thick (4 ounces each)

4 slices homemade-style white bread, trimmed into 2 ½-inch rounds

2 cups skim milk

CHEF'S TIP Salt cod should look white in color, with an even, tight texture to the flesh. Pass over any specimens that are brittle, flaky, or gray or yellow. All salt cods have different levels of salinity, so be sure to taste the cod after soaking. If it still tastes unbearably salty, change the water and soak it for another few hours. When it's done, it will taste pleasantly, rather than overly, salted. You need to soak the salt cod in water overnight, so plan ahead.

1. Rinse the **salt cod** under running water and put it in a bowl. Cover with water and refrigerate overnight. Place half the cubed butter in the freezer.

2. Drain the salt cod and rinse well. Place it in a saucepan with the **whole milk** and simmer over low heat for 1 hour. Drain the cod and let cool.

3. Meanwhile, preheat the oven to 400°F. Prick the potatoes all over with a fork and place them in a baking pan. Bake until very tender, 50 to 60 minutes. When the potatoes are cool, peel and lightly crush them with a fork.

4. To **make the brandade,** put the drained salt cod in a food processor with 2 tablespoons of the olive oil and the garlic, and puree. Add ⅓ cup of the crushed **potato** and pulse until the mixture is just smooth, taking care not to over-process. Put half the remaining potatoes in a small saucepan with the unfrozen 2 tablespoons butter. Heat the mixture, stirring gently, until the butter is melted and the potatoes are hot. Mix in the brandade, taste, and add more salt if necessary. Cover and keep warm, or reheat gently before serving (see Melissa's Tips).

5. If you've turned the oven off, preheat it again to 400°F. Brush the fresh cod all over with 2 tablespoons of the olive oil, place on a baking sheet, and sprinkle with salt. Roast the cod until it turns opaque, 7 to 10 minutes.

6. Meanwhile, brush the bread rounds on both sides with 2 tablespoons of the olive oil. Place in one layer on a baking sheet. Bake the bread at the same time as the cod, until toasted, about 7 minutes, turning after 4 minutes.

7. Just before serving, prepare the sauce. Put the skim milk and the remaining 2 teaspoons of olive oil in a small saucepan and bring to a simmer. Add the remaining potatoes, allowing them to warm up if they are cold, then take the pan off the heat. Using an immersion blender or hand-held mixer (or transfer to a standing mixer), whip the mixture, adding the frozen butter cubes gradually. Continue to whip until the mixture is very foamy, about 2 minutes.

8. To **serve,** dab a small amount of the brandade mixture on the bottom of 4 serving plates. Top each dab with a crouton, then spoon the remaining brandade mixture over the croutons. Place the cod fillets on top, and cover the cod with the foamy potato sauce. Serve immediately.

MELISSA'S TIPS Using skim milk in the sauce keeps the texture very light, but be sure to use **whole milk** for cooking the cod, since it will absorb the salt more effectively.

You can **make the brandade** the day before and store it, covered, in the refrigerator. Reheat it gently in the microwave, or in a saucepan over very low heat (stirring constantly).

In a food processor, **potatoes** go from fluffy and mashed to gluey in seconds, so make sure to pulse, rather than process, the brandade mixture.

This dish is supposed to look like a paragon of whiteness, but if it seems too plain-Jane to **serve** to company, feel free to garnish with chopped fresh herbs, the aforementioned black truffles if you should have some, or even coral-colored beads of salmon caviar.

ANITA LO, Anissa, New York

Miso Black Cod with Roe

I simply love Anissa, Anita Lo and Jennifer Scism's understated yet enchanting restaurant in the Village. Unlike many chefs in this book, whose ornate cooking needs toning down, the dishes at Anissa are minimalist and pure, though the techniques can get a little involved. When I asked Anita for this extraordinary miso cod recipe—my absolute favorite on the menu—I wasn't surprised to find that it had way more steps than I was prepared for. To simplify it, I eliminated the dashi broth and a few of the garnishes. But I didn't touch the heart of the dish: the miso marinade for the cod. It's quick to put together in terms of active kitchen time (you'll need just a few minutes to make the marinade), but the fish does require at least two days to cure. It's utterly worth it, and is in fact convenient for a dinner party since all the work is done ahead. Then the fish broils up to its crisp-edged perfection in under 10 minutes. PREPARATION TIME: 25 MINUTES, PLUS 2 TO 3 DAYS CURING

SERVES 4

½ cup mirin

½ cup sake

1 cup sweet white miso (Saikyo)

4 sable fish (black cod) fillets (6 ounces each)

4 scallions, whites and greens separated and thinly sliced

Salmon roe and/or tobiko, for garnish (see Melissa's Tip)

MELISSA'S TIP Tobiko—flying fish roe —are a popular garnish because the small salty eggs have a slight brininess and they retain their pleasing crunch

1. In a saucepan over high heat, combine the mirin and sake and bring to a boil. Simmer for 15 minutes to evaporate the alcohol. Turn off the heat and let cool before whisking in the miso.

2. Arrange the fillets in a shallow dish and coat them liberally with the marinade on both sides. Sprinkle the scallion whites on top of each fillet (save the greens for garnish). Cover the fish tightly, place in the refrigerator and allow to cure for 2 or 3 days.

3. Preheat the broiler and position a rack 5 inches from the heating element. Oil a baking sheet. Wipe the scallions and any excess marinade off the fish fillets and place them on the pan. **Broil** under high heat until the fish is caramelized at the edges and just cooked through in the center, 8 to 10 minutes. Place a fillet on each of 4 plates and top with scallion greens and a heaping teaspoon of salmon roe and/or tobiko.

SAKE AND MIRIN

Sake is a fermented Japanese rice wine that varies greatly according to region of origin and quality. Ask at a good wine shop for a sake that you can also enjoy drinking, or buy cooking sake at an Asian market, which has a lower alcohol content and will be just fine in this sauce.

Mirin is a sweet, sherry-like Japanese rice wine used in cooking to add sweetness and depth of flavor. In recipes where the sauce is broiled, like this one, the mirin helps the sauce caramelize. Cheap shin-mirin is a pale replica that consists of alcohol (usually only about 1 percent alcohol, whereas authentic mirin is closer to 17 percent) and sweeteners, which will sweeten the recipe without adding much flavor. If you can obtain the superior "hon-mirin" imported from Japan, which is amber in color, it is worth the expense (www.asianfoodgrocer.com, 1-877-360-1855).

even when exposed to heat. Look for the orange colored, unflavored kind for this recipe (green tobiko is flavored with wasabi). **Salmon roe** are like deep orange baubles that pop emphatically when you crush them with your tongue. They are both salty and a little slippery and very fun to eat. Look for these at a good fish market or an appetizing or gourmet store. You can use either one, or a combination of the two, for garnish.

CHEF'S TIPS Miso is an aged fermented paste of soybeans and other grains such as barley, rice, or wheat. It is used most commonly as a soup base, but also as a seasoning. There are many different misos available in this country, ranging from the young pale miso with a high proportion of rice in it (usually called sweet white miso), used here, to a dark, aged red-brown paste with more barley in it. The Saikyo miso called for here is made in Kyoto, but any sweet white miso is okay. Buy a fresh (not pasteurized) miso and store it in the refrigerator. Sweet white miso is available at www.asianfoodgrocer.com, 1-877-360-1855.

Don't let the fish get too close to the **broiler** or the sugars in the marinade will burn.

WYLIE DUFRESNE, WD-50, New York

Halibut with Pickled Shiitake Mushrooms and Red Pepper Oil

Interrupting recipes from chefs like Wylie Dufresne is, to me, the most fun and challenging part of this book. A disciple of Spanish chef Ferran Adrià and his restaurant, El Bulli, Wylie makes food that is complex, layered, highly imaginative, and unexpected, and he uses all kinds of nontraditional techniques and equipment to get it that way. My job is to bring his recipe back down to earth without losing the essential qualities that make it specifically and brilliantly Wylie's. For example, here, instead of dehydrating and grinding red peppers for red pepper oil, I use sweet paprika, which is essentially ground red peppers (albeit of another type). In place of making the garnish of dried, crisped halibut skin, I simply cook the fish in a way that crisps the skin to achieve a similar texture. And in lieu of smoking the potatoes before mashing, I just mash them normally, which does remove one layer of flavor but saves a lot of trouble if you don't happen to be well versed in stovetop smoking. But even with my tweaks, this recipe, with its unusual combination of pickled, sweet, and savory flavors and slippery, crisp, and creamy textures, still comes together beautifully and recognizably as Wylie's. **PREPARATION TIME:** 1½ HOURS PLUS AT LEAST 24 HOURS MARINATING

SERVES 4

PICKLED MUSHROOMS

½ cup sugar

4 cups champagne or white-wine vinegar

1 tablespoon cumin seed, toasted (see Chef's Tips, page 57)

1 tablespoon fennel seed, toasted (see Chef's Tips, page 57)

1 tablespoon coriander seed, toasted (see Chef's Tips, page 57)

1 tablespoon coarse sea salt or kosher salt

¼ teaspoon crushed red pepper flakes

1½ cups julienned shiitake mushroom caps

4 shiso leaves or ¼ cup cilantro leaves (see Melissa's Tip)

RED PEPPER OIL

1 tablespoon sweet paprika

½ cup grapeseed or canola oil

FISH AND POTATOES

3 baking potatoes, peeled

Coarse sea salt or kosher salt

4 tablespoons unsalted butter

Cayenne pepper

4 halibut fillets, skin on (7 ounces each)

Freshly chopped tarragon, for garnish

CHEF'S TIPS Plan ahead: the **mushrooms** must marinate for 24 hours.

1. Prepare the **mushrooms:** In a large saucepan over high heat, cook the sugar, swirling the pan occasionally, until it caramelizes and turns a deep amber brown, about 7 minutes. Add 4 cups of water (stand back, the caramel might spit); the vinegar;

cumin, fennel, and coriander seeds; salt; and red pepper flakes. Bring to a boil, then turn off the heat and let steep for 15 to 20 minutes. Place the mushrooms in a bowl and pour the liquid through a strainer over them. Add the **shiso** leaves, cover, and refrigerate for at least 24 hours and up to 1 week.

2. Prepare the red pepper oil: Heat the paprika in a small dry saucepan over high heat for 30 seconds to 1 minute to draw out the flavor. Pour the powder into a bowl and whisk in the oil. Cover and set aside at room temperature for up to 24 hours.

3. Just before serving, prepare the potatoes. Boil them in well salted water until tender, about 20 minutes. Drain and return the potatoes to the pan. Set over low heat and let the potatoes dry out for about 3 minutes, tossing them occasionally. Add 2 tablespoons of the butter and a large pinch of salt and a pinch of cayenne and mash the potatoes with a potato masher or fork until very smooth. Cover to keep warm.

4. Preheat the oven to 400°F. Season the **halibut** with salt and cayenne pepper to taste. In a large, preferably nonstick, oven-proof skillet over medium heat, melt the remaining 2 table-spoons butter and place the halibut skin side down in the pan. Cook until the skin is golden, about 3 minutes. Flip the fillets and place the pan in the oven for 5 minutes. If desired, flash the pan under the broiler for a minute or two (watch carefully so it doesn't burn) to get the skin even crisper.

5. Warm the marinated mushrooms in a saucepan over low heat or in the microwave. Place the mashed potatoes on the plate, with the mushrooms to one side. Sprinkle the chopped tarragon over the mushrooms. Place the fish on top of the potatoes and drizzle the red pepper oil around the plate.

MELISSA'S TIP Shiso is a green leafy herb sometimes called Japanese mint or Japanese basil, though it has a tarter, less minty flavor. I've also seen it referred to as Japanese beefsteak plant or perilla. Look for fresh shiso from summer through fall in Japanese markets, or use cilantro for a different flavor.

CHEF You can substitute cod for the **halibut** in this recipe, since both are firm, white-fleshed fish.

CHARLIE TROTTER, Charlie Trotter, Chicago

Five-Spice–Crusted Tuna with Roasted Carrots and Rutabaga Puree

Charlie Trotter is one of those celebrity chefs who I know only by his reputation and cookbooks rather than personally. That didn't stop me from including him, though I admit to using his cookbooks rather than my own experience as a starting point. I chose this recipe because I was intrigued by the way he coats the fish with the kinds of assertive spices you'd more likely find coating meat or poultry. But given tuna's full, meaty flavor, it works perfectly. The accompaniments—a sweet rutabaga puree that acts like a velvety sauce, and roasted carrots—are edited down and streamlined from a longer list of glazed baby vegetables, but are so outstanding in flavor they can stand alone with the fish. It's a winning dish that tastes like haute cuisine for a lot less effort. PREPARATION TIME: 20 MINUTES, PLUS 50 MINUTES ROASTING TIME

SERVES 4

1 pound (about 6 medium) carrots, peeled and sliced on the bias ½ inch thick

4 tablespoons extra-virgin olive oil

Coarse sea salt or kosher salt and freshly ground black pepper

1 rutabaga, peeled and cut into 1-inch wedges

3 garlic cloves, peeled

½ cup vegetable broth, low-sodium if canned

¼ teaspoon ground cinnamon

¼ teaspoon ground star anise

¼ teaspoon ground cloves

¼ teaspoon ground allspice

¼ teaspoon pink peppercorns, crushed (see Melissa's Tips)

4 tuna steaks (1¼ inches thick, about 6 ounces each)

1 tablespoon grapeseed or canola oil

1½ tablespoons chopped fresh chives

MELISSA'S TIPS Rutabagas look like yellow-tinted overgrown turnips, and they're sweet and rooty tasting. You can substitute 2 medium parsnips for the rutabaga.

CHEF'S TIP For the puree, you want the rutabaga and garlic to roast until tender without getting any color. **Keep them covered** and check halfway through the cooking, adding more broth if necessary to ensure they are in a moist environment.

1. Preheat the oven to 375°F. On a rimmed baking sheet, toss the carrots with 3 tablespoons of the olive oil and salt and pepper. Place the **rutabaga** and garlic in a small ovenproof dish, drizzle with the remaining olive oil, and season with salt and pepper. Add a few teaspoons of vegetable broth and **cover the dish with foil.** Roast the rutabaga and garlic until tender, about 40 minutes, and the carrots until nicely browned, about 50 minutes.

2. Transfer the rutabaga and garlic (not the carrots) to a blender and puree with enough of the remaining broth to make a loose puree. Season with salt and pepper and keep warm, or reheat gently before serving.

3. In a bowl, combine the ground spices and **crushed pink peppercorns.** Season the tuna well with salt and pepper, then sprinkle the spice mix all over the tuna.

4. Heat the grapeseed oil in a large pan over high heat. Add the tuna and sear until golden brown outside and medium inside, about 4 minutes on the first side and 3 minutes on the second side, or longer to taste. Serve the tuna with rutabaga puree and roasted carrots, garnished with the chives.

MELISSA When a recipe calls for **crushed** or coarsely ground spices, if you don't have a mortar and pestle or clean coffee grinder, use the side of a knife or a heavy can or jar.

Pink peppercorns are berries that are unrelated to black pepper, but their sweet, slightly fruity, peppery flavor and shape and size make them comparable. Pink peppercorns get along particularly well with fish like the rosy seared tuna in this recipe, or with red-fleshed poultry like duck.

DAVID BOULEY, Danube, New York

Slow-Cooked Salmon with Chive Oil and Apple–Rosemary Puree

Once you make salmon this way, you'll never want to use another technique. It seems almost too easy: the fish fillets get rubbed with butter, wrapped in plastic, and put into a very low oven for 10 minutes. In that time, the flesh barely firms up and doesn't change color, yet is rendered into something silky and melt-in-your-mouth tender. This is all because of the plastic wrap, which creates a vacuum around the fish, cooking it evenly from the inside out. At Danube, David serves it with several complicated sauces and various garnishes. I've streamlined the dish and chosen the simplest and best accompaniments: a verdant chive oil, sweet apple–rosemary sauce, and fresh horseradish. However, the salmon is an extremely flexible recipe, and you could serve it with just about anything: sautéed wild mushrooms, roasted tomatoes, or even just a shower of fresh herbs.

But before you decide to abandon all the garnishes, make the apple–rosemary puree at least once. I really think it's the hidden jewel of the whole dish. It has incredible flavor from heating fresh rosemary sprigs in brown butter before adding the apples. No matter how many times I make it, I never get tired of the moment when the rosemary hits the butter in the pan and releases its scent; it smells so good you just have to stop for a second and breathe deep. This recipe makes plenty and the leftovers are divine in yogurt or even by itself. PREPARATION TIME: 1 1/2 HOURS

SERVES 4

3 Granny Smith apples, peeled, cored, and thinly sliced

2/3 cup dry white wine

1 tablespoon sugar

1 whole clove

1/2 cinnamon stick

4 tablespoons unsalted butter, softened

1 sprig of fresh rosemary

Fine sea salt and freshly ground black pepper

1 1/4 cups chives (about 1 bunch), cut into 1-inch lengths

1/2 cup grapeseed or canola oil

1 tablespoon freshly squeezed lemon juice (from 1/2 lemon), or to taste

8 skinless wild salmon fillets (3 ounces each)

2-inch knob of fresh horseradish, peeled (optional, see Chef's Tips)

MELISSA'S TIPS You can make both the **chive oil** and **apple–rosemary puree** ahead. The chive oil will last for a week tightly sealed in the refrigerator; bring it to room temperature before using (this will take about 30 minutes). The apple–rosemary puree can be made the day before (refrigerate this, too); gently reheat it.

1. Prepare the **apple–rosemary puree:** Put the apples, wine, sugar, clove, and cinnamon stick in a large saucepan and stir. Cover and cook over medium heat for 10 minutes. Uncover and cook, stirring frequently, until the liquid has been absorbed and the apples are very soft, about 30 more minutes.

2. Meanwhile, melt 2 tablespoons of the butter in a small saucepan over medium heat. Cook without stirring until the white milk solids fall to the bottom of the pan and turn nut-brown, about 5 minutes. Add the rosemary and shake the pan so that the butter foams up around it. Remove from the heat and let steep for at least 5 minutes.

3. When the apples have finished cooking, remove the cinnamon stick and clove and discard. Remove the rosemary from the butter and discard. Place the apple mixture and the melted butter in a food processor or blender and puree until completely smooth. Season with salt and pepper to taste.

4. Place the **chives** in a clean blender and cover with a few tablespoons of the oil. Process until the oil is green, slowly drizzling in the rest of the oil while the motor is running. Season the chive oil with salt, pepper, and lemon juice to taste.

Other herb oils also go well with this dish, if you happen to have a surfeit of fresh herbs around. Use a combination, or substitute dill, cilantro, or basil for the **chives.**

5. To prepare the **salmon,** preheat the oven to 250°F. Season both sides of the fillets with salt and pepper. Spread ½ tablespoon of the butter over each of 2 large ovenproof plates, lay 4 of the fillets on each plate, and top each fillet with more butter (use another ½ tablespoon of butter per plate). Wrap the plates in plastic wrap to form a tight seal. Place on the middle rack in the oven and cook for 10 minutes. The fish will still look raw but will have taken on a silky, firm texture and will be heated through. Season with salt and pepper.

CHEF'S TIPS It's very important to bring the fish to room temperature before cooking; this will take 30 minutes to an hour in a warm kitchen. The **salmon** is at its best served directly after cooking, but you can wrap the fish on the plates and refrigerate them for up to 6 hours before you start cooking.

6. To serve, spoon some of the apple puree in the center of each plate. Arrange 2 salmon fillets over the puree and drizzle the chive oil around the salmon. Grate a dusting of fresh **horseradish** over all, if desired.

If you can't get fresh **horseradish,** it's better to leave it out entirely than to use the vinegary prepared kind sold in jars. (For more on fresh horseradish, see Sidebar, page 167.)

CORY SCHREIBER, Wildwood, Portland, Oregon

Fennel-Baked Salmon with Summer Tomatoes

Wild salmon is one of my favorite types of the fish, and I eat it whenever I can find it, in season (see Melissa's Tip). Since it has such an intense flavor on its own, I don't usually like to do too much to enhance it. Thus James Beard–designated "Best Chef of the Pacific Northwest," Cory Schreiber, has an ideal recipe — just ripe summer tomatoes, herbs, and mayonnaise, either homemade or jarred depending upon your comfort level and timeframe. (If you want to make your own mayo, see the sidebar.) PREPARATION TIME: 45 MINUTES, PLUS 1 HOUR MARINATING TIME

SERVES 4

SALAD

2 tablespoons red wine vinegar

1 teaspoon coriander seeds, toasted and ground (see Chef's Tips, page 57), or 1 teaspoon ground coriander

Coarse sea salt or kosher salt and freshly ground black pepper

¼ cup extra-virgin olive oil

6 ripe tomatoes of any variety (about 4 pounds), halved, cored, and cut into 6 or 8 wedges, depending on their size

1 fennel bulb, trimmed, halved, cored, and thinly sliced crosswise

1 small red onion, thinly sliced

1 carrot, peeled and thinly sliced

¼ cup fresh cilantro leaves

4 cups tender arugula leaves (about 4 ounces), washed and dried

SALMON

4 wild salmon fillets (6 ounces each)

1 tablespoon coarsely ground fennel seeds (see Chef's Tips, page 57)

1 tablespoon grated lemon zest

Coarse sea salt or kosher salt and freshly ground black pepper

2 tablespoons extra-virgin olive oil

Mayonnaise, either homemade or jarred, for serving (optional)

CHEF'S TIP This is a summer recipe, for summer **tomatoes** that are ripe and have as much flavor and fragrance as possible. Though the recipe is great with any ripe tomato that smells like a tomato, the best ones to use are heirloom tomatoes, which are increasingly available at farmers' markets from midsummer through early fall. These tomatoes, from seed varieties that have been around for at least 50 years, hark back to the time before tomatoes were bred for durability, when sweet, interesting flavor and wonderful fragrance and

1. Make the salad dressing: In a small bowl, whisk together the vinegar, coriander, and a generous pinch of salt and pepper. Drizzle in the oil, whisking constantly. Set aside.

2. In a medium bowl, combine the **tomatoes,** fennel, onion, carrot, and cilantro. Toss with the vinaigrette and marinate for 1 hour.

3. Preheat the oven to 325°F. Rub the **salmon** fillets with the fennel seeds, lemon zest, salt, and pepper. Drizzle the olive oil over the fillets and arrange them on a baking sheet. Bake for 15 to 20 minutes, until done to taste. Tent with foil and let rest for 10 minutes.

4. Just before serving, toss the arugula with the dressed vegetables and season with more salt and pepper if necessary. Place a salmon fillet on each of 4 plates. Spoon some of the salad over the top of each fillet and finish with a dollop of mayonnaise if desired.

HOMEMADE MAYONNAISE

1 large egg
1 large egg yolk
¼ teaspoon Dijon mustard, plus additional to taste
1 teaspoon freshly squeezed lemon juice, plus additional to taste
½ teaspoon salt, plus additional to taste
¾ to 1 cup grapeseed oil or extra-virgin olive oil, or a combination

In a blender or food processor, process to combine the egg, egg yolk, and mustard. Add the lemon juice and salt and process for about 2 minutes in a blender or 10 seconds in a food processor. With the motor running, gradually drizzle in the oil, beginning with one drop at a time and increasing the flow to a thin stream when the mixture begins to thicken, until the sauce is the desired thickness. Adjust the salt, lemon juice, and additional mustard to taste. Refrigerate, covered, for up to 2 days.

texture were paramount. Buy a variety of yellow, green, orange, red, and striped heirlooms to really dress up this recipe.

MELISSA'S TIP Like supermarket tomatoes, farmed **salmon** has lost a lot in translation. Wild salmon has a higher oil content, which means the fish has more healthy Omega-3 fatty acids; it's also incomparably better tasting, and it's worth seeking out at good fish markets. Wild Alaskan salmon range from the prized Copper River sockeyes that become available in the late spring to cohos that appear in late summer to the incredible though rare Yukon Kings, which show up briefly in specialty markets in midsummer.

CORNELIUS GALLAGHER, Oceana, New York

Pastrami-Stuffed Trout with Green Cabbage, Pickled Blueberries, and Walnuts

Cornelius Gallagher's recipe for skate stuffed with pastrami and served with cabbage, huckleberries, and a Devonshire cream emulsion is full of restaurant staples like duck fat and beef *jus*. But pared down, it's really just a great recipe for fish with an innovative stuffing of salty pastrami set off by crunchy cabbage and tart blueberries. As long as you can get to a fish counter and a deli counter, you can make this recipe. Using whole trout instead of skate makes the cooking much simpler (skate is one of those testy fish that is tough if undercooked and rubbery if overcooked), as long as you don't mind handling a whole fish.

PREPARATION TIME: 1 HOUR

SERVES 4

¼ cup blueberries

¼ cup champagne or white wine vinegar

7 tablespoons extra-virgin olive oil

1 tablespoon unsalted butter

1 small carrot, peeled and coarsely chopped

1 small celery stalk, coarsely chopped

1½ cups thinly sliced green cabbage

¼ cup walnuts, chopped and toasted (see Sidebar, page 51)

2 tablespoons chopped fresh flat-leaf parsley

1 tablespoon walnut oil, optional (see Chef's Tip)

Coarse sea salt or kosher salt and freshly ground black pepper

1 cup heavy cream

½ cup sour cream

2 tablespoons Dijon mustard

4 whole trout (8 ounces each)

2 ounces thinly sliced pastrami

CHEF'S TIP Look for French **walnut oil** that is a nice amber color—it will have a toasty nut flavor (available at www.zingermans.com, 1-888-636-8162). Store your oil in the fridge and taste and smell before using to make sure it is still fresh and hasn't gone rancid. I use the oil sparingly here, just to back up the walnuts in the cabbage, but you could also leave it out.

1. In a bowl, combine the berries and vinegar and let sit at room temperature for 1 hour.

2. Meanwhile, in a large sauté pan over medium heat, warm 1 tablespoon of the olive oil with the butter. Add the carrot and cook, stirring, for 1 minute. Add the celery and cook, stirring, until the vegetables begin to soften but don't take on any color, about 8 more minutes. Add the cabbage, walnuts, and parsley and continue cooking until the cabbage has wilted, about 5 more minutes. Drizzle in the **walnut oil** if using, season with salt and pepper, and keep warm (or reheat gently before serving).

3. In a saucepan, bring the cream to a boil and simmer until reduced by half, about 5 minutes. Whisk in the sour cream and mustard and keep warm (or gently reheat); don't let it boil.

4. Season the trout with salt and pepper inside and out. Stuff the cavity of each trout with a quarter of the **pastrami.**

5. In a large nonstick skillet over medium-high heat, warm the remaining 6 tablespoons of olive oil until lightly smoking. Place the fish in the pan and cook, sliding the fish in the pan so that the oil surrounds them, until golden on the bottom, about 4 minutes. Flip and cook until golden on the second side, 3 to 4 more minutes.

6. Lay a serving of cabbage in the center of each plate, drizzle the cream sauce around it, then top with a trout. Spoon some of the vinegar-soaked berries over the trout and serve immediately.

MELISSA'S TIP If you've never tackled a 5-inch-thick **pastrami** sandwich at New York's Second Avenue Deli, you may not have fully taken in the beauty of this pink salty-smoky meat. Pastrami makes a mean sandwich, but what exactly is it? It's actually corned (salted) beef that has been smoked to further preserve it. In this recipe, the pastrami functions a little like a smoked pork product, as in the classic bacon-wrapped trout.

Vanilla-Poached Shrimp with Rhubarb and Pea Tendrils

In his elegant recipe, Terrance Brennan, the genius chef of the 3-star Picholine and the more casual Artisanal, uses lobster. I almost kept it that way except that lobster, in my mind, is a special-occasion crustacean. Yet Terrance's gorgeous rhubarb, vanilla brown butter, and pea tendril garnishes are something I'd want to eat more than once or twice a year. So I tried it with shrimp and the results were amazing. It's a straightforward quick-cooking dish that ends up with nuanced, out-of-the-ordinary flavors and a very pretty presentation in shades of pink and green. PREPARATION TIME: 50 MINUTES

SERVES 4 TO 6

COMPOTE

2 pounds rhubarb, trimmed and cut into ½-inch pieces (about 6 cups)

6 tablespoons sugar, plus additional to taste

Freshly squeezed juice of 1 lemon

SHRIMP

1½ pounds extra-large shrimp, peeled and deveined

Coarse sea salt or kosher salt and freshly ground black pepper

½ cup (1 stick) unsalted butter, cut into cubes

½ vanilla pod, split lengthwise and scraped (see Melissa's Tips, pages 260–261)

1 tablespoon aged balsamic vinegar, plus additional to taste

5 cups pea tendrils (about 5 ounces)

CHEF'S TIPS You can make the **compote** 2 days ahead. Store it in the fridge and reheat it gently before serving.

MELISSA'S TIPS Hothouse **rhubarb,** which appears in late winter, has thinner stalks that are more tender and sweet than garden rhubarb, which appears in the spring. Since the degree of tartness can vary a lot, and you don't want to end up with a dessert sauce for your shrimp, the recipe calls for a restrained quantity of sugar—you can always sprinkle in a little more to taste while the compote is still warm.

1. Make the **compote:** In a small saucepan over medium heat, combine the **rhubarb,** sugar, and lemon juice. Cook, stirring occasionally, for about 10 minutes, until the rhubarb melts. Taste and add up to 2 more tablespoons sugar if the rhubarb is very sour. The compote should be on the tart side but not puckering.

2. In a large bowl, toss the **shrimp** with salt and pepper. In a large skillet over medium heat, cook the butter with the vanilla seeds until the milk solids fall to the bottom of the pan and turn deep amber brown, about 5 minutes. Stir in the vinegar. Add the shrimp and sauté until just cooked through, about 5 minutes, stirring occasionally. At the last moment, toss in 4 cups of the **pea tendrils** and cook until just heated through, no more than 1 minute. Taste and add more salt, pepper, and vinegar if desired.

3. To serve, spoon the compote into bowls, arrange the shrimp on top, and spoon the butter sauce over them. Garnish with the remaining cup of pea tendrils.

CHEF You can use this recipe as a general approach to seafood, substituting small medallions of any seafood like crab, lobster, or scallops for the **shrimp.** Taste to be sure the flesh is just cooked through, since the cooking time may vary.

For more information about making brown butter, see Chef's Tip, page 131.

MELISSA Pea tendrils, also sold as pea shoots, are a delicacy that can be found in Chinese vegetable markets. They are the topmost leaves of pea plants, with curling tendrils, soft, small leaves, and crunchy stalks, all of which have a gentle, nutty pea flavor. Other microgreens can be substituted in a pinch.

KERRY HEFFERNAN, Eleven Madison Park, New York

Sea Scallops "Grenobloise" with Lemon, Caperberries, and Croutons

This recipe is based on a classic skate dish that Kerry Heffernan serves at his very classic New York institution, Eleven Madison Park. The traditional recipe for a Grenobloise calls for regular capers, but Kerry cleverly substitutes caperberries, which have a jammier, more luscious texture and fruitier taste. In turn, I substituted scallops for the skate since I think they are easier to find and cook. In any case, it's a marvelous recipe that's timeless—in both senses of the word. PREPARATION TIME: 45 MINUTES

SERVES 4

3 slices homemade-style white bread

2 lemons

4 tablespoons grapeseed or canola oil

2 pounds fresh spinach, stemmed, washed, and spun dry

10 tablespoons unsalted butter, at room temperature

Coarse sea salt or kosher salt and freshly ground black pepper

2 pounds sea scallops

Wondra flour, for dredging

⅓ cup thinly sliced caperberries (see Melissa's Tips)

¼ cup chopped fresh flat-leaf parsley

1. Preheat the oven to 300°F. Cut the bread into ½-inch cubes and spread them in a single layer on a rimmed baking sheet. Toast, tossing halfway through, until crisp and golden, about 15 minutes.

MELISSA'S TIPS Supreme is a French term for a technique that involves removing the juicy sections of a citrus fruit without any of the membrane that surrounds them.

2. Supreme the lemons: Use a serrated knife to slice the top and bottom off each lemon, exposing the fruit. Stand a lemon on its base and cut the rest of the peel off, working with the curve of the fruit, so that the whole lemon is free of all peel, pith, and membrane. Holding the lemon over a bowl to catch the juices, slice the segments free and let them fall into the bowl. Repeat with the other lemon and set aside.

3. In a large sauté pan over high heat, warm 1 tablespoon of the oil. Add half of the spinach along with 1 tablespoon of butter and salt and pepper to taste. Cook until wilted, about 2 minutes. Transfer to a bowl, cover to keep warm, and repeat with the remaining spinach.

4. Season the scallops with salt and pepper and dredge lightly in the **flour.**

5. Add another tablespoon of oil to the pan and place it over high heat. Working in batches, arrange the scallops in a single layer in the pan (do not crowd) and cook until golden brown, about 1½ to 2 minutes per side. Transfer the cooked scallops to a warm plate, tent with foil to keep warm, and repeat with the remaining scallops and oil.

6. Add the remaining butter to the pan and cook, stirring, until the solids separate and the **butter browns,** about 5 minutes. Take the pan off the heat and add the lemon segments with their juice to stop the cooking process. Add the **caperberries,** parsley, croutons, and salt and pepper to taste.

7. To serve, mound some spinach in the center of each plate, arrange the scallops on top, and drizzle the sauce over all.

MELISSA Wondra **flour** is a lower-protein flour that dissolves quickly in liquids and so is often used in gravies. It is sold in canisters in grocery stores and has a light, nonstarchy texture when used as a breading, as it is here for the sautéed scallops.

CHEF'S TIP The **brown butter** in this recipe is made by cooking butter until the liquid in it has evaporated and the milk solids have fallen to the bottom of the pan and browned. The amount of time this process takes will vary depending on the amount of liquid in the butter to begin with. Since the butter will froth as it bubbles, stir the foam so that you can monitor the browning process below. Don't be afraid to let the butter go pretty brown, but be sure to have your liquid on hand to stop the browning as soon as you add it to the pan; the darker the butter gets, the more flavor it will have (as long as it doesn't burn).

MELISSA Caperberries are the round green fruits (and capers are the buds) of a wild bush that grows on the Mediterranean coast. They are sold pickled, in jars, and they have a milder, more mellow flavor than capers. However, a smaller quantity of rinsed, chopped capers is an appropriate substitute.

MICHELLE BERNSTEIN, formerly of Azul, Miami

Crispy Soft-Shell Crab with Pickled Watermelon, Arugula, and Feta Salad

Soft-shell crabs are only intimidating to some home cooks because of having to clean them, which involves, among other things, snipping off their little faces. Luckily, you can avoid this confrontation and have your fishmonger do it for you. Or, if you want to emulate my mother, don't clean them at all — she thinks they're juiciest this way, if you can get over the slightly spongy texture of the gills. In any case, if you haven't already, you should absolutely add soft shells to your repertoire because they fry up in minutes and really need very little embellishment. In this recipe, Michelle Bernstein pairs them with an interesting and offbeat garnish of quickly pickled watermelon and feta cheese, two great counterpoints to the crabs' crispy shell and sweet flesh. PREPARATION TIME: 1 HOUR AND 15 MINUTES, PLUS 20 MINUTES PICKLING

SERVES 4

PICKLED WATERMELON

3 cups seedless (or seeds removed) watermelon flesh, cut into 1 by 1 ¹/₂-inch pieces (from about ¹/₄ small watermelon)

¹/₂ cup red wine vinegar

¹/₄ cup sugar

¹/₈ teaspoon fennel seed

¹/₈ teaspoon pink peppercorns (see Melissa's Tip, page 121)

¹/₈ teaspoon black peppercorns

1 bay leaf

SALAD AND CRABS

6 cups arugula (or watercress)

¹/₂ cup crumbled feta cheese (about 2 ounces)

3 tablespoons extra-virgin olive oil

Coarse sea salt or kosher salt and freshly ground black pepper

1 cup all-purpose flour

8 large soft-shell crabs, cleaned, washed, and patted dry

Grapeseed or canola oil, for pan-frying

CHEF'S TIP If you want to clean soft-shell crabs yourself, lift and fold back the tapering points that are found on each side of the back shell, and remove the spongy substance that lies under them. Turn the crab on its back and, with a pointed knife, remove the small piece at the lower part of the shell (including the eyes), which terminates in a point. Rinse well.

1. Place the watermelon in a shallow bowl. In a medium saucepan over medium heat, combine ¹/₄ cup water with the vinegar, sugar, fennel seed, pink and black peppercorns, and bay leaf. Heat, stirring, until the sugar dissolves, about 2 minutes. Let cool for about 15 minutes, then strain the liquid over the watermelon. Chill the watermelon in the pickling liquid for about 20 minutes, then drain and keep cold until ready to serve. You can keep the drained watermelon in the refrigerator for up to 4 hours.

2. Prepare the salad just before cooking the crabs: In a large bowl, toss the arugula with the feta and olive oil and season with salt and pepper.

3. Place the flour in a bowl. Season each crab with salt and pepper, and dredge it in a little flour. Heat a large, heavy skillet over medium-high heat for 1 to 2 minutes, then fill the pan with about ¼ inch of grapeseed or canola oil. Heat the oil until it shimmers. Add the crabs and fry until golden brown, about 1½ to 2 minutes per side, then transfer them to a plate lined with paper towels. Season again with salt and pepper.

4. To serve, divide the salad among 4 plates and top each salad with 2 crabs. Scatter some watermelon pieces on each plate and serve.

Poultry

Mongolian Barbecued Chicken
with Chinese Eggplant
NORMAN VAN AKEN, Norman's

Braised Basque Chicken with
Tomatoes and Paprika
DANIEL BOULUD, Daniel

Pollo al Forno with Panzanella
JONATHAN WAXMAN, Barbuto

Oven-Poached Poussin in Buttermilk
and Herbs
SHEA GALLANTE, Cru

Chicken with Pancetta,
Oyster Mushrooms, Asparagus,
and Sherry Vinegar
JOHN SCHAEFER, Gramercy Tavern

Duck Confit Salad with
Candied Kumquats, Medjool Dates,
and Pistachios
TRACI DES JARDINS, Jardinière

Seared Duck Breast with
Port Wine, Red Plums, Cucumber,
and Scallions
CYRIL RENAUD, Fleur de Sel

Honey-Glazed Duck with Braised
Red Cabbage and Apples
KURT GUTENBRUNNER, Wallsé

Grilled Quail with Tomato,
Cucumber, and Farro Salad
MARCO CANORA, Hearth

Coffee and Cardamom Spiced Squab
LAURENT GRAS, formerly of Fifth Floor

NORMAN VAN AKEN, Norman's, Coral Gables, Florida

Mongolian Barbecued Chicken with Chinese Eggplant

I took a rather large liberty with this recipe. In Norman Van Aken's original, he uses veal. But I loved the spicy, potent sauce so much that I knew I'd want to eat it often, which with veal can be prohibitive. Luckily, it's perfect on chicken, whose mild flesh readily absorbs all the heady chile and garlic flavors, and broils up with a crisp skin to boot. After I made that swap, I pared down the garnishes to the essentials, skipping various salsas, slaws, and salads. As it is now, the chicken, in its gloriously unctuous sauce, served on a bed of slippery eggplant, is the happy center of attention. If you aren't afraid of starch, add a bowl of rice. PREPARATION TIME: 50 MINUTES, PLUS AT LEAST 6 HOURS MARINATING

SERVES 4 TO 6

CHICKEN AND MARINADE

½ cup sherry vinegar

½ cup peanuts, coarsely chopped, plus
    additional for garnish

⅓ cup soy sauce

⅓ cup Asian (toasted) sesame oil

⅓ cup plum sauce

⅓ cup honey

⅓ cup sriracha (see Melissa's Tips)

¼ cup hoisin sauce

3 tablespoons hot chile oil

2 tablespoons minced shallot

2 tablespoons chopped fresh cilantro leaves,
    plus additional for garnish

1½ tablespoons minced gingerroot

6 garlic cloves, minced

3½ pounds chicken thighs and legs

EGGPLANT

4 Japanese or other small eggplant, trimmed
    and sliced lengthwise ¼ inch thick

2 tablespoons extra-virgin olive oil

Coarse sea salt or kosher salt and freshly
    ground black pepper

CHEF'S TIP If you want to go back to my original recipe and use veal, this amount of **marinade** is enough for six 12-ounce veal chops. Marinate them as directed for the chicken, then grill or broil until done to taste.

1. Make the **marinade:** Combine all of the ingredients except the chicken and mix well. Pour the marinade over the chicken, cover, and refrigerate for 6 to 12 hours.

2. Preheat the broiler or the grill. Remove the **chicken** pieces from the marinade and wipe off any clinging pieces of garlic. Grill or broil the chicken, turning the pieces from time to time, until cooked through, about 25 to 30 minutes.

3. Meanwhile, prepare the eggplant: Brush the slices with olive oil and sprinkle with salt and pepper. If you have room, grill or broil the slices along with the chicken, about 2 minutes per side. Or wait until the chicken is done, then cook the eggplant immediately.

4. Serve the chicken on top of the eggplant, garnished with cilantro and chopped peanuts.

MELISSA'S TIPS Sriracha is a smooth red chile and garlic paste used as a condiment and sauce ingredient in Southeast Asian cooking. Look for it in Asian groceries. If you can't find it, Chinese chile–garlic paste can be substituted.

Since there are few things I love more than crisp **chicken** skin, it would never occur to me to use skinless pieces. But if you'd rather, go right ahead, the recipe works equally well.

DAVID WONDRICH, MIXOLOGIST INTERRUPTED

Don't toss the raspberries from the syrup. They are great over ice cream or in fruit salad.

RED LACQUER PUNCH

Serves 10

Over a low flame, stir together 1 cup turbinado or Demerara sugar, 1/2 cup water and 2/3 cup raspberries until the sugar has melted. Run the resulting syrup through a fine-meshed strainer and let it cool. Juice 8 limes, running the liquid through a fine-meshed strainer.

Combine the lime juice with the raspberry syrup in a large bowl and add 1 bottle 100% agave reposado tequila. Refrigerate. Half an hour or so before you're ready to serve it, slide a large block of ice (this can be purchased or made at home by simply freezing a bowl of water overnight) into the bowl. Just before serving, add a quart of seltzer and garnish with thin wheels of lime and more fresh raspberries.

DANIEL BOULUD, Daniel, New York

Braised Basque Chicken with Tomatoes and Paprika

Although I've known Daniel Boulud for years, he and I didn't really work together until I helped him write his cookbook *Global Braise* (Ecco Books, 2006). Meetings with Daniel Boulud always took place in the sky box—his windowed office suspended above the kitchen. That's Mission Control of the Daniel empire. The books are but a small part of it all, a well-oiled machine that includes the restaurants, television appearances, charity benefits, designing a line of pots and pans and a line of knives, the catering . . . just being in that room made my head spin, and not just because it's high up. Daniel can multitask like no one I know. I've seen him simultaneously talk on his cell phone to Japan, edit a recipe, and notice a sloppy bit of garnishing on the line from twelve feet above. For him, it's all about the details; he and I wrangled over them incessantly for the book—with me wanting to cut corners to make a recipe more home-cook friendly and him wincing at the prospect of, say, not covering a braised chicken dish with a round of parchment paper. Whenever I did win a point in the end, it's because he let me. For this recipe, well, since this is my book, he had no choice. But even he would agree that my shortcut version of his original dish is nearly as delectable. PREPARATION TIME: 40 MINUTES, PLUS 25 TO 30 MINUTES BRAISING

SERVES 6

4 ounces Spanish chorizo, sliced ¼ inch thick (see Melissa's Tip)

3 pounds chicken legs and thighs

Coarse sea salt or kosher salt and freshly ground black pepper

2 red bell peppers, stemmed, seeded, and cut into ½-inch-thick strips

2 small red onions, sliced

6 garlic cloves, thinly sliced

2 large sprigs of fresh thyme

¾ cup dry sherry

1 cup halved cherry tomatoes (or diced plum tomatoes)

2 teaspoons sweet paprika (see Melissa's Tips, page 86)

¾ teaspoon crushed red pepper flakes, or to taste

Thinly sliced fresh basil leaves, for garnish

MELISSA'S TIP Chorizo is a Spanish pork sausage spiced with smoked paprika. The Spanish chorizo called for in this recipe can be eaten as is, with bread and cheese, or used in dishes like paella; Mexican chorizo is raw and has to be cooked before use. High-quality imported Spanish chorizo that is well marbled with fat will have better flavor and will crisp up nicely in the pan, as opposed to the shrink-wrapped kind available in most grocery stores. You

1. Preheat the oven to 350°F. In a large ovenproof sauté pan over medium heat, cook the **chorizo** on both sides until it begins to brown and render its fat, about 5 minutes. Use a slotted spoon to transfer the chorizo to a plate. Season the chicken well with salt and pepper, then brown the chicken pieces in the pan in two batches, for about 10 minutes per batch; transfer the browned chicken to plates lined with paper towels.

2. Pour off all but about 2 tablespoons of the fat from the pan. Add the bell peppers, onions, garlic, and thyme, season

can order this, and other Spanish products, from La Tienda (888-472-1022; *www.tienda.com*).

with salt, and sauté until soft, about 5 minutes. Add the sherry, tomatoes, paprika, and red pepper flakes and simmer for 1 minute, stirring to scrape up the browned bits from the bottom of the pan.

3. Return the chicken and chorizo to the pan, **cover,** and place in the oven until the chicken is cooked through, 25 to 30 minutes, turning the chicken occasionally. Adjust the seasoning, garnish with basil, and serve.

CHEF'S TIP If you don't have a pan with a **cover,** you can cover the pan with a circle of parchment paper, wax paper, or foil. It will work just as well.

JONATHAN WAXMAN, Barbuto, New York

Pollo al Forno with Panzanella

Although I wish I were too young to remember Jams, Jonathan Waxman's seminal American restaurant on the Upper East Side, I'm not. I ate there once when I was in college, and that dinner has stayed with me all these years. The centerpiece of the meal, of course, was Jonathan's justly famous, crisp-skinned, ridiculously tender and flavorful roast chicken, which he's reproduced with some variation at every restaurant he's opened since. Currently, at Barbuto, he goes Italian, pairing the burnished bird with panzanella, a bread and tomato salad. You can vary the garnishes to suit your taste and what's in season, once you master Jonathan's absolutely perfect technique for cooking a chicken. PREPARATION TIME: 1 HOUR 20 MINUTES

SERVES 4

2 chickens (4 pounds each), butterflied (ask your butcher to do this for you, or see Melissa's Tip)

6 tablespoons extra-virgin olive oil, plus additional for brushing the chickens

Coarse sea salt or kosher salt and freshly ground black pepper

4 garlic cloves, minced

¾ pound day-old rustic Italian bread, cut into 1-inch cubes

1½ pounds string beans, trimmed

2 pints cherry tomatoes, halved crosswise

2 small shallots, minced

¼ cup fresh flat-leaf parsley leaves

Freshly squeezed juice of 1 lemon

CHEF'S TIPS If you have access to a good butcher, I think it's worth seeking out organic, free-range, all-natural **chickens** that have never been frozen or plastic wrapped.

MELISSA'S TIP If you prefer, you can butterfly the **chickens** yourself. Rinse and pat them dry. With a good pair of scissors, remove the backbone from each bird. Cut each bird in half and pull out the breastbones. Then proceed with the recipe as directed.

1. Rinse and dry each **chicken.** Place a flat, heavy pan or cutting board on top of the chicken and press down hard to flatten the pieces. Brush the chickens on both sides with olive oil and season well with salt and pepper. Place the chicken skin side up in one or two large cast-iron skillets or a heavy roasting or jelly-roll pan (the lower the sides, the better), and let rest while you prepare the bread salad.

2. Preheat the oven to 375°F. In a large bowl, make a sauce with 3 tablespoons of the olive oil, half of the minced garlic, and salt and pepper. Add the bread cubes and toss to coat evenly. Arrange the bread cubes on a baking tray and toast them in the oven, tossing halfway through, until golden and crunchy, about 10 minutes. Set aside to cool.

3. Raise the oven temperature to 500°F. **Roast** the chicken until the juices run clear when the thigh is pierced, 25 to 30 minutes.

4. Meanwhile, bring a large pot of salted water to a boil. Add the string beans and cook until al dente, about 3 minutes. Drain and run cold water over the beans to cool them, then drain well.

5. When the chicken is cooked, preheat the broiler and broil the chicken until the skin is crisp and burnished, 2 to 3 minutes (watch carefully so it does not burn). Tent with foil until serving time.

6. In a large bowl, toss the bread and blanched beans with the tomatoes, shallots, parsley, lemon juice, the remaining minced garlic, the remaining 3 tablespoons of olive oil, and salt and pepper to taste. Drizzle some of the chicken pan juices over the salad. Serve the chicken with the salad on top.

CHEF I make this recipe in a wood-burning oven (that's what *al forno* means); **roasting** the chicken is a good alternative or, during grilling season, you can grill the chicken over a medium (preferably wood) fire.

SHEA GALLANTE, Cru, New York

Oven-Poached Poussin in Buttermilk and Herbs

If I could afford it, I'd eat at Cru, Shea Gallante's elegant wine-focused restaurant in the Village, about three times a week. I just can't imagine growing tired of Shea's cutting-edge-but-not-annoyingly-creative cuisine, which walks a perfect line between the familiar and something you've never seen before—without crossing over into something you'd never want to see again. For example, in this recipe, he poaches a poussin (or you could use regular chicken) in buttermilk, which sounds like a recipe for bland and boring but in fact is one of the most delightfully tender and flavorful ways to prepare a bird. The slow cooking breaks down the flesh until it's practically spoonable, while the herbs and garlic amply season it. Of all his many garnishes, I've kept only one, carrots in a vivacious carrot- and orange-juice sauce, mostly because I love the way the color pops next to the pale meat on the plate. But if you'd prefer, just skip it. A dark green salad of watercress or arugula will certainly do the trick. PREPARATION TIME: 45 MINUTES, PLUS 2 HOURS MARINATING AND 2 HOURS POACHING

SERVES 8

1 quart buttermilk

1 pint (2 cups) heavy cream

2 garlic cloves, sliced

1 tablespoon chopped fresh tarragon

1 tablespoon fresh thyme leaves

1 tablespoon chopped fresh flat-leaf parsley

Coarse sea salt or kosher salt and freshly ground black pepper

4 poussins (about 1¼ pounds each), halved, or 1 large chicken, quartered (see Chef's and Melissa's Tips)

1 tablespoon honey

1 teaspoon sweet paprika (see Melissa's Tips, page 86)

½ cup freshly squeezed orange juice

1 cup carrot juice, preferably fresh

3 tablespoons plus 1 teaspoon extra-virgin olive oil

1 tablespoon unsalted butter

2 bunches of baby carrots, cut into ½ by 2-inch sticks

1 large parsnip, cut into ½ by 2-inch sticks

1 star anise (see Melissa's Tips, page 000)

Freshly ground nutmeg to taste

CHEF'S TIP Poussins are nothing fancier than baby chickens between four and six weeks old, large enough to feed two people. They are very tender and have a delicate taste. You can also substitute regular chicken, though you may need to increase the cooking time by 15 minutes or so.

1. In a large baking dish, combine the buttermilk, cream, garlic, and fresh herbs (reserving a pinch of thyme for garnish) with 2 teaspoons of salt and generous grindings of pepper. Add the **poussins** or **chicken,** cover, and let marinate in the refrigerator for about 2 hours.

2. Preheat the oven to 200°F. Place the baking dish with the buttermilk and chicken in the oven, uncovered. Cook for about 2 hours, checking, stirring, and turning every 10 to

20 minutes, until the legs are approximately 160°F. (Use a thermometer to make sure the buttermilk never climbs above 180°F.) Remove the pan from the heat, cover, and let rest for 15 minutes.

3. While the chicken is cooking, in a small saucepan over high heat, bring the honey to a boil. When it begins to brown, after a minute or two, add the paprika and then pour in the orange juice immediately. Lower the heat to medium and simmer until the liquid is reduced by half, about 7 minutes. Add the **carrot juice** and reduce by half again, another 15 to 20 minutes. Season with salt and pepper and slowly whisk in 3 tablespoons of the oil. Keep warm.

4. In a skillet over medium-low heat, warm the remaining teaspoon of oil and melt the butter. Add the carrots, parsnip, star anise, a light grating of nutmeg, and a pinch of salt. Cook, stirring and adjusting the heat as necessary to keep the vegetables from browning, until they start to become soft, about 20 minutes. Add the orange–carrot sauce and cook gently over low heat until tender, about 5 more minutes. Keep warm or reheat gently.

5. When the poussin is cooked and has rested, pull the skin off the meat, then pull the meat off the legs and slice the breast. Arrange the meat, carrot mixture, and sauce on warm plates. Garnish with the reserved thyme.

MELISSA'S TIPS If you use one large **chicken** cut into four pieces instead of the poussins, and if your guests are big eaters, feel free to use a few extra legs as well. There will be enough room in the pot.

Unless you have a juicer, pick up some **carrot juice** at a health food store for this recipe (you can order the orange juice there too, if you like, or squeeze your own).

JOHN SCHAEFER, Gramercy Tavern, New York

Chicken with Pancetta, Oyster Mushrooms, Asparagus, and Sherry Vinegar

Behind every good celebrity chef is a good executive chef, and Tom Colicchio at Gramercy Tavern is no exception. Executive chef John Schaefer has both internalized Tom's style of cooking and created his own, which adheres to the restaurant's mission of seasonality, originality, and accessibility. In this dish, John starts with a classic technique—cooking the chicken parts separately, then reuniting them in a quickly made pan sauce using the livers. I've combined several steps and the result is a perfect chicken-for-company recipe: it's elegant and unexpected, and most of the work can be done ahead. PREPARATION TIME: 2 HOURS

SERVES 6

CHICKEN

2 tablespoons extra-virgin olive oil

3 pounds chicken legs

1 onion, diced

1 head of garlic, split in half through the equator

1 carrot, diced

1 celery stalk, diced

3 cups chicken broth, low-sodium if canned

4 boneless chicken breast halves (about 2 pounds) with the skin on (see Melissa's Tips)

Coarse sea salt or kosher salt and freshly ground black pepper

16 thin slices pancetta (about ¹/₃ pound)

SHERRY VINEGAR SAUCE

1 tablespoon extra-virgin olive oil

¹/₂ pound chicken livers

1 shallot, minced

1 garlic clove, minced

1 sprig of fresh thyme

¹/₃ cup sherry vinegar

2 tablespoons unsalted butter

Coarse sea salt or kosher salt and freshly ground black pepper

VEGETABLES

2 tablespoons unsalted butter

1 bunch of asparagus, trimmed and cut into 1-inch pieces (about 1¹/₂ cups)

¹/₂ pound oyster mushrooms

Coarse sea salt or kosher salt and freshly ground black pepper

CHEF'S TIPS This recipe can be replicated using most white-meat poultry, such as guinea hen, capon, or turkey.

1. Make the chicken: Preheat the oven to 325°F. In a large Dutch oven or casserole over high heat, warm the oil. Add the chicken legs, onion, garlic, carrot, and celery, and brown the legs for about 15 minutes, turning to brown all sides. Add the broth (it should come about halfway up the chicken; if it is substantially lower, add more broth or water). Bring to a simmer, cover, and place in the oven until the meat is falling-off-the-bone tender, about 50 minutes.

2. Take the garlic out of the pot and let cool. Transfer the chicken legs to a plate and let cool. Squeeze the garlic flesh out of the skins, mash it in a bowl, and set aside. Pull off all the chicken meat from the bones and reserve. Strain the broth left in the pan, reserving both the broth and the vegetables.

3. Raise the oven temperature to 400°F. Season the chicken breasts generously with salt and pepper and rub them with the garlic puree. Wrap each breast in 4 slices of pancetta and arrange them on a baking sheet. Cook for 9 minutes on each side, then finish under the broiler for about 1 minute per side, to crisp the pancetta. Tent with foil to keep warm.

4. Make the sauce: Heat the tablespoon of olive oil in a small skillet over high heat. Add the livers and brown well on all sides, about 5 minutes. Add the shallot, garlic, and thyme and sauté until translucent, about 4 minutes. Pour in the vinegar and scrape up the browned bits from the bottom of the pan. Add the reserved broth and bring to a boil. Reduce the heat to medium and simmer for 2 minutes, until the livers are cooked through. Transfer to a blender and puree. Strain the sauce through a fine-mesh sieve into a large skillet. Stir in the 2 tablespoons butter and season with salt and pepper.

5. Prepare the **vegetables:** In a skillet over medium-high heat, melt the 2 tablespoons butter. Add the asparagus and cook until it begins to soften, 3 minutes. Add the mushrooms and sauté until soft, 5 minutes longer. Season with salt and pepper.

6. To serve, warm the sauce gently. Add the chicken leg meat and vegetables and warm through. Portion into shallow bowls and place a chicken breast (sliced or whole) on top. Spoon some asparagus and mushrooms on the side.

MELISSA'S TIPS Buying skin-on boneless chicken breasts from the supermarket is nearly impossible, but you can easily find them at a butcher. Or, buy skin-on, bone-in chicken breasts and bone them yourself. It's extremely easy: Just cut the breast down the middle to separate the two halves, then slide a knife between the meat and the bone. It doesn't have to be perfect, so don't worry if it looks a little messy. It will still taste good.

Except for broiling the chicken breasts, which should be done at the last minute, you can make all the components for this dish ahead and then just reheat everything before serving. It's best to cook the chicken breasts within 3 hours of serving, then leave them at room temperature. Slide them under the broiler to warm them up and crisp the skin while you reheat everything else.

CHEF Change the **vegetables** as the seasons change. This recipe works well in the spring, but you can use Brussels sprouts and black trumpet mushrooms in the fall and winter.

TRACI DES JARDINS, Jardinière, San Francisco

Duck Confit Salad with Candied Kumquats, Medjool Dates, and Pistachios

Purchased duck leg confit is probably one of the most brilliant shortcuts in this entire book. No chef worth his or her *fleur de sel* would ever use it because it's not at all economical — for them. But for us home cooks, it's a godsend. First of all, though making duck confit isn't hard, it is one of those stand-in-front-of-the-stove-all-day kinds of endeavors that none of us should enter into lightly. But once you have it on hand, it will keep for weeks in the fridge, and it becomes the building block for all kinds of dishes, including salads and, of course, cassoulet. Buying it isn't cheap, but the vacuum-packed legs you can find at specialty markets or mail-order from D'Artagnan (800-327-8246; www.dartagnan.com) are of excellent quality and will last forever in the freezer (well, at least a year). All you have to do is unwrap it, crisp the skin under the broiler or in a skillet, then use the velvety meat as you please. I particularly love it in salads, where its richness is cut by crisp greens and a sharp vinaigrette. In Traci Des Jardins's version, she adds candied kumquats and dates for a bit of welcome sweetness that works really well with the gamy meat. It's a gorgeous combination that is all the better when you consider how incredibly easy it is to make. PREPARATION TIME: 1 HOUR, PLUS ½ HOUR INFUSING

SERVES 4 TO 6

KUMQUATS

1½ cups sugar

5 slices fresh gingerroot, about ⅛ inch thick

Zest of 1 orange, removed with a vegetable peeler

½ stick cinnamon

1 star anise (see Melissa's Tips, page 35)

2 cups (8 ounces) kumquats, sliced into ⅛-inch rounds

DUCK CONFIT SALAD

3 duck legs confit

2 tablespoons freshly squeezed orange juice

1 tablespoon sherry vinegar

Coarse sea salt or kosher salt and freshly ground black pepper

3 tablespoons extra-virgin olive oil

2 cups arugula, washed and dried

1 head of frisée, washed, dried, and torn

4 pitted Medjool dates, thinly sliced

1 tablespoon diced shallot

¼ cup salted pistachios, toasted (page 51), for garnish

1 tablespoon chopped fresh mint, for garnish

MELISSA'S TIPS The **kumquats** can be dispensed with without too big a disruption to the salad. If you like, substitute orange or tangerine segments, though it's not strictly necessary.

1. Make the **kumquats:** In a saucepan, combine the sugar, ginger, orange zest, cinnamon, and star anise with 1½ cups water. Bring to a boil, stirring until the sugar dissolves. Remove the pan from the heat and let the mixture infuse for 30 minutes.

2. Use a slotted spoon to remove and discard the solids from the syrup. Add the kumquats and bring to a boil. Reduce the heat and simmer for 5 minutes, then let the kumquats cool in the syrup.

3. Make the duck: Preheat the oven to 425°F. Preheat an oven-proof skillet over medium-high heat. Place the **duck legs** skin side down in the skillet and reduce the heat to medium. Cook for 3 to 4 minutes, then place the pan in the oven and cook until the skin is nicely crisped, about 9 minutes. Transfer to a cutting board and let rest.

4. Meanwhile, prepare the vinaigrette. Whisk together the orange juice and vinegar, and season with salt and pepper. Gradually whisk in the olive oil.

5. Cut the duck meat off the bone and slice it. In a large bowl, combine the arugula, frisée, dates, shallot, and about ¼ cup drained kumquats. Toss the salad with enough of the vinaigrette to lightly coat everything. Serve the salad on plates topped with the duck. Garnish with pistachios and mint and drizzle with more vinaigrette, if desired.

If you do decide to use them, the **kumquat** recipe makes extra that will keep for weeks. Just store the kumquats in their syrup in a covered container in the fridge. I love them with yogurt (full-fat, please) for breakfast, though they are also splendid over ice cream or mixed with lemon curd, if you happen to have that on hand.

CHEF'S TIP If you do want to make your own **duck leg** confit, it's not hard: Use duck legs with the thighs attached and rub them all over with kosher salt, pepper, and, if you like, some chopped shallot, garlic, and thyme. Refrigerate, covered, for a day or two. Rub off some of the seasonings and lay the duck snugly in a baking dish. Pour melted duck fat (available from specialty markets and via mail order from D'Artagnan: 800-327-8246; www.dartagnan.com) over the meat to cover (about 1 cup per duck leg). Bake at 225°F. until the duck is falling-off-the-bone tender, 2 or 3 hours. Cool and store in the duck fat for up to several weeks. The fat itself can be strained and used for future cooking—it has great flavor. Try it when you sauté potatoes, shrimp, scallops, and fish.

CYRIL RENAUD, Fleur de Sel, New York

Seared Duck Breast with Port Wine, Red Plums, Cucumber, and Scallions

No matter what the season, at Fleur de Sel, Cyril Renaud's cozy little jewel of a restaurant, there is always some kind of duck on the menu. Cyril is a genius with duck, changing the trappings but always preparing it so that the skin is potato-chip crisp and the meat of the breast ruby red and juicy. In this recipe, he works within the classic duck-with-fruit paradigm, using Chinese red dates instead of the more familiar orange or cherry. I've substituted red plums, which have a similar acidity but are much easier to find. The watercress, scallion, and cucumber garnishes reflect the Asian influence of the dates, but work equally well with plums. It's an unusual—and unusually compelling—way to gild duck breast. **PREPARATION TIME: 1 1/2 HOURS**

SERVES 4

4 teaspoons plus 1 tablespoon extra-virgin olive oil

2 red onions, sliced

1 teaspoon brown sugar

Coarse sea salt or kosher salt and freshly ground black pepper

4 red plums, pitted and coarsely chopped

4 whole Long Island or 3 whole magret duck breasts (see Chef's Tip), split, skin scored into a crosshatch pattern

2 bunches of fresh watercress

1/4 cup port wine

2/3 cup veal or chicken broth, low-sodium if canned

Skin of 1 cucumber, cleaned, carefully removed, and thinly sliced, for garnish

2 scallions, thinly sliced, for garnish

CHEF'S TIP There are a few different **duck** breeds available in the United States, and they vary in flavor and size. I use Long Island, or Pekin, duck breasts here, which are small, tender, and mild, and are therefore ideal for roasting and serving individually. Magret de canard, the richer, more gamy, full-flavored breast from Moulard ducks (a Pekin–Muscovy cross raised for foie gras), is sometimes easier to find, however. If you cannot find Long Island duck breast, use 3 whole magrets de canard to serve 4 people, and increase the roasting time by a few minutes.

1. In a skillet over medium heat, warm 2 teaspoons of the oil. Add the onions, brown sugar, and salt and pepper, and cook until the onions are soft, about 15 minutes. Add the plums and cook until they too are soft, about 10 minutes longer.

2. Preheat the oven to 450°F. Season the **duck** breasts with salt and pepper on both sides. In a large ovenproof skillet over medium-high heat, warm 2 teaspoons of oil. Add the duck breasts, skin side down, and cook until the skin is golden brown and the duck nearly cooked through, about 10 minutes. Place the entire skillet in the oven and roast the duck, without turning, until done to taste (it should be rare, either red or pink, but not cooked through), about 5 to 10 minutes longer. Transfer the breasts to a plate and tent with foil to keep warm. Scoop the fat from the pan and reserve for another use, or discard.

3. Meanwhile, in another skillet over medium heat, warm the remaining 1 tablespoon of the olive oil. Add the watercress and stir as it wilts. When the watercress is soft, stir in the plum mixture. Adjust the seasonings to taste and set aside.

4. In the same pan that you used for the duck, bring the port to a boil and simmer until syrupy, about 3 minutes. Add the broth and cook for 5 minutes more.

5. To serve, spoon the watercress–plum mixture in the middle of each plate. Slice the duck breasts and place the slices on top. Drizzle some sauce over the duck and garnish with the **cucumber skin** and scallions.

MELISSA'S TIPS Scoring the skin on the **duck** allows some of the fat to drain off as you cook it and makes it crisper.

Since you'll be using the **skin of the cucumber,** choose one that has not been coated in wax, or wash it well. Or substitute thinly sliced cucumber—less elegant but easier.

KURT GUTENBRUNNER, Wallsé, New York

Honey-Glazed Duck with Braised Red Cabbage and Apples

This is a simple but supremely elegant recipe for an Austrian roast duck with braised red cabbage. At the charming Wallsé in the West Village, Kurt Gutenbrunner starts with this rather classic recipe, then adds cheffy touches like a *jus* and extra garnishes. But stripped down to its soul, it's an incredibly satisfying, wintry dish that deserves more play than it gets in the United States. In fact, roasting a duck is not much harder than roasting a chicken, though finding one in the supermarket is, I suppose. Still, once you have your duck on hand, all you really need to do is pop it in the oven and baste. Note that while the skin on this duck does get golden and caramelized, it doesn't turn wafer thin and crisp like a Peking duck. But the soft, tasty layer of fat clinging to it more than makes up for the loss of crunch. PREPARATION TIME: 1 HOUR AND 45 MINUTES, PLUS 1½ HOURS ROASTING TIME

SERVES 4

RED CABBAGE

2 tablespoons extra-virgin olive oil

2 tablespoons unsalted butter

3½ tablespoons sugar

1 small onion, sliced

1 head of red cabbage (about 2¼ pounds), finely grated

2 tart apples such as Granny Smith, grated

1 cup dry red wine

1 cup beef broth, low-sodium if canned

3 tablespoons lingonberry jam

Coarse sea salt or kosher salt and freshly ground black pepper

HONEY-GLAZED DUCK

One 6-pound duck, trimmed

3½ tablespoons unsalted butter, softened

1 to 2 cups chicken broth, low-sodium if canned, for basting

1 tablespoon chopped fresh oregano

Coarse sea salt or kosher salt and freshly ground black pepper

2 tart apples such as Granny Smith, quartered

1 orange, cut into 6 wedges

2 small onions, peeled and quartered

1 tablespoon honey

CHEF'S TIP You can prepare the **cabbage** up to 5 days ahead of time and reheat it, or let it simmer while the duck is roasting.

1. Prepare the red **cabbage:** In a large skillet over medium-high heat, cook the oil, 2 tablespoons butter, and sugar, swirling the pan occasionally, until the mixture is a dark caramel color, about 15 minutes.

2. Add the sliced onion and fry until golden, about 7 minutes. Add the cabbage, grated apples, red wine, and beef broth and simmer, partially covered, until the cabbage is soft, about

45 minutes. Stir in the **lingonberry** jam and season with salt and pepper.

3. Prepare the duck: Preheat the oven to 375°F. Rub the outside of the duck with the 3½ tablespoons butter. Place it, breast down, on a rack in a roasting pan. Pour ½ cup of the broth over it, then sprinkle with the oregano and salt and pepper. Stuff the abdominal cavity of the duck with the pieces of apple, orange, and onion.

4. Roast the duck for about 40 minutes, basting repeatedly with the cooking juices. Then very carefully turn it over (use tongs)—the fat will pop. Roast for another 30 minutes, until the meat is nearly cooked through (about 155°F. on an instant-read thermometer), continuing to baste every 10 minutes or so, using more broth if the pan is dry.

5. When the meat is tender, raise the oven temperature to 500°F. Brush the duck skin with the honey, return it to the oven, and roast for another 10 to 15 minutes, turning once, until the skin has turned crisp.

6. Remove the duck from the oven, tent with foil, and let rest for 10 minutes. Discard the apples, onions, and orange from the cavity of the duck, carve it, and serve with the cabbage.

MELISSA'S TIP Lingonberries are a relative of cranberries used often in German, Austrian, and Scandinavian cooking. Lingonberry jam is a tart red preserve similar to cranberry sauce—look for it in stores that stock Scandinavian or Eastern European goods or order it from Far Away Foods (650-344-1013; www.farawayfoods.com).

MARCO CANORA, Hearth, New York

Grilled Quail with Tomato, Cucumber, and Farro Salad

I love serving quail. Although they seem grand in a polish-the-silver way, they are in fact incredibly speedy and easy to cook, and all the preparation is done by the butcher. Once you get your little, partially boned birds home, all you do is marinate and broil them for no longer than it takes to cook a chicken breast, and the result is so much more deluxe. Here, I've adapted Marco Canora's recipe for glazing the birds with balsamic vinegar and serving them with a farro salad. I've kept the recipe pretty true to what he does at Hearth, though I did combine a few steps to save time. But the flavors of the herby, charred quail, paired with the nutty, nubby-grain salad dotted with nuggets of salty pancetta, are entirely his. **PREPARATION TIME: 1 HOUR 15 MINUTES, PLUS 2 TO 4 HOURS MARINATING**

SERVES 6

FARRO SALAD

2 ounces pancetta, diced

1 small yellow onion, diced

1 small carrot, peeled and diced

1 celery stalk, diced

1 sprig of fresh thyme

1 sprig of fresh rosemary

Coarse sea salt or kosher salt and freshly ground black pepper

1½ cups farro, rinsed (see Melissa's Tips, page 214)

1 large tomato, seeded and diced

1 cucumber, peeled, seeded, and diced

½ red onion, finely diced

½ cup chopped fresh basil leaves

6 tablespoons extra-virgin olive oil

2 tablespoons red wine vinegar

QUAIL

6 partially boned quail (see Melissa's Tips)

¾ cup extra-virgin olive oil

¼ cup balsamic vinegar

6 garlic cloves, sliced

1 sprig of fresh thyme, plus additional for garnish

1 sprig of fresh rosemary, plus additional for garnish

Finely grated zest of 1 lemon

Coarse sea salt or kosher salt and freshly ground black pepper

MELISSA'S TIPS You can prepare the farro **salad** through step 1 (the most time-consuming) as much as 2 days ahead and store it in the refrigerator. Just bring it to room temperature, add the remaining ingredients, and toss before serving. Or, start the quail marinating, then prepare the salad and keep it covered at room temperature until serving time.

1. Prepare the **salad:** In a very large skillet or a wide pot over medium-high heat, cook the pancetta until it has released its fat, about 5 minutes. Add the diced yellow onion, carrot, and celery and the thyme, rosemary, and salt and pepper. Cook until the vegetables begin to soften, about 15 minutes. Add 4 cups of water and bring to a boil. Add the farro and simmer for 20 to 25 minutes, until al dente. Drain the excess liquid and remove and discard the thyme and rosemary sprigs. Let cool.

2. Transfer the farro to a serving bowl. Add the tomato, cucumber, red onion, basil, olive oil, and vinegar. Toss well. Adjust the seasonings just before serving (you will likely want to add more salt).

3. Prepare the **quail:** Arrange the quail on a roasting pan. In a small bowl, mix together the remaining ingredients and pour over the quail. Let marinate in the refrigerator for at least 2 hours, or up to overnight.

4. To cook the quail, preheat the broiler or light the grill. Broil or grill at high heat for 6 minutes, turn the birds over, and cook for 6 minutes more, or until **brown and crispy.**

5. Transfer to a platter and serve with the farro salad, garnished with sprigs of thyme and rosemary.

You can buy partially boned **quail** (the rib cage will be removed but not the leg or wing bones) at your butcher. Often they will be frozen, so make sure to plan ahead and thaw them overnight in the fridge.

CHEF'S TIP The sweetness of balsamic vinegar gives these quail a delicious **browned crust.** But since the sugars can easily burn, watch the quail carefully as they cook so that they taste caramelized and are beautifully burnished, not blackened and bitter.

LAURENT GRAS, formerly of Fifth Floor, San Francisco

Coffee and Cardamom Spiced Squab

There was a lot of interrupting necessary for this squab recipe. Award-winning chef Laurent Gras, a master of combining different flavors, textures, and techniques, did not hold back when he created this fragrant dish. He adds to the flavors of coffee and cardamom to also include a foie gras and squab *jus,* an asparagus salad, and what he calls a "palette of flavor," involving a lemon marmalade, a caramelized almond paste, a bitter chocolate milk, and a cocoa cream.

Here, I left but the essence—that is, squab that's quickly but effectively marinated in cardamom-spiced coffee, then brushed with cardamom oil and roasted. The acidity of the coffee and the haunting flavor of the spice nicely underscore the rich, gamy meat of the squab. It's a rather exotic dish for a dinner party, but it's as easy to make as Cornish game hen and just as adorable. PREPARATION TIME: 1 HOUR, PLUS 20 MINUTES MARINATING AND 25 MINUTES ROASTING

SERVES 4 TO 6

½ cup grapeseed oil (see Melissa's Tips)

Seeds from 10 cardamom pods (see Melissa's Tips)

4 squab (1 pound each) (see Melissa's Tips)

4 cups coffee brewed with 15 cardamom pods (see Chef's Tip)

Coarse sea salt or kosher salt

4 tablespoons extra-virgin olive oil

MELISSA'S TIPS Grapeseed oil is a flavorless vegetable oil made from— surprise—grape seeds. It has a pretty high smoking point, so it's good for cooking at high temperatures, and I find it more neutral and lighter than other vegetable oils. Look for it at good groceries or substitute another neutral oil like canola.

To remove the tiny black seeds from the pale **cardamom** pods, pinch each one open with your fingers and release the seeds into a bowl.

1. In a blender, whirl the **grapeseed oil** with the **cardamom** seeds, then strain through a fine-mesh sieve into a small bowl. Set aside.

2. Preheat the oven to 400°F. Place the **squab** in a heavy-duty Ziploc bag or two, depending upon the size of the bags you have, then add the **coffee,** dividing it between the two bags if necessary. Squeeze out all the air and seal the bags. Let sit for 10 minutes, then turn the bags and let rest for another 10 minutes. Pat the squab dry with a towel and place them in a roasting pan.

3. Season the squab with salt, drizzle each with 1 tablespoon of the olive oil, and roast for 25 minutes, flipping the squab after 10 minutes. The meat should still be a little rare; that's okay for squab.

4. When you remove the squab from the oven, brush them all over with the cardamom oil, and preheat the broiler.

5. To finish the dish, broil the squab until the skin turns crisp, about 2 minutes per side. You can serve each guest a whole squab or carve and portion them out.

Squab are baby pigeons (once they can fly, they are called pigeons). These dark-meat birds are tender and intensely flavorful, and they cook quickly. You can often find them in Asian markets. Otherwise, order them from a good butcher, either whole or partially boned, which makes them easier to eat.

CHEF'S TIP Brewing the **coffee** with the cardamom pods mixed in with the grounds gives it just the right, subtle cardamom flavor. This is a nice way to spice up your after-dinner espresso, too.

Meat

Flatiron Steak Rendang with
Spiced Coconut Sauce
ZAK PELACCIO, 5 Ninth

Red Wine–Braised Beef Short Ribs
DANIEL BOULUD, Daniel

Wine-Poached Filet Mignon
with Aromatics
GUIDO HAVERKOCK, Ristorante Castello Banfi

Filet Mignon Pot au Feu with
Horseradish Cream
DAN SILVERMAN, Lever House

Tagine of Lamb Shanks with Prunes,
Ginger, and Toasted Almonds
ANDREW CARMELLINI, formerly of Café Boulud

Rack of Lamb with a Cumin and
Salt Crust, Lemon, and Cilantro
DAVID WALTUCK, Chanterelle

Fennel-Crusted Lamb Loin
with Vinegar Sauce
SCOTT CONANT, L'Impero and Alto

Roasted Pork Loin with Juniper
and Herbs
SARA JENKINS, formerly of 50 Carmine

Citrus-Braised Pork Shank with
Bread-Crumb Gremolata
TOM DOUGLAS, Dahlia Lounge

Roasted Pork Chops with Peaches
and Basil
CHRIS DOUGLASS, Icarus

Spicy Pork Ribs with Garlic and
Tomatoes
FRANK PROTO, Landmarc

Braised Pork Belly with Red
Cabbage–Parsley Salad
PAUL KAHAN, Blackbird

Dolcetto-Braised Veal Cheeks with
Porcini Mushrooms
SCOTT BRYANT, Veritas

Veal Ricotta Meatballs
AKHTAR NAWAB, Craftbar

Venison Loin Adobada with Chipotle
Black Beans
JANOS WILDER, Janos

Crispy Sweetbreads with Capers
and Green Beans
MARC MURPHY, Landmarc

ZAK PELACCIO, 5 Ninth, New York

Flatiron Steak Rendang with Spiced Coconut Sauce

When I first met Zak Pelaccio, he was cooking at the Chicken Bone Café in hipster central—Williamsburg, Brooklyn. His menu, which he characterized as "Brooklyn eclectic," included things like Vietnamese sandwiches (with pâté, pickles, and pork roast) and locally made brioche stuffed with gelato. Since then, he's moved to Manhattan's Meatpacking District to cook at 5 Ninth. But other than the name (*Brooklyn eclectic* is no longer apropos), nothing about his quirky and compelling style has changed, thank goodness. This classic coconut curry, like much of his repertoire, was inspired by a trip he took to Indonesia. I've cut out the turmeric vegetables he serves with it and adapted the sauce slightly, but the end result tastes pretty close to his original—which is spicy, fragrant, rich, and gingery. The sauce is terrific on the steak, but if you are like me, you'll want to spoon it on top of everything within reach. Rice works particularly well.

PREPARATION TIME: 2 HOURS

SERVES 6

RENDANG SAUCE

- **1 tablespoon coriander seed, toasted (see Chef's Tips, page 57)**
- **1 teaspoon black peppercorns, toasted (see Chef's Tips, page 57)**
- **5 Thai bird or jalapeño chiles (see Melissa's Tips), minced**
- **4 garlic cloves, minced**
- **One 2-inch piece fresh gingerroot, minced**
- **1 stalk lemongrass, chopped**
- **1 tablespoon ground turmeric**
- **2 tablespoons grapeseed or canola oil**
- **2⅔ cups (1½ cans) coconut milk**
- **4 kaffir lime leaves, torn (see Melissa's Tips)**

Coarse sea salt or kosher salt

Freshly squeezed lime juice, to taste

STEAK

- **1 tablespoon extra-virgin olive oil**
- **2 pounds flatiron or rib-eye steak**
- **Coarse sea salt or kosher salt and freshly ground black pepper**
- **4 garlic cloves, peeled and left whole**
- **2 tablespoons unsalted butter**
- **1 cup grated unsweetened coconut, toasted (see Melissa's Tips), for garnish**
- **2 kaffir lime leaves, thinly sliced, for garnish**

MELISSA'S TIPS Shaped like a skinny jalapeño, the Thai bird **chile** is a hottie. It is available fresh in green or red, and its flavor is similar to that of fresh árbol or cayenne peppers. Two less hot but more common substitutes that work here are serrano and jalapeño peppers. Look for fresh chiles that are glossy and tight-skinned. Always wear rubber

1. Make the rendang sauce: With a mortar and pestle or using a food processor, grind together the toasted coriander and black pepper. Add the **chiles,** garlic, ginger, lemongrass, and turmeric, and pound or process to a paste.

2. In a skillet over high heat, warm the grapeseed oil. Add the rendang paste and cook until aromatic, about 5 minutes. Add

RECIPE CONTINUES

gloves when handling them, and wash the knife and cutting board afterward, since potent chile juices will spread like wildfire.

Kaffir **lime leaves** are used in Southeast Asian cooking, where their fragrant citrus flavor is infused into sauces, broths, and stews. Look for the fresh leaves, which have much more flavor than dried or frozen ones, at Asian specialty stores. Or do like I do, and keep a kaffir lime tree in a pot in a sunny spot (but watch out for its thorns—mine attacks passersby!).

CHEF'S TIPS Rib eye is an excellent, albeit more expensive, alternative to flatiron **steak,** but it's easier to find.

MELISSA To prepare the **coconut** flakes for the garnish, toast them in a dry skillet over medium heat for a minute or two, stirring constantly, then transfer them immediately to a plate to cool. Be sure to use unsweetened coconut flakes.

CHEF This dish goes nicely with plain jasmine rice. I always rinse my rice in cold water three times to remove the excess starch. I also prefer to use a rice cooker, which not only frees up the stovetop but also cooks rice more evenly and gently and keeps it warm until ready to serve.

the coconut milk and 4 **lime leaves** and bring to a boil. Reduce the heat to medium-low and simmer for 1 hour.

3. Pass the sauce through a fine-mesh strainer, pushing vigorously to extract all the flavor, and season to taste with salt and lime juice. The sauce can be made ahead and reserved in the refrigerator for up to 3 days.

4. Make the **steak:** Preheat the oven to 400°F. In an ovenproof skillet over high heat, warm the olive oil. Season the steak all over with salt and pepper. Place the steak in the pan and sear it well, about 3 minutes per side. Transfer the entire pan to the oven and cook for 4 to 8 minutes, until done to taste. Remove the pan from the oven, add the garlic and butter to the pan, and baste the steak. Let the meat rest for 5 minutes before slicing.

5. To serve, reheat the sauce on the stove over low heat or in the microwave. Slice the steak and spoon some sauce on top. Garnish with the toasted **coconut** and the 2 lime leaves.

DANIEL BOULUD, Daniel, New York

Red Wine–Braised Beef Short Ribs

Daniel Boulud is a chef who loves to braise, especially rich, fatty cuts of meat like short ribs. At Daniel, this substantial dish is a cold-weather mainstay, which he pairs with a roster of varying garnishes including anything from marrow to porcini to a mustard, red wine, and beef *jus* and glazed celery. My minimalist, ungarnished version is no less hearty but much simpler to make. I like it served on top of mashed potatoes or buttered egg noodles. But if you wanted to go all out, a scattering of sautéed wild mushrooms would not be out of place. PREPARATION TIME: 1½ HOURS PLUS 2½ HOURS BRAISING

SERVES 8

3 bottles dry red wine (see Melissa's Tip, page 164)

2 tablespoons vegetable oil

8 short ribs (about 8 pounds), trimmed of excess fat

Coarse sea salt or kosher salt

1 teaspoon whole black peppercorns, crushed

2 tablespoons all-purpose flour, for dredging

10 garlic cloves, peeled and left whole

8 shallots, trimmed and halved

2 carrots, peeled and cut into 1-inch lengths

2 celery stalks, cut into 1-inch lengths

1 medium leek, white and light green parts only, coarsely chopped

6 sprigs of fresh flat-leaf parsley

2 sprigs of fresh thyme

2 bay leaves

2 tablespoons tomato paste (see Melissa's Tips)

3 quarts beef broth, low-sodium if canned

Freshly ground white pepper

MELISSA'S TIPS This recipe begins with a little pyrotechnics, to speed the evaporation of the alcohol in the wine by lighting it on fire. Don't worry: the flames will be tame and contained in the pot—they'll die out on their own.

1. In a large saucepan over medium heat, warm the wine. When the wine is hot, stand back and carefully set it aflame with a long match. Let the flames die out, then increase the heat and bring the wine to a boil. Boil until it is reduced by about half (you'll be left with about 5 cups), about 20 minutes, then remove from the heat.

2. Position a rack in the middle of the oven and preheat to 350°F.

3. In a Dutch oven or large flame-proof casserole over medium-high heat, warm the oil. Season the ribs all over with salt and the crushed pepper. Dust half of the ribs with 1 tablespoon of flour. Slip the ribs into the hot oil and sear for

RECIPE CONTINUES

4 to 5 minutes per side, until well browned. Transfer the browned ribs to a plate and repeat with the remaining ribs.

4. Spoon out all but 1 tablespoon of fat from the pot, lower the heat to medium, and add all the vegetables and herbs. Sauté the vegetables until they are lightly browned, 5 to 7 minutes. Stir in the **tomato paste** and cook for 1 minute.

5. Add the reduced wine, browned ribs, and broth to the pot. Bring to a boil, cover the pot tightly, and place it in the oven. **Braise** for 2½ hours, or until the ribs are tender enough to be easily pierced with a fork. Every 30 minutes or so, lift the lid and skim off any fat that has risen to the top. (You can stop cooking at this point, store in the refrigerator overnight, and, the next day, skim off the fat, and reheat before continuing.)

6. Carefully transfer the meat to a warm serving platter and cover with foil to keep warm. Place the pan over high heat and boil until the liquid thickens and reduces to a nice sauce-like consistency, about 10 minutes. Season with salt and freshly ground white pepper and pass through a fine-mesh strainer, discarding the solids. Pour the sauce over the ribs and serve immediately. (Alternatively, the ribs and sauce can be combined and kept covered in the refrigerator for 2 to 3 days. To serve, reheat gently, basting frequently, on top of the stove or in a 350°F. oven.)

MELISSA Whenever you add **tomato paste** to a recipe, give it a little bit of a sauté before you add more liquid to the pan. Stirring it over direct heat for a minute (until it just begins to deepen in color) will mellow the tinny, raw flavor and impart a slightly caramelized richness. Have your liquid ready to add, and do so in time to keep the tomato paste from darkening and burning, or it will become bitter.

CHEF'S TIP These ribs are cooked the way I had them growing up in France, by starting with a traditional base of aromatics and fresh herbs and slowly **braising** the meat until tender. The success of this dish depends on browning the meat well at the start and diligently skimming off the fat that rises to the surface throughout the braising time.

GUIDO HAVERKOCK, Ristorante Castello Banfi, Montalcino, Italy

Wine-Poached Filet Mignon with Aromatics

This is the only recipe in the book from a European chef still living in Europe (it's slightly harder to interrupt a chef whose first language isn't English and who lives thousands of miles away). At its soul is a very simple technique that involves poaching tender filet mignon in plenty of red wine (the venerable Banfi estate, producers of Brunello and other wines, certainly has plenty on hand) and aromatics. The meat is taken out of the pot when it's still rosy inside, and the wine is reduced further, making a heady sauce. Of course Guido's original dish includes a veal demi-glace and a caramel as the base of the sauce, and black truffles on top. But honestly, it doesn't need the bells and whistles. Serve this lovely dish with your favorite special-occasion red wine; it doesn't have to be the same wine you used for cooking (see Melissa's Tip).
PREPARATION TIME: 45 MINUTES, PLUS 45 MINUTES INFUSING

SERVES 4

3 bottles dry red wine (see Melissa's Tip)

2 celery stalks, coarsely chopped

2 carrots, peeled and coarsely chopped

1 large onion, coarsely chopped

4 garlic cloves, coarsely chopped

2 sprigs of fresh thyme

2 sprigs of fresh rosemary

1 bay leaf

1 teaspoon black peppercorns

4 filet mignons (about 1 ½ inches thick)

Coarse sea salt or kosher salt

1 tablespoon extra-virgin olive oil

4 tablespoons (½ stick) unsalted butter, chilled and cubed

3 tablespoons all-purpose flour

Freshly ground black pepper

MELISSA'S TIP The oft-repeated chestnut about not cooking with any **wine** you wouldn't drink is not really the most practical advice for, say, a person who likes to drink only grand cru Burgundy, nor for a recipe like this one, in which 3 bottles of wine are used as a poaching liquid. A recipe like this is actually a good place to use that tacky bottle of red someone brought to your last party, along with a bottle or two of decent table wine. As long as it's dry and red, it will be fine here.

1. In a large, nonreactive pot, bring the **wine** to a boil over high heat. Boil until reduced by half, about 25 minutes.

2. Add the celery, carrots, onion, garlic, thyme, rosemary, bay leaf, and peppercorns. Boil for 5 more minutes. Turn off the heat, cover, and let infuse for 30 minutes. Strain out the solids.

3. Bring the wine back to a simmer. Warm a skillet over medium-high heat for a few minutes. Season the steaks all over with a generous amount of salt. Add the olive oil to the preheated skillet and sear the steaks in the oil, just until browned on all sides, about 3 minutes total. Use tongs to transfer the steaks to the simmering wine, turn the heat off, and let infuse, covered, until done to taste, 12 to 14 minutes for medium-rare. Reserve the skillet.

4. While the steaks are infusing, use your hands to mash together the butter and flour into a paste. Place the skillet over medium-high heat and add 1 cup of the strained wine; simmer until reduced by half, about 5 minutes. Reduce the heat to medium-low and whisk in the butter–flour paste a little at a time, whisking until each piece has been incorporated before adding another. Simmer for a minute or two after all the butter paste is added. Season the sauce with salt and pepper. Slice the steaks and serve them with the red-wine pan sauce.

CHEF'S TIPS You can also use filet mignon of veal for this recipe—veal has a slightly milder flavor that will absorb the wine and aromatics even more readily.

After poaching, you can freeze and reuse the strained cooking wine one more time. Just add a little bit of fresh wine, simmer it for a few minutes, then add new vegetables.

Olive Oil Mashed Potatoes

Guido likes to serve these filets over olive oil–enriched mashed potatoes. Use the best olive oil you can find. PREPARATION TIME: 20 MINUTES

SERVES 4

3 Russet potatoes, peeled and quartered
Coarse sea salt or kosher salt

¼ cup extra-virgin olive oil
Freshly ground black pepper

Boil the potatoes in salted water until tender, about 15 minutes. Drain and return the potatoes to the pan. Set over low heat and let the potatoes dry out for about 3 minutes, tossing them occasionally. Add the olive oil and a pinch of salt and pepper, and mash the potatoes with a potato masher or fork until very smooth.

DAN SILVERMAN, Lever House, New York

Filet Mignon Pot au Feu with Horseradish Cream

Dan Silverman, the executive chef at Lever House, is a scholarly, adventuresome chef, the kind whose bookshelves buckle under the weight of first-edition and obscure cookbooks. Need a recipe for turtle soup or deviled duck kidneys or a medieval lamb preparation with fifty spices? Dan's your man.

So when Dan and his wife, Susan Gross, invited me over for dinner I was prepared for something out of the ordinary. I wasn't disappointed. Simmering on the stove, fragrant steam fogging the windows, was an authentic *bollito misto*, a stockpot of homemade broth filled with bobbing meats: ridiculously tender chicken and boneless short ribs and, as a centerpiece, a whole cow's tongue, velvety and soft when sliced. A pungent fresh horseradish cream sauce was the accompaniment, along with ladlefuls of broth and coarse sea salt for sprinkling. Not your average meal; I still salivate when I think of it.

For this book, I wanted a recipe that would reflect Dan's unique sensibility and refer to that memorable meal, but something that was simpler and less obscure. (Tongue is risky dinner-party fare; you really need to be secure in your friendships before attempting it.) He gave me the recipe below. It's every bit as compelling as the original *bollito misto* and more elegant, thanks to the filet mignon. You can serve it as it is—with a pristine garnish of good olive oil, a sprinkle of coarse sea salt, and some chopped leafy herbs. Or try it with the fresh horseradish sauce (opposite) that recalls Dan's original dinner, though without the tongue. PREPARATION TIME: 2 HOURS AND 45 MINUTES

SERVES 6

4 teaspoons extra-virgin olive oil, plus additional for drizzling

2 large onions, peeled and halved

6 cups beef broth, low-sodium if canned

4 pounds chicken wings, necks, back, feet, or other scrap parts

4 celery stalks, cut into 1-inch lengths

3 turnips, peeled and cut into 1-inch pieces

3 leeks, white part only, cleaned and sliced

2 carrots, peeled and cut into 1-inch lengths

2 tomatoes, diced

2 garlic cloves, smashed and peeled

1 tablespoon whole black peppercorns

2 sprigs of fresh thyme

2 sprigs of fresh flat-leaf parsley

2 star anise (see Melissa's Tips, page 35)

1 whole clove

1 bay leaf

Coarse sea salt or kosher salt and freshly ground black pepper

6 filet mignon steaks (about 1¼ inches thick)

Fleur de sel (or coarse sea salt), for serving (see Melissa's Tips)

3 tablespoons chopped fresh herbs such as flat-leaf parsley, chives, basil, and tarragon, for garnish

Horseradish Cream, for serving (optional, see Sidebar, opposite)

1. In a stockpot over high heat, warm 1 teaspoon of the oil. Add the onions, cut side down, and cook without stirring until they are dark brown and well caramelized on the cut side, about 10 minutes.

2. Add the beef broth, chicken parts, celery, turnips, leeks, carrots, tomatoes, garlic, peppercorns, thyme, parsley, star anise, clove, bay leaf, and a generous pinch of salt and pepper. Add enough water to cover everything by 2 inches, and bring to a simmer. Cook the mixture, adjusting the heat to maintain a low simmer, for 2 hours. Let cool slightly, then strain the broth through a colander set over a clean pot, pressing down on the solids. Discard the solids. Let cool completely and refrigerate until serving, up to 3 days, or freeze for up to a month.

3. Bring the broth to a simmer over medium-high heat. Add the **steaks** and let poach in the barely simmering liquid until done to taste, 9 to 11 minutes for rare (see Chef's Tip). Use a slotted spoon to transfer the meat to a cutting board and tent with foil to keep warm. (After cooking the meat, don't discard the broth. Either serve it as a first course, maybe with croutons topped with some delicacy like pâté or good melted cheese or caramelized onions. Or cook tortellini in the broth and serve them with plenty of chopped fresh herbs. Or save it for another use, anywhere beef broth is called for.) Let rest for 5 minutes, then cut the filets in half horizontally. Place two filet halves in each of six shallow bowls, ladle a little broth on top, and garnish with the remaining olive oil, *fleur de sel,* herbs, and horseradish cream, if desired.

HORSERADISH CREAM

This creamy, biting sauce can be prepared up to 6 hours in advance, though it will mellow as it sits. Fresh horseradish root is easiest to find in the spring and late fall, and is easiest to grate in a food processor, though you can grate it by hand—just open a window to let out the tear-inducing fumes. In a bowl, stir together 1 cup *fromage blanc* or whole-milk yogurt, 1 cup crème fraîche or sour cream, and ½ cup freshly grated horseradish, and season with sea salt and freshly ground black pepper.

CHEF'S TIP Filet mignon is tender and expensive, and the last thing you want to do is cook away its rosiness and dry it out. So be ready to pull the **steaks** from the broth as soon as they're done (and bear in mind that smaller steaks will cook faster, so some might finish cooking first). I wouldn't cut into a steak to test for doneness, since it releases the juices that you want to get to the plate, and it mutilates a nice-looking piece of meat. Instead, use an instant-read thermometer or the "palm method": For a rare steak, the meat, when pressed in the center, will feel like the soft, spongy part of your palm below your thumb, and will register about 120°F. For medium-rare, stretch out your palm and feel the center, where it feels firmer but there is still some spring (it will register about 130°F). For medium-well, feel your outstretched palm toward the area where your pinky is—it will have very little give (and will register about 155°F). I personally would encourage you to cook it to the rarer side of your preference for this recipe.

MELISSA'S TIP *Fleur de sel* ("flower of salt") is a rarefied snowflake-shaped sea salt that forms naturally when the sun bleaches the salt flats on the shores of Provence and Brittany. This top layer of white salt is raked and gathered by hand. It has a complex, slightly mineral taste and a mild salinity, along with a pleasant crunch, making it a great garnish for everything from a baked potato to a chocolate tart (try it!). Like fine extra-virgin olive oil, fleur de sel is too expensive and nuanced to use in cooking, so always add it off the heat, just before serving. Most gourmet stores sell a variety of sea salts, or you can order it from Zingerman's (888-636-8162; www.zingermans.com).

ANDREW CARMELLINI, formerly of Café Boulud, New York

Tagine of Lamb Shanks with Prunes, Ginger, and Toasted Almonds

Unlike the happily and decidedly French restaurant Daniel, where chef Daniel Boulud serves his take on the classics, Café Boulud, his more casual restaurant uptown, espouses a more global perspective. Former executive chef Andrew Carmellini used ingredients and techniques from around the world, which he melded with Daniel's refined European sensibility. For instance, in this tagine, Andrew uses a cross-cultural mix of Middle Eastern and North African seasonings, from herbaceous *zahtar* to sesame seeds and almonds, as well as the subtle, intriguing flavor of Earl Grey tea. He serves it with a rather French garnish of caramelized artichokes with carrots and onion, but it's not essential to the dish. However if you feel like making it, it is fitting and delightful, so I've included it in a sidebar. PREPARATION TIME: 1 HOUR AND 20 MINUTES, PLUS 2 TO 2 1/2 HOURS BRAISING

SERVES 4

SPICE MIX

1 1/2 teaspoons Jordanian *zahtar* (see Melissa's Tips)

1 teaspoon *ras al hanout* (see Melissa's Tips)

1 teaspoon hot paprika (see Melissa's Tips, page 86)

1 teaspoon freshly ground white pepper

1/2 teaspoon coarse sea salt or kosher salt

LAMB SHANKS

2 tablespoons extra-virgin olive oil

4 lamb hind shanks (about 3 pounds total)

1 onion, coarsely chopped

1 carrot, peeled and coarsely chopped

5 garlic cloves, peeled and left whole

One 2-inch piece of fresh gingerroot, peeled and sliced

Coarse sea salt or kosher salt and freshly ground white pepper

1 tablespoon tomato paste (see Melissa's Tips, page 163)

1 large tomato, diced

1 tablespoon all-purpose flour

3 cups unsalted veal or lamb broth, or low-sodium beef broth

2 sprigs of fresh thyme

2 Earl Grey tea bags

8 dates, pitted

GARNISH

24 pitted prunes

2 tablespoons golden raisins

2 tablespoons sesame seeds, toasted (see Melissa's Tips)

2 tablespoons toasted sliced almonds (see page 51)

Caramelized artichokes (optional, see page 171)

1. Preheat the oven to 400°F. In a small bowl, combine all the ingredients for the spice mix.

2. In a roasting pan or Dutch oven over high heat, warm the olive oil. Season the lamb shanks all over with some of the spice mix. When the oil is very hot, add the shanks and brown well on all sides, about 20 minutes total. Transfer the lamb to a plate for the moment and lower the heat under the pan.

3. Add the onion, carrot, garlic, and ginger to the pan, season with salt and pepper, and cook, stirring, for 3 to 5 minutes, until the vegetables are lightly browned. Stir in the tomato paste and tomato and cook for 2 minutes more. Add the flour and cook, still stirring, for 1 minute. Return the lamb shanks to the pan, pour in the broth, and add the thyme. Bring to a boil, cover with a lid or a piece of foil, and transfer the pan to the oven. Braise, basting every 20 minutes or so, for 2 to 2½ hours, until very tender.

4. In a small saucepan, bring 2 cups of water to a boil. Remove from the heat and add the tea bags. Cover and infuse for 5 minutes, then discard the tea bags. Soak the dates in the tea until they are soft, about 5 minutes. Drain the dates, reserving the tea to use for the garnish. Puree the dates in a food processor or blender.

5. When the lamb is finished braising, stir in the date puree. Transfer the lamb shanks to a warm platter and place the pan over high heat. Reduce the liquid by half, about 10 minutes. Season with some of the spice mixture and salt and pepper, then strain over the lamb shanks.

MELISSA'S TIPS *Zahtar* is a spice mix that varies in its components depending upon whether you are talking to cooks in North Africa, Turkey, Syria, Jordan, or Iran. The Jordanian mix usually includes sesame seeds, thyme or marjoram (or zahtar, an herb very similar to thyme), and sumac, a tart red spice, and it is used on meats. Look for it at Middle Eastern markets or order it from Penzey's Spices (800-741-7787; www.penzeys.com).

Ras el hanout is a Moroccan spice mix that includes a variety of sweet, savory, and hot spices, including cinnamon, nutmeg, ginger, cardamom, cumin, pepper, cayenne, and sometimes dried lavender. It can be found in Middle Eastern and gourmet shops or you can order it from Kalustyan's (800-352-3451; www.kalustyans.com).

RECIPE CONTINUES

Sesame seeds can be bought hulled or unhulled—the unhulled ones are a little bigger and browner and have more crunch, but you can use either here. Just make sure your seeds taste fresh, with no bitter, rancid aftertaste, since seeds are high in oil and can go bad after a few months. Store fresh sesame seeds in a cool, dry place and toast them to bring out their flavor and enhance their crunch. The easiest way to toast the tiny seeds without the risk of forgetting them for a second and burning them is to toss them continuously in a dry pan over medium heat until fragrant and lightly browned, about 3 minutes. Immediately transfer the seeds to a plate to cool.

At Café Boulud, this recipe is served in **tagines,** which are Moroccan lidded serving dishes with little chimney-type tops, traditionally used for stews. Of course, you can serve this in any warmed dish. But if you happen to have a collection of tagines or other lidded dishes (even a soup tureen!) it's lovely to bring the covered dish to the table and open it with a flourish, releasing the fragrant steam to oohs and aahs.

CHEF'S TIP If you prefer to make this recipe a day in advance, the flavors will benefit from resting overnight in the fridge, and you will be able to easily remove the fat once it has hardened at the surface. After skimming, reheat the pot in a 350°F. oven for about ½ hour or give it a gentle simmer on the stove, then proceed with the garnish.

6. To prepare the garnish, bring the reserved tea to a simmer and add the prunes and raisins. Let them plump off the heat until softened, about 5 minutes. Drain and then roll the prunes in the **sesame seeds.** Serve the *tagine* topped with the prunes, raisins, and almonds. Garnish with Caramelized Artichokes, if using.

Caramelized Artichokes

SERVES 4

3 tablespoons extra-virgin olive oil

3 fresh artichoke hearts, cleaned, each cut
into 8 wedges

1 onion, thinly sliced

1 carrot, sliced on the bias ¼ inch thick

Coarse sea salt or kosher salt and freshly
ground black pepper

In a large skillet over medium heat, warm the olive oil. Add the artichokes, onion, and carrot, season with salt and pepper, and cook, stirring regularly, for about 10 minutes, until the vegetables are well caramelized and the artichokes are fork-tender.

DAVID WALTUCK, Chanterelle, New York

Rack of Lamb with a Cumin and Salt Crust, Lemon, and Cilantro

Over the past twenty-five years that Chanterelle has been open, David Waltuck's cuisine has gone from pretty straight-ahead French-American to more global in scope, including influences from Asia and the Mediterranean. In this recipe for rack of lamb, he combines ingredients from them all, with the lemon and garlic sauce recalling Greece, the cilantro from Southeast Asia, and the rack of lamb from France. This twist on a classic offers flavors that are both familiar and compelling; it's the kind of dish you'll want to make over and over. And now that I've simplified it (eliminating a separate sauce, combining several steps, and making the eggplant flans optional), you can. PREPARATION TIME: 1 HOUR AND 15 MINUTES, PLUS 30 MINUTES RESTING

SERVES 4 TO 6

3 tablespoons ground cumin

1 tablespoon coarse sea salt or kosher salt, plus more to taste

2 teaspoons freshly ground black pepper, plus more to taste

2 racks of lamb (about 1¼ pounds each)

1 head of garlic, separated into cloves and peeled

½ cup plus 3 tablespoons extra-virgin olive oil

½ cup chicken broth, low-sodium if canned

¼ cup dry white wine

2 tablespoons freshly squeezed lemon juice (from 1 lemon)

3 tablespoons unsalted butter

¼ cup fresh cilantro leaves, for garnish

Eggplant Flans, for serving (optional; see page 176)

CHEF'S TIP The average **rack of lamb** has about seven ribs, which will feed two or three, depending on what else you're serving. If you aren't that familiar with rack of lamb, make sure to notice which side has the layer of fat before you coat it with the spice mixture. This is the side that needs to go into the pan first to brown.

1. Preheat the oven to 500°F. and place a heavy-duty metal roasting pan in the oven to heat up.

2. In a bowl, combine the cumin, salt, and pepper. Rinse the lamb and shake it dry, but don't dry it completely—you want the seasoning to stick. Put the **lamb** on a plate and rub it all over with the cumin mixture. Let sit for about 20 minutes while the oven and pan preheat.

3. Meanwhile, put the **garlic** in a pan and cover with ½ cup of the olive oil. Bring the mixture to a bare simmer (there should be only a bubble or two) and let cook gently until the cloves are very soft, 20 to 30 minutes. Set aside.

RECIPE CONTINUES

MELISSA'S TIPS This recipe calls for poaching a whole head of **garlic** in oil, which yields more than you'll need — the lamb calls for only 2 cloves, and, if you make them, the eggplant flans use another 4. The remaining oil-poached garlic can be kept in the refrigerator for up to a week. It's excellent spread on crostini or added to salad dressing.

If you aren't making the **flans** and you don't want to bother roasting garlic, just press 2 raw cloves into the sauce instead. It will have a sharper, more pungent garlic flavor but will be no less delicious.

4. When the roasting pan is very hot, carefully add the remaining 3 tablespoons of the olive oil (it may splatter) and place the lamb, fat side down, into the pan. Roast the lamb until nicely browned on the bottom, about 10 minutes, then flip the racks and cook about 5 minutes on the other side for rare (about 120°F. on an instant-read thermometer), or cook it more or less to taste. If the fat side is not as brown as you would like at this point, turn the broiler to high and broil until really brown, 2 to 3 minutes longer. Transfer the lamb to a carving board and let rest for about 10 minutes.

5. Place the roasting pan on the stovetop over high heat. Add the chicken broth and use a wooden spoon to scrape up the browned bits from the bottom of the pan. Pass 2 of the roasted garlic cloves through a garlic press into the sauce, or smash them in a bowl and add the paste to the sauce. Add the wine and lemon juice and simmer until slightly thickened, about 6 minutes. Whisk in the butter and season with salt and pepper.

6. Serve the lamb with the pan sauce, garnished with cilantro leaves, accompanied by eggplant flan, if desired.

Eggplant Flans

These flans can be made up to two days in advance and reheated in a microwave or 250°F oven, or steamed briefly in a pot over simmering water.

SERVES 6

2 medium-size eggplants, pricked with a fork

Extra-virgin olive oil, for drizzling

4 cloves of roasted garlic (see lamb recipe on preceding pages)

1 cup heavy cream

2 large eggs

1 large egg yolk

Coarse sea salt or kosher salt and freshly ground black pepper

Pinch of cayenne pepper

1. Preheat the oven to 400°F. Put the eggplants in a foil-lined baking dish and drizzle them with olive oil. Bake until the eggplants implode, 30 to 40 minutes, then let them cool slightly.

2. Scrape the eggplant flesh out of the skin. In a blender, puree 2 cups of the cooked eggplant with the roasted garlic, cream, eggs, yolk, and salt, pepper, and cayenne to taste. Run the blender until everything is completely smooth. Pour the mixture into six 8-ounce ramekins and bake in a hot water bath (in a roasting pan that's filled halfway with hot water and covered with foil—see Melissa's Tips, page 230) until just set in the center, about 1 hour.

Fennel-Crusted Lamb Loin with Vinegar Sauce

Scott Conant is famous around New York for his amazing handmade pastas. But when I was thinking about which recipe to request for the book, his juicy, fennel-rubbed lamb loin immediately came to mind. Covered in spices and quickly cooked so the outside is crusty while the center stays rare, then paired with a tangy vinegar-based sauce, it's the kind of dish that I just can't stop eating. Scott changes the garnish seasonally, but I decided to leave it off altogether. All this dish needs is a fork, a knife, and your undivided attention. PREPARATION TIME: 1 HOUR AND 10 MINUTES, PLUS AT LEAST 4 HOURS RESTING

SERVES 6

SPICE RUB

2 tablespoons fennel seeds

1/2 tablespoon coriander seeds

1 teaspoon crushed red pepper flakes

1/2 tablespoon sweet paprika

1/2 teaspoon cayenne pepper

LAMB AND VINEGAR SAUCE

1 lamb loin (about 2 1/2 pounds)

4 tablespoons extra-virgin olive oil

Coarse sea salt or kosher salt and freshly ground black pepper

2 shallots, thinly sliced

3 sprigs of fresh thyme

Pinch of crushed red pepper flakes

6 tablespoons red wine vinegar

2 1/2 cups chicken broth, low-sodium if canned

1 tablespoon unsalted butter, chilled

MELISSA'S TIP The **lamb loin** is from the saddle (sort of like the lower back of the animal) and can be cut into loin chops, which are thick and tender, or into a lamb loin roast, which is what's called for here. The roast is boned and rolled, just like a pork loin, and it's both easy to serve and extremely flavorful. All you need to do is sear the meat, roast it (it should stay rosy inside), snip away the strings that help the roast keep its shape in cooking, then carve it up into thick, pink slices. It's an expensive piece of meat but certainly company-worthy and simple to deal with.

1. Prepare the spice rub: Place the fennel, coriander, and red pepper flakes in a dry sauté pan. Warm over low heat, stirring constantly with a wooden spoon, until very fragrant, about 6 minutes. Add the paprika and cayenne and let heat for 30 seconds. Transfer to a plate to cool, then grind fine in an electric coffee grinder or using a mortar and pestle.

2. Prepare the **lamb:** Coat the lamb with 2 tablespoons of the olive oil, season it generously with salt and pepper, and rub the spice mixture all over its surface. Wrap well with plastic and refrigerate for at least 4 hours and up to 24 hours.

3. When ready to cook the lamb, preheat the oven to 350°F. Preheat a heavy, ovenproof pan over high heat for a couple of minutes, then add a tablespoon of the oil. Sear the lamb well

on all sides, about 5 minutes. Place the pan in the oven and roast until the center of the loin registers 120°F. on an instant-read thermometer for rare, 35 to 40 minutes.

4. Meanwhile, prepare the **vinegar** sauce: In a small saucepan over medium-high heat, warm the remaining tablespoon of olive oil and sauté the shallots, thyme, and pinch of red pepper flakes with a little salt until the shallots begin to brown, 5 to 7 minutes. Add the vinegar and stir to scrape up the browned bits from the bottom of the pan. Bring to a boil and simmer rapidly until thick and reduced, about 3 minutes. Pour in the broth and simmer for another 20 minutes. Strain the sauce into another pan and whisk in the butter. Cover to keep warm or reheat gently before serving.

5. Transfer the lamb to a carving board and let rest for 10 minutes before slicing. Slice and serve with the vinegar sauce.

CHEF'S TIPS I like to let the lamb marinate in the spices for a good 24 hours before I cook it, so plan to prepare the meat a day before you will be serving it.

Since the flavor of the sauce depends on it, use a good-quality red wine **vinegar**—I always use one made in the traditional, slow, Orleans method (the label will indicate this).

SARA JENKINS, formerly of 50 Carmine, New York

Roasted Pork Loin with Juniper and Herbs

I adore the flavors of Sara Jenkins's slow-roasted pork roast, which she cooks with juniper, plenty of herbs, garlic, and red wine until it's meltingly tender. What I don't love is the seemingly unending six-hour cooking time. Instead, I raised the heat from 250° F., the temperature she roasts at, to 500°F., and was able to interrupt the recipe at the one-hour mark. The taste is just as savory as Sara's version, but so much quicker. She serves it with white beans and sautéed mustard greens, two perfect accompaniments; if you're culling from this book, Polenta (page 187) and Brussels Sprouts à la Plancha (page 200) would also work well.

PREPARATION TIME: 1 HOUR AND 10 MINUTES

SERVES 6 TO 8

3 garlic cloves

2 tablespoons chopped fresh rosemary

2 tablespoons chopped fresh sage

1 tablespoon juniper berries

1 tablespoon coarse sea salt or kosher salt

1 teaspoon black peppercorns

1 boneless pork loin (3½ to 4 pounds)

3 tablespoons extra-virgin olive oil

1 cup dry red wine

MELISSA'S TIPS Purple-black, pea-sized **juniper berries** are the flavoring in gin, which has their piney-sweet flavor. They're generally available in the spice section of supermarkets. If you have a choice in the matter, look for berries that are still somewhat soft rather than hard and shriveled.

CHEF'S TIP For the best flavor, marinate the **pork** in the herb paste overnight in the fridge.

MELISSA Sara uses red **wine** for her recipe, but white wine works equally well, though the flavor will be different. Use whichever you have on hand or feel like opening.

Leftover pork roast makes the best sandwiches, which you probably already know.

1. Preheat the oven to 500°F.

2. In an electric coffee grinder or the smallest work bowl of a food processor or a blender, grind the garlic, rosemary, sage, **juniper berries,** salt, and peppercorns until they form a rough paste.

3. Using a sharp knife, stab the **pork** loin about ten times at even intervals. Stuff the holes with a few teaspoons of the spice paste, then smear the rest of the paste over the top of the loin.

4. Place the pork in a roasting pan and drizzle the oil over it. Roast for 10 minutes, then pour the **wine** over the meat (make it fast, then stand back, as the fat in the pan will spit). Continue to roast, basting with the wine in the pan every 15 minutes, until the internal temperature of the roast reaches 140°F. on an instant-read thermometer, about 1 hour total (or longer, if you prefer not to eat juicy, pink-tinged pork). Let rest, loosely covered, for 15 minutes. Cut away the strings, slice the meat, and serve at once.

TOM DOUGLAS, Dahlia Lounge, Seattle

Citrus-Braised Pork Shank with Bread-Crumb Gremolata

Unlike veal shanks or lamb shanks, which have been handily embraced by chefs in upscale restaurants all over the country, pork shanks are still usually considered rustic, low-down fare, more along the lines of pig's feet than, say, osso buco. But not to Tom Douglas. At Dahlia Lounge, he slow-braises pork shanks with lemon juice and zest until they are falling-off-the-bone tender, then sprinkles them with a toasted bread-crumb gremolata—his adaptation of the typical parsley-and-garlic garnish for osso buco. It's an elegant touch that makes the presentation feel much more silver spoon than greasy spoon, but, happily, doesn't change the gutsy, porky taste of the shanks one bit. **PREPARATION TIME: 45 MINUTES, PLUS 2½ HOURS BRAISING**

SERVES 6

PORK SHANKS

6 fresh pork shanks (see Chef's Tips)

Coarse sea salt or kosher salt and freshly ground black pepper

¼ cup extra-virgin olive oil

2 medium onions, coarsely chopped

2 carrots, peeled and coarsely chopped

2 celery stalks, chopped

4 sprigs of fresh thyme

4 to 6 cups chicken broth, low-sodium if canned

Zest and freshly squeezed juice of 2 lemons (see Melissa's Tip)

BREAD-CRUMB GREMOLATA

1 teaspoon extra-virgin olive oil

½ cup fresh, coarse bread crumbs (see Sidebar, page 19)

¼ cup chopped fresh flat-leaf parsley

Grated zest of 2 lemons

Coarse sea salt or kosher salt and freshly ground black pepper

CHEF'S TIPS We like to use 4-inch center-cut **pork** shanks, which you will have to order from a butcher. But regularly cut shanks will work here, too.

MELISSA'S TIP Make sure to grate the **zest** off the lemons before you juice them. It's much easier than trying to grate the spent lemon halves.

1. Preheat the oven to 350°F. Season the **pork** with salt and pepper. In an ovenproof pot or Dutch oven (it should have a lid) over medium-high heat, warm the ¼ cup oil until hot but not smoking. Add the pork shanks and sear on all sides until well browned, about 5 minutes per side. (Work in batches if necessary to avoid overcrowding the pan.) Transfer the browned shanks to a large plate.

2. Add the onions and carrots to the fat remaining in the pan and sauté until softened and starting to caramelize, about 12 minutes. Add the celery and thyme and sauté a few minutes more. Return the shanks to the pot, pour in enough broth to cover the meat by about three quarters, add the lemon zest and juice, and bring to a boil. Cover the pan and place it in the oven to braise until the meat is very tender and pulling away from the bone, about 2½ hours.

3. Meanwhile, prepare the bread-crumb gremolata. In a small skillet over medium-high heat, warm the teaspoon of olive oil. Add the bread crumbs and stir until they begin to brown and get crunchy, about 5 minutes. Transfer the crumbs to a small bowl to cool, then stir in the parsley and lemon **zest,** and season with salt and pepper.

4. Transfer the shanks to a platter and tent with foil to keep warm. Pour the braising liquid through a sieve into a clean, heavy saucepan. Skim off the fat, then bring the liquid to a boil over medium-high heat. Simmer until the liquid is reduced to a slightly thickened sauce, about 8 minutes. Season to taste with additional salt and pepper.

5. To **serve,** place the pork shanks on warm plates, ladle some of the sauce over each shank, and generously scatter the bread-crumb gremolata over the top.

CHEF In the restaurant, to finish the shanks for service, we sear the cooked pork shanks in a very hot pan, which browns and caramelizes them even more, then we pour on the sauce. You could do the same at home, or **serve** them straight from the oven.

CHRIS DOUGLASS, Icarus, Boston

Roasted Pork Chops with Peaches and Basil

At Icarus, Boston's darling Chris Douglass roasts a pork loin to serve with softly cooked peaches and fragrant, fresh basil. I substituted pork chops because I find them both quicker to cook and juicier, even if you don't brine them; and I love the way the salty, fatty pork drippings mix with the sweet peaches on the plate. This was created as a very summery dish, perfect when peaches and basil are in abundance, and it should really stay that way; substitute apples and sage in the fall or winter rather than using cottony, out-of-season peaches. PREPARATION TIME: 1½ HOURS, PLUS UP TO 1½ HOURS BRINING

SERVES 4

¾ cup kosher salt, plus additional to taste

½ cup sugar

Four 1-inch-thick pork chops

Freshly ground black pepper

4 tablespoons grapeseed or canola oil

4 ripe peaches, pitted and quartered

2 tablespoons sherry vinegar

2 shallots, diced

4 tablespoons (½ stick) unsalted butter, chilled and cubed

½ cup fresh basil leaves, torn into pieces, for garnish

MELISSA'S TIP People talk about new **pork** and old pork because a lot has changed in the way pigs are bred for meat in this country. And the reputation of pork has changed as a result, going from a fatty, succulent delicacy to a dry, healthful, so-called "white meat." Chefs, of course, are not in favor of fat-robbing, and they have been a major proponent of retro pork—that is, heritage breeds and farming practices that humanely and sustainably produce natural, flavorful, old-fashioned meat with enough fat to insulate it during cooking. Ask your butcher to help you find well-marbled pork, or look for products from Niman Ranch, one of the biggest and best names in this field (see www.nimanranch.com for more info).

1. In a deep, nonreactive bowl or pan, dissolve the salt and sugar in 8 cups of warm tap water. Add the **pork** chops (they should be completely submerged) and refrigerate for 1 to 1½ hours.

2. Remove the pork from the **brine,** rinse, and pat dry. Season the chops liberally with black pepper. Cover loosely with plastic wrap and let rest at room temperature while the peaches are cooking.

3. Preheat the oven to 350°F. Spread 2 tablespoons of the oil evenly over a shallow roasting pan that will comfortably fit the peaches in a single layer. Arrange the peaches in the pan and roast until soft and just cooked through, about 20 minutes. Remove from the oven (do not turn the oven off) and let cool slightly before carefully removing the skins. Set aside the 12 nicest-looking pieces of peach for garnish, and return the other peach quarters to the pan. Pour the sherry vinegar into the pan and scrape up the browned bits to deglaze the pan.

Pour the contents of the pan into a blender and puree for the sauce.

4. Transfer the peach puree and the diced shallots to a heavy saucepan over medium-low heat, and simmer until reduced by half, about 7 minutes. Turn down the heat and add the butter 1 piece at a time, stirring constantly. Pass the sauce through a sieve and cover to keep warm.

5. In an ovenproof skillet over medium heat, warm the remaining 2 tablespoons of oil. Add the chops and brown them on all sides, about 5 minutes per side. Place the pan in the oven and roast for 25 to 35 minutes, until the chops reach an internal temperature of 140°F. (pink) to 150°F. (less pink). Remove the pan from the oven, add the reserved peach wedges, cover loosely with foil, and set aside to rest for 10 minutes.

6. Pour the peach sauce into the pan, season with salt and pepper, and heat gently. To serve, transfer the pork chops and peaches to plates. Spoon the sauce over and around the pork and scatter the torn basil leaves over the top.

CHEF'S TIP Brining—soaking in salt-water—is a great way to improve the flavor and moistness of meats like pork and turkey, which can become dry and bland. The salt not only seasons the meat but also increases its ability to hold moisture when cooked. These pork chops need to brine for 1 to 1½ hours, so plan accordingly.

FRANK PROTO, Landmarc, New York

Spicy Pork Ribs with Garlic and Tomatoes

Frank Proto is Marc Murphy's chef de cuisine at Landmarc, one of my favorite casual Tribeca spots. Frank has a different take on the usual rib preparation. Instead of smoky, barbecued-all-day-in-a-pit ribs, or lacquered, slightly sweet Chinese-style spareribs, Frank cooks ribs Italian style, with tomatoes, garlic, and crushed red pepper. It's a pretty easy dish to begin with, though I had my work cut out scaling down the proportions. One of the most popular dishes on the menu, the original recipe makes enough for 30 to 40 servings; this version comfortably feeds eight. At Landmarc, Frank serves the ribs over polenta to absorb all that good sauce. PREPARATION TIME: 1 HOUR, PLUS UP TO 3 HOURS BRAISING

SERVES 8

2 racks St. Louis–cut pork ribs (about 3 pounds each)

Coarse sea salt or kosher salt and freshly ground black pepper

Two 28-ounce cans plum tomatoes

¼ cup fresh basil leaves, plus additional chopped basil for garnish

½ pound bacon, diced

10 garlic cloves, coarsely chopped

3 red onions, sliced

2½ cups dry white wine

¼ cup extra-virgin olive oil

¼ cup sherry vinegar

4 teaspoons crushed red pepper flakes

MELISSA'S TIP St. Louis–style **ribs,** cut from the sparerib and trimmed so there is less waste, are particularly meaty and succulent. The racks are pretty large, so you'll need a great big roasting pan for this recipe.

CHEF'S TIPS If the **bacon** is especially fatty, pour off some of the fat before you add the onions.

The ribs can be cooked up to two days ahead (store them in their tomato sauce in the fridge). Then warm them up when you finish the sauce.

1. Preheat the oven to 350°F. Season the **ribs** with salt and pepper and lay them in a large, flame-proof roasting pan. Pour the tomatoes over the ribs and scatter the basil on top.

2. In a skillet over medium-high heat, sauté the **bacon** until slightly crisp, about 4 minutes. Add half the garlic and all the onions and cook until browned, about 7 minutes. Pour in the wine and let the mixture simmer until it's reduced by half, about 10 minutes. Pour the onion mixture over the ribs, cover the pan tightly with foil, and bake until the meat is literally falling off the bone, 2½ to 3 hours. Transfer the ribs but not the sauce to a plate.

3. Just before serving, in a skillet over high heat, warm the oil. Add the remaining garlic and sauté until fragrant and lightly golden, about 2 minutes. Add the vinegar and red pepper flakes and bring back to a simmer. Pour the garlic mixture into the pan with the sauce from the ribs, place it over heat high, and let it reduce by about a third, about 10 minutes. Add the ribs to the pan and toss them around to coat them in the sauce and reheat them. Serve them hot, garnished with more basil, if desired.

POLENTA

This is also excellent with the roasted pork loin on page 180.

1 teaspoon coarse sea salt or kosher salt

1 cup medium-grind cornmeal or quick-cooking polenta

3 tablespoons unsalted butter, cut into pieces

Bring 3½ cups of water to a boil in a heavy-bottomed saucepan. Add the salt, then slowly pour in the polenta while stirring. Reduce the heat and simmer, stirring frequently, until done, about 15 minutes for quick-cooking polenta. Stir in the butter and serve.

035

PAUL KAHAN, Blackbird, Chicago

Braised Pork Belly with Red Cabbage–Parsley Salad

You're probably most familiar with pork belly that has been cured and sliced into bacon, but it is also available fresh. Fresh pork belly is an inexpensive cut with a good amount of fat on it that has long been used in Chinese kitchens and is beginning to get more attention by chefs of all persuasions, as people begin to notice that the new breeds of lean pork are, shall we say, rather lacking. The fat content of pork belly, combined with a long, slow braise, yields melt-in-the-mouth results. This simplified version of Paul Kahan's fabulous recipe is reduced to the unctuous meat and a bright, crunchy slaw of cabbage and parsley that perfectly balances the richness of the dish. PREPARATION TIME: 1 HOUR AND 20 MINUTES, PLUS OVERNIGHT RESTING AND UP TO 3 HOURS BRAISING

SERVES 4 TO 6

BRAISED PORK BELLY

2 pounds fresh (unsalted) pork belly

1 tablespoon coriander seeds

1 tablespoon fennel seeds

1/2 teaspoon cumin seeds

Coarse sea salt or kosher salt and freshly
    ground black pepper

8 garlic cloves, finely chopped

2 celery stalks, coarsely chopped

2 carrots, peeled and coarsely chopped

1 medium onion, coarsely chopped

1 cup dry white wine

3 cups chicken broth, low-sodium if canned

1 large sprig fresh thyme

RED CABBAGE–PARSLEY SALAD

1 cup very thinly shaved red cabbage

1 cup flat-leaf parsley leaves

4 teaspoons extra-virgin olive oil

Splash of champagne or white wine vinegar

Coarse sea salt or kosher salt and freshly
    ground black pepper

MELISSA'S TIPS This is a recipe with an **overnight** resting step, so plan accordingly.

CHEF'S TIP Scoring the fat on a pork belly has three functions: it allows the flavors of the spice rub to penetrate better, seasoning the meat; when you are browning the meat, the fat is better rendered (released) into the pan; and the scoring increases the amount of surface area that becomes crisp and caramelized. Try scoring any fatty cut of meat, including duck and goose, to melt the fat away, leaving the crackling skin.

1. The **night** before you plan to serve the pork, trim it: Slice the skin off the fat, leaving 1/4 inch of fat (alternatively, you can ask your butcher to do this, as the skin is somewhat tough). **Score the fat** in a crosshatch pattern.

2. In a dry skillet over low heat, lightly toast the coriander, fennel, and cumin seeds, stirring constantly, until fragrant, about 4 minutes. Transfer the spices to a plate to cool, then coarsely grind them in an electric coffee grinder or using a mortar and pestle. Cover the pork on the top and bottom with the spices. Wrap well in plastic, place in a bowl, and refrigerate overnight.

3. The next day, preheat the oven to 325°F. Scrape the seeds off the fat side of the pork and season well with salt and pepper. In a large, heavy-bottomed skillet over medium heat, sear the pork, fat-side down. When the fat is a nice brown color, about 5 minutes, transfer the pork to a roasting pan, fat side up. Pour most of the fat out of the skillet and add the garlic, celery, carrots, and onion. Sauté the vegetables until just tender, about 12 minutes. Season with salt and pepper, add the wine, and cook until reduced by two thirds, about 5 minutes.

4. In a small saucepan, bring the broth to a boil. Pour the vegetable mixture over the pork, add the hot broth and thyme, and season generously with salt. Place the pan in the oven and braise, uncovered, until the pork is extremely tender when pierced, 2½ to 3 hours, basting occasionally with the pan juices.

5. To make the salad, simply toss together all the ingredients, seasoning with salt and pepper to taste. Serve the pork with the salad and, if desired, the pan juices.

MELISSA If you own a mandoline or a Japanese slicer like a Benriner, you'll be able to use that to shave the red cabbage for the salad. Otherwise, quarter and core the cabbage and then slice it thin with a knife—you only need a cup, so you will probably use less than a quarter of a cabbage.

SCOTT BRYANT, Veritas, New York

Dolcetto-Braised Veal Cheeks with Porcini Mushrooms

When 3-star chef Scott Bryant packed up his pantry at Indigo, where he was the chef before opening Veritas, he left certain things behind: fiery chile peppers, Szechwan peppercorns, fermented black beans, Asian fish sauce, artichokes—anything that would numb, confuse, or overwhelm the palate was out. At Veritas, the telephone book–sized wine list is set on the table before the menu, indicating their priority. So now Scott's rule is to keep his cooking simple and wine-friendly, leaving all culinary frippery to restaurants where the cocktail menu is longer than the list of wines by the glass. This dish is a perfect example of Scott's newfound conservatism, in the very best sense. The veal cheeks are simmered in wine, rosemary, and tomatoes, which reduces to a thick, flavorsome sauce, then matched with mushrooms—all classic, wine-friendly flavors that are delightful no matter what you are drinking with the food. It's a failsafe, make-ahead company dish, even if you substitute veal stew meat for the hard-to-find cheeks (see Melissa's Tips). Polenta (page 187) or Olive Oil Mashed Potatoes (page 165) make a soft, tasty bed to absorb all that good sauce. PREPARATION TIME: 1 HOUR 20 MINUTES, PLUS 2 HOURS BRAISING

SERVES 4

18 veal cheeks, cleaned (or 2¹⁄₂ pounds veal stew meat)

Coarse sea salt or kosher salt and freshly ground black pepper

2 tablespoons extra-virgin olive oil

6 garlic cloves, chopped

4 plum tomatoes, cored, seeded, and diced

1¹⁄₂ bottles dry red wine, preferably Dolcetto

2 sprigs each of fresh rosemary, thyme, and sage

3 tablespoons unsalted butter

1 medium onion, diced

2 large carrots, peeled and diced

1 cup diced celery (about 2 stalks)

8 ounces fresh porcini mushrooms, wiped clean with a towel and sliced (see Melissa's Tips)

Snipped fresh chives, or fresh rosemary sprigs, for garnish

MELISSA'S TIPS If you don't have a butcher who will procure—and clean—**veal cheeks** for you, then use veal stew meat instead, because cleaning the little guys is very labor intensive. Veal cheeks are divine, but this is a nice stew recipe, and there's no need to spend hours trimming the meat.

1. Preheat the oven to 350°F. Season the **veal cheeks** well with salt and pepper. Preheat a large Dutch oven over high heat for a couple minutes. Add half the oil to the pan and then add half of the veal cheeks. Sear the veal until very well browned on all sides, about 12 minutes. Transfer the browned veal to a plate lined with paper towels and sear the second batch, transferring it to a plate when browned.

2. Reduce the heat to medium and add the garlic to the pan. Stir and cook for about 45 seconds, then add the tomatoes. Cook, stirring, until the tomatoes are soft, about 3 minutes.

Pour in the **wine** and bring to a boil, then add the browned veal and fresh herbs. Cover and braise in the oven until the meat is meltingly tender, about 2 hours, uncovering the pot for the last ½ hour.

3. Meanwhile, in a sauté pan over medium heat, melt 1 tablespoon of the butter. Add the onion, carrots, and celery and season with salt and pepper. Cook without browning, stirring occasionally, until tender, about 20 minutes. Adjust the heat to ensure that the vegetables do not take on any color. Transfer the vegetables to a pot large enough to eventually hold all the stew.

4. Add the remaining 2 tablespoons of butter to the pan and raise the heat to medium-high. When the butter foams, add the **porcini** and sauté until the slices are golden on both sides, about 10 minutes. Season with salt and pepper and add to the pot with the other vegetables.

5. When the meat is cooked, use tongs to transfer the veal cheeks to the pot with the vegetables. Place the Dutch oven over medium-high heat and bring the liquid from the meat to a boil. Simmer until it is reduced and thickened to a nice sauce consistency, about 7 minutes.

6. Strain the sauce over the meat and vegetables, stir to combine, and reheat slowly before serving. Serve garnished with snipped fresh chives or rosemary sprigs.

CHEF'S TIP Although *dolcetto* means "little sweet one" in Italian, Dolcettos are actually fruity yet dry, medium-bodied red **wines** from the Piedmont region of Italy. They're definitely food wines. A natural partner to the white truffles from the same region, Dolcettos are equally well suited to wild mushrooms like the porcini here. But other medium-bodied dry reds with a fair amount of acidity will work too, such as a Beaujolais or Pinot Noir.

MELISSA If fresh **porcini** are not an option (they're available in season only, and not exactly cheap), substitute another full-flavored wild mushroom; you could also add a few slices of dried porcini to round out the flavor of the stew. To do so, about ½ hour before the stew is done, place a few dried porcini in a dish and cover with hot water. Let the mushrooms hydrate for about 15 minutes, then take them out of the liquid, wipe them free of grit, and cut them into slivers. Stir the soaked porcini and strained soaking liquid back into the stew for the last 15 minutes of braising.

AKHTAR NAWAB, Craftbar, New York

Veal Ricotta Meatballs

I was never a meatball fan until I tasted Akhtar Nawab's light-as-a-cloud version at Craftbar. The secret is the ricotta cheese, which gives them a fluffy, dissolve-on-the-tongue texture, rather than the usual Spalding bounce. Although the recipe wasn't hard when I finally got my hands on it (it took several weeks of begging, but he finally gave it up), it did take a few tries to get them not to fall apart in the sauce. I adjusted the proportions slightly and handled the mixture as gently as if it were made of live butterfly wings, and that seemed to do the trick. But even if one or two of the meatballs *do* fall apart in the sauce, serve it with a spoon or over pasta. It's so good that no one will complain. PREPARATION TIME: 30 MINUTES, PLUS UP TO 1 HOUR BRAISING

SERVES 4 TO 6

1 1/2 **pounds ground veal**

4 **cups ricotta cheese (see Chef's Tip)**

1/3 **cup freshly grated Parmesan cheese (about 1 ounce), plus additional for serving**

1 **large egg**

1/8 **teaspoon freshly grated nutmeg**

3/4 **teaspoon coarse sea salt or kosher salt, plus more to taste**

1/4 **teaspoon freshly ground black pepper, plus more to taste**

All-purpose flour, for dusting

Olive oil, for frying

1 **can (28 ounces) whole San Marzano tomatoes (see Chef's Tips, page 85)**

1/2 **cup (1 stick) unsalted butter**

1/4 **bunch of fresh basil, plus additional for garnish**

1 **garlic clove, chopped**

CHEF'S TIP Ricotta from the grocery store is okay in this recipe, but fresh ricotta from a good Italian deli or cheese store is superlative.

MELISSA'S TIP These meatballs are as delicate as possible, meaning they aren't full of binders like bread crumbs or so many eggs they taste like breakfast. You need to handle them gently to keep them from falling apart. Keeping the ingredients chilled until the last minute also helps.

1. Preheat the oven to 325°F. In a large bowl, mix together the veal, **ricotta,** Parmesan, egg, nutmeg, 3/4 teaspoon salt, and 1/4 teaspoon pepper. Dust your hands with flour and form the mixture into balls about 1 1/2 inches in diameter.

2. Pour about 1 inch of oil into a large skillet and warm it over high heat. Add the meatballs and sear until nicely browned on all sides, about 3 minutes total (work in batches if necessary to avoid overcrowding). Transfer the browned meatballs to plates lined with paper towels.

3. In a stockpot over medium-high heat, bring the tomatoes to a simmer. Stir in the butter, basil, and garlic. Add the seared meatballs, cover, and braise in the oven until the sauce is thick and the meatballs are cooked through, 45 minutes to 1 hour. Season with salt and pepper to taste.

4. Serve the meatballs and sauce sprinkled with finely chopped basil and grated Parmesan.

JANOS WILDER, Janos, Tucson

Venison Loin Adobada with Chipotle Black Beans

Interrupting this recipe was a tough one because Janos Wilder's original dish, though many-stepped and rarefied (it involved smoking tomatoes over mesquite), was magnificent to eat. Figuring out which components to do away with made me feel like I do when I edit down an article from 5,000 words to, say, 750 (no, not that paragraph!). But once I get into slash-and-burn mode, I know it's for the best. And so it was with this recipe. After I got used to the idea of trimming away three quarters of the ingredients and steps, I realized how good it was in its most basic, unadorned state: just the assertively spiced, tender venison loin served with a smoky black bean coulis. Compared to the original version, which contained sweet potato and mushroom chilaquiles (a casserole), smoked tomato salsa, shiitake escabeche, and venison sauce, it's about two days quicker to make. And unlike one of my unedited 5,000-word articles, which won't ever see the light of day, you can still sample Janos's original recipe at his eponymous restaurant, always chosen in *Zagat* as one of Tucson's favorites. PREPARATION TIME: 1 HOUR AND 10 MINUTES, PLUS 24 TO 48 HOURS MARINATING

SERVES 4

¼ cup mild chili powder

7 garlic cloves, 4 cloves crushed and 3 cloves chopped

3 tablespoons freshly squeezed lime juice (from 1½ limes)

2 tablespoons dark brown sugar

1 tablespoon balsamic vinegar

4 boneless venison loins (6 ounces each)

1 tablespoon extra-virgin olive oil

½ small onion, chopped

2 tablespoons red wine vinegar

8 plum tomatoes, halved, seeded, and diced

1 to 2 chipotle chiles in adobo sauce (see Melissa's Tips), to taste

2 tablespoons fresh oregano leaves, plus additional for garnish

Coarse sea salt or kosher salt and freshly ground black pepper

3 cups black beans, cooked and drained (canned is fine)

1 cup chicken broth, low-sodium if canned

1 cup finely chopped pecans

2 tablespoons grapeseed or canola oil

MELISSA'S TIPS Unless you know a hunter, your best bet is to ask a good butcher for either wild **venison** from Scotland or Ireland, or farmed American venison (I find the ubiquitous farmed venison from New Zealand to have a mushy texture). Farmed venison is a little milder and less gamy than wild, which some people may prefer.

1. In a large bowl, mix the chili powder, the 4 crushed garlic cloves, the lime juice, brown sugar, and balsamic vinegar to form a paste. Rub the **venison** loins all over with the paste, wrap with plastic, and refrigerate for **at least 24** and up to 48 hours.

2. Prepare the chipotle black beans: In a skillet over medium heat, warm the olive oil. Add the 3 chopped garlic cloves and the onion and sauté until lightly browned, about 7 minutes.

CHEF'S TIP The venison marinates for **at least 24 hours,** so make sure you begin at least a day in advance.

Add the red wine vinegar and bring to a simmer, then add all but ½ cup of the tomatoes, all the **chipotle chiles,** the oregano, and a generous pinch of salt and pepper. Cook until the tomatoes break down, about 10 minutes. Stir in the black beans and broth and bring to a simmer. Cook over low heat for 5 minutes, then taste and add more salt and pepper, if necessary.

3. Working in batches, puree the black bean mixture in a blender until smooth. Cover to keep warm (or reheat gently before serving).

4. Preheat the oven to 350°F. Roll the venison in the pecans. Warm the grapeseed oil in an ovenproof skillet (or two, depending upon the size of your pan) over medium-high heat. Add the venison loins and sear until browned on all sides, about 8 minutes, taking care not to burn the pecans. Place the pan in the oven and finish cooking the venison until done to taste, about 6 minutes for rare.

5. Serve the venison with the black bean coulis, garnished with the reserved tomatoes and oregano.

MELISSA Chipotle chiles in adobo sauce are a great canned food. Chipotles are smoked jalapeño peppers, and the adobo sauce is a thick, dark red, tangy tomato sauce that takes on some of the smokiness of the peppers. The spice is mostly inside the peppers, in the veins and seeds, which you could remove if you're spice-sensitive (wear rubber gloves when handling the spiciest part of the pepper). But these are only moderately hot, so most people won't mind the heat. Look for canned chipotles in adobo sauce in stores that cater to Mexican cooks (or order them online from www.mexgrocer.com).

MARC MURPHY, Landmarc, New York

Crispy Sweetbreads with Capers and Green Beans

Though this is one of my favorite recipes in the entire book, my guess would be that it might also be the least made dish. Most home cooks tend to consider raw sweetbreads with trepidation, even those who always order them in restaurants. I can understand. Sweetbreads are both relatively labor intensive (compared to, say, a steak) and they have a high ick quotient in terms of cleaning and handling. But if I can possibly convince you to give these luscious, crispy yet soft-centered little treats a try, you won't be sorry. And the street cred you'll gain will surely trump cooks at every other dinner party you attend, ever — worth every trimmed vein and membrane. PREPARATION TIME: 50 MINUTES

SERVES 6

1½ pounds veal sweetbreads

4 cups chicken broth, low-sodium if canned

1 fresh bay leaf

1 pound French green beans, trimmed and halved crosswise

Coarse sea salt or kosher salt

3 tablespoons extra-virgin olive oil

2 shallots, thinly sliced (½ cup)

2 anchovies

7 tablespoons unsalted butter, chilled and cubed

2 tablespoons chopped fresh flat-leaf parsley

Freshly ground black pepper

1 cup all-purpose flour

½ cup capers

Lemon wedges, for garnish

MELISSA'S TIPS Sweetbreads are the thymus of young animals (here we use veal, but lamb sweetbreads are also wonderful). This recipe is a pretty straightforward outline of the sweetbread cooking process, which includes boiling until firm, then cleaning away the veins and membrane before sautéing lightly. Avoid overcooking, both when boiling and sautéing, or the result can be a little chalky.

CHEF'S TIP To keep the nice white color of the **sweetbreads,** you can soak them in a large bowl of water acidulated with the juice of 1 lemon. Keep the bowl in the refrigerator for an hour or two, changing the water and lemon juice about once every half hour.

1. Prepare the **sweetbreads:** In a saucepan over high heat, combine the sweetbreads, broth, and bay leaf, and bring to a boil. Reduce the heat to low and simmer for 7 to 8 minutes, until the sweetbreads feel firm to the touch. Transfer the sweetbreads to a plate to cool and reserve ¼ cup of the broth.

2. Meanwhile, prepare the green beans: Bring a large pot of salted water to a boil. Drop in the green beans and cook until crisp-tender, about 4 minutes. Drain well.

3. In a sauté pan over medium-high heat, warm 1 tablespoon of the olive oil. Add the shallots and sauté until light brown, about 5 minutes. Add the anchovies, and stir until they begin to dissolve, 3 minutes longer. Add the reserved ¼ cup of broth and cook for about 3 minutes. Lower the heat to medium and swirl in 4 tablespoons of the butter, piece by piece. Add the green beans, parsley, and salt and pepper, and cook for 1 minute longer. Cover to keep warm.

4. Trim away all the veins and membranes from the sweet-breads and cut them into 1 ½-inch pieces. Toss the pieces in the flour and sprinkle with salt and pepper to taste.

5. In a skillet over high heat, warm the remaining 2 tablespoons of olive oil and remaining 3 tablespoons of butter. Add some of the sweetbreads (do not crowd the pan) and some of the **capers** and sauté until the sweetbreads are well browned, about 6 minutes. Transfer to a plate, tent with foil to keep warm, and repeat with the remaining sweetbreads and capers. Serve immediately with the green beans and lemon wedges.

MELISSA Capers are the buds of a Mediterranean flowering shrub that have been pickled and then either jarred in brine or salted. Use the brined capers sold in jars here (they are much easier to find). If you've always found the taste of capers a tad strong, give them a quick rinse under cold water before adding them to the pan.

Vegetables and Sides

Brussels Sprouts à la Plancha
ANDY NUSSER, Casa Mono

Fennel Slaw with Salsa Verde
TONY MANTUANO, Spiaggia

Quick Sauté of Zucchini with
Toasted Almonds and Pecorino
JIMMY BRADLEY, Red Cat

Herb and Lemon Stuffed Eggplant
with Fennel
DANTE BOCCUZZI, Aureole Restaurant

Spring Vegetables in an Iron Pot
ALAIN DUCASSE, Alain Ducasse

Fried Artichokes with Taleggio
SARA JENKINS, formerly of 50 Carmine

Elote Loco
(Roasted Corn with Lime and Cheese)
JOSÉ ANDRÉS, Café Atlantico

Asparagus Flan with Parmesan
MARK VETRI, Vetri

Three-Cheese Potato Gratin
WALDY MALOUF, Beacon

Farro with Spicy Cauliflower Ragù
MARK LADNER, Lupa

Buckwheat Polenta with
Porcini Mushrooms, Garlic,
and Parsley
FORTUNATO NICOTRA, Felidia

ANDY NUSSER, Casa Mono, New York

Brussels Sprouts à la Plancha

How do you interrupt a recipe for Brussels sprouts that has four ingredients, not counting the salt and pepper? You don't—or at least, I didn't. And even without my help, it's probably one of the simplest things in the book. But I wanted to include it because it's my favorite way to prepare one of my favorite vegetables. Andy Nusser sears and caramelizes the cut side of the sprouts while the middle takes on a texture that's as soft and tender as a baked potato. Then he holds back on the seasonings, adding just enough to complement the natural sweetness of the crucifer. If you like Brussels sprouts (and if you don't, try them at least once prepared this way to make sure), this will likely become your favorite recipe for them, too. I like to toss these sprouts with ¼ cup grated manchego, Parmesan, or Pecorino Romano cheese at the end.

PREPARATION TIME: 20 MINUTES

SERVES 6

Coarse sea salt or kosher salt

1½ pounds Brussels sprouts, ends trimmed

3 tablespoons extra-virgin olive oil

Freshly ground black pepper

1 tablespoon freshly squeezed lemon juice (from ½ lemon)

1½ tablespoons fresh thyme leaves

MELISSA'S TIPS Like many maligned vegetables, **Brussels sprouts** have gotten a bad rap because they aren't always served fresh. Buy them in cold weather (frost makes them sweeter) and avoid large, loose-leaved or tough, yellowed specimens. Some markets offer sprouts still on their stalk, a thick green trunk from which the sprouts protrude like gnarls on a tree. Cut the sprouts off the stalk and always peel off a couple of the tough outer leaves. When buying sprouts loose, look for smaller ones that are all about the same size for even cooking, and then trim a slice from their base to expose a fresh surface.

CHEF'S TIP The **iron skillet** is ideal for this recipe. Since it heats very thoroughly and uniformly, the Brussels sprouts brown evenly on their cut side. It gives them fantastic flavor.

1. Bring a large pot of salted water to a rolling boil and fill a bowl with water and ice. Add the **Brussels sprouts** to the boiling water and blanch for 1½ minutes. Immediately drain and transfer to the ice bath for a minute or two to cool, then drain well.

2. Place your largest **cast-iron skillet** over medium heat and let preheat for 10 minutes. Meanwhile, slice each sprout in half through the stem end and toss with the olive oil, salt, and pepper. Arrange a single layer of the sprouts cut side down in the skillet and cook until crisp, brown, and slightly charred, about 6 minutes. Transfer to a plate and keep warm. Repeat with the remaining sprouts.

3. Finish the sprouts by drizzling the lemon juice over the top and sprinkling with fresh thyme. Serve while hot.

Fennel Slaw with Salsa Verde

At the genteel Spiaggia, James Beard Award–winning chef Tony Mantuano serves an appetizer of grilled sardines with salsa verde and fennel salad. I loved the combination of the crisp and cool anise-flavored fennel with the sharp, tangy sauce, but sardines are a hard sell for a lot of people and often hard to find. So here I simply leave them out, turning Tony's elegant appetizer into a simple side dish or salad course. Or, for an unusual hors d'oeuvre, pile the slaw onto garlic-rubbed crostini.

SERVES 6

½ cup minced fresh tarragon

½ cup minced fresh chives

⅓ cup minced fresh Italian parsley

1 hard-boiled egg, peeled and chopped

½ teaspoon Dijon mustard

⅓ cup extra-virgin olive oil

1½ tablespoons capers, rinsed, drained, and chopped

Sea salt and freshly ground pepper to taste

3 fennel bulbs, with the feathery fronds

Freshly squeezed lemon juice

CHEF'S TIP The **salsa** can be made up to a week ahead and stored in the refrigerator. It's great served with any kind of grilled fish, meat, or even vegetables.

MELISSA'S TIP If you have one, you can also use a mandoline or a Japanese benriner to get perfectly thin, delicate slices of **fennel**. It's both easier and faster than slicing by hand.

1. Make the **salsa:** In a bowl, combine the tarragon, chives, parsley, egg, mustard, olive oil, and capers. Stir to mix thoroughly and let stand for at least one hour to allow the flavors to blend. Taste and season with salt and pepper.

2. To prepare the **fennel,** use a sharp knife to trim off the hard root end and the stalks, reserving the fronds. Halve the fennel lengthwise, and peel off the woody outer layer and discard it. Place the fennel cut side down on a cutting board and slice into very thin half-moons. Chop 2 tablespoons of the fronds.

3. In a medium bowl, toss the fennel with enough salsa to lightly coat it. Season with lemon juice, salt, and black pepper to taste, garnish with the reserved fronds, and serve.

JIMMY BRADLEY, Red Cat, New York

Quick Sauté of Zucchini with Toasted Almonds and Pecorino

The Red Cat, which opened on the western edges of Chelsea before that neighborhood became all that, was Jimmy Bradley's and Danny Abrams's first collaboration. It's the kind of convivial place with good cocktails and great food that everyone would want in their neighborhood and is, in fact, almost worth moving for, except that I'm too late, given west Chelsea's real estate value. This dish might not seem like much, but in fact it's the one thing on Jimmy's oft-changing menu that is a constant, and that I always have to order. Cutting the zucchini into matchsticks before sautéing them means they cook in about a minute, with crisp browned spots in places while still al dente in the center. And the addition of toasted almonds and salty Pecorino cheese is simple yet spot-on. PREPARATION TIME: 15 MINUTES

SERVES 4

3 tablespoons extra-virgin olive oil

½ cup sliced almonds

1 pound zucchini (3 to 4 small), sliced lengthwise into ⅛-inch-thick slices, then crosswise into matchsticks (about 5 cups)

Coarse sea salt or kosher salt and freshly ground black pepper

4 ounces Pecorino Romano, shaved with a cheese slicer or vegetable peeler

MELISSA'S TIP This recipe is so fast and easy, but since it relies on the highest heat and the most surface area in the pan, you do need to have **two pans** going at once. Be sure every ingredient is set out in advance and you're good to go. While I recommend measuring 1½ tablespoons of oil into each pan (or if you'd rather estimate, at least make sure you use enough oil to really coat each pan), you can halve the other ingredients by eye.

CHEF'S TIP This sauté is worth taking the trouble to **serve** on warmed plates. To warm plates, place them in a low oven for a few minutes or run scalding tap water over them, then dry them. Remember to handle the warm plates carefully. Or warm a platter if you are serving family style. Just make sure to get it while it's hot.

1. Divide the oil between **2 large skillets** set over high heat. When the oil is hot enough to shimmer but not yet smoking, add half the almonds to each pan. Cook, tossing constantly, until the almonds are golden-brown, about 30 seconds. Add half the zucchini to each pan and toss well to coat in oil. Take both pans off the heat, season the zucchini with salt and pepper, then return the pans to the heat for another 30 seconds to warm and distribute the seasoning.

2. Divide the sauté among 4 salad plates and arrange 3 shavings of Pecorino in a pyramid over each serving. **Serve** immediately while it's nice and hot.

DANTE BOCCUZZI, Aureole Restaurant, New York

Herb and Lemon Stuffed Eggplant with Fennel

At Aureole, Dante Boccuzzi's obsession with seasonal vegetables has led him to offer one of the most interesting and diverse vegetarian tasting menus in the city. This gorgeous eggplant dish, fragrant with fennel and lemon, is a mainstay on the menu during the late summer and early autumn, when the eggplant and fennel seasons overlap. In Dante's original recipe, he makes the eggplant slices into roulades, frying them until crisp. I saved several steps and some mess by broiling all the components stacked on top of one another. It's a more vertical, less complicated presentation that still captures the same herbaceous and lemony flavors. PREPARATION TIME: 45 MINUTES

SERVES 8

2 medium eggplants (about 14 ounces total), trimmed and cut crosswise into ½-inch rounds

Freshly squeezed juice of 2 lemons

Coarse sea salt or kosher salt

½ cup extra-virgin olive oil

8 shallots, peeled and thinly sliced

1 fennel bulb, quartered, cored, and thinly sliced, fronds finely chopped

Freshly ground black pepper

2 cups finely chopped mixed fresh herbs such as savory, oregano, flat-leaf parsley, and basil

Freshly grated zest of 4 lemons

⅓ cup heavy cream

⅓ cup grated Parmesan cheese

CHEF'S TIP Fresh **eggplants** have glossy, tight skins and should feel heavy for their size, so you know they have dense flesh and aren't dry and spongy inside. Eggplants are sweetest in the late summer and early fall, and small or medium-size ones are always sweeter than the mammoth ones they sell at many supermarkets. Treat eggplants like tomatoes, avoiding the refrigerator, and use before they turn soft or begin to dry out and shrivel. Soaking the slices in salt and lemon juice gets rid of their slight bitterness, and extracts water, making them firmer in the end. Broiling brings out a sweet, caramelized flavor, though you can also achieve this by grilling.

1. In a large bowl, toss the **eggplant** rounds with the lemon juice and a generous pinch of salt. Set aside for 30 minutes.

2. In a sauté pan over medium heat, warm ¼ cup of the olive oil. Add the shallots, sliced **fennel,** a pinch of salt, and pepper. Cook, stirring, until tender, about 8 minutes. Add the fennel fronds, herbs, and lemon zest, and cook for 4 more minutes. Add more salt and pepper to taste.

3. Preheat the broiler. Drain the marinated eggplant slices, then toss them with the remaining ¼ cup of olive oil and a pinch of salt and pepper. Line a rimmed baking sheet with foil and lay the eggplant slices out in a single layer on the baking sheet. Broil until well browned, then turn the slices over and brown the bottoms, about 2 minutes per side. Let cool briefly. Leave the broiler on.

4. To assemble, transfer an eggplant round to another foil-lined baking sheet. Top the round with about 2 tablespoons of the shallot and fennel mixture, then place a second eggplant round on top. Repeat, ending with a third eggplant round. Repeat with the remaining eggplant rounds and the rest of the filling. Drizzle a little of the cream over each stack, then sprinkle the tops with Parmesan. Broil the stacks until the cheese has browned, about 2 minutes (watch them carefully to make sure the cheese doesn't burn). Serve warm or at room temperature.

MELISSA'S TIP Fennel is a bulbous, licorice-tasting vegetable (also sold as anise) with a celery-like crunchiness. A fennel bulb should be white and crisp without blemishes, and ideally it should have a nice healthy shock of dill-like fronds still attached. For the licorice-wary, fennel is definitely best served cooked, when it takes on a soft sweetness that is much less intense (licorice lovers, on the other hand, can enjoy raw fennel as a crudité with dips, or shaved into a slaw-like salad tossed with lemon and olive oil). Wild fennel is also available at some markets; it is smaller and tougher, and often has even more flavor. To trim a fennel bulb, cut off the tough sprouting arms, reserving the fronds to use as an herb; trim the base; use a vegetable peeler to remove any of the outer area that seems tough and fibrous; halve it lengthwise and cut out the white core at the base; and slice.

Spring Vegetables in an Iron Pot

This is a takeoff on one of Alain Ducasse's signature dishes. His ever-so-heavily-truffled version, served in individual covered iron pots, is more complicated and rarefied than what I offer here, and is absolutely worth going to his restaurant to sample if you have the expendable income. But this modified version is worth making at home. It's exactly the kind of dish to serve to those people in your life (and we all have at least one) who think they don't like vegetables. This gorgeous mélange will show them. PREPARATION TIME: 1 HOUR

SERVES 4

½ cup extra-virgin olive oil

8 small carrots, peeled, or 4 regular carrots, peeled and quartered

8 small turnips, peeled, or 4 regular turnips, peeled and halved

8 small red radishes, trimmed

4 spring onions or scallions, trimmed

2 Swiss chard leaves, leaves and ribs separated

2 to 3 cups chicken broth, low-sodium if canned

16 baby artichokes, trimmed and quartered (you do not have to remove the chokes—see Melissa's Tip, page 208)

8 asparagus spears, tips separated, stalks trimmed and halved crosswise

4 small zucchini blossoms, pistils removed (see Melissa's Tip)

1 cup fresh or frozen peas (see Melissa's Tips, page 84)

1⅛ teaspoons coarse sea salt or kosher salt, plus additional to taste

Freshly squeezed juice of ½ lemon

Freshly ground black pepper

CHEF'S TIPS In the fall, you can substitute chestnuts, celery, fennel, and leek for the spring onions, zucchini blossoms, asparagus, and radishes, and replace the lemon juice with aged red wine vinegar.

MELISSA'S TIP Look for **squash blossoms** in the summer at markets that cater to Mexican or Italian cooks or at farmstands and specialty produce markets. (Or pluck them from the ends of your homegrown summer squash!) The blossoms can be refrigerated for a few hours or even overnight, but it's best to plan on using them the day you buy

1. In a large cast-iron or other heavy pot over medium-high heat, warm 3 tablespoons of the olive oil. Add the carrots, turnips, radishes, spring onions, and Swiss chard ribs, stir well, and cook for 3 to 4 minutes. Add ¼ cup of the chicken broth and cook, stirring frequently, until the vegetables are lightly browned but still firm, 8 to 10 minutes. (When you prick the vegetables with the tip of a sharp knife, you should feel a slight resistance.) Pour more chicken broth into the pot as the liquid evaporates, adding just enough each time to moisten the vegetables and cover the bottom of the pot.

2. Add the artichokes, asparagus stalks, and **zucchini blossoms,** and cook, stirring gently a few times, for 7 minutes more, adding chicken broth as necessary.

3. Add the asparagus tips, Swiss chard leaves, peas, ¼ cup of the chicken broth, 2 tablespoons of the olive oil, and 1 teaspoon salt, stirring to combine. Cook, adding chicken broth as necessary, until all the ingredients are meltingly tender, about 7 minutes.

4. Take the pan off the heat and add the lemon juice, the remaining 3 tablespoons of olive oil, ⅛ teaspoon salt, and pepper to taste. Stir well and serve immediately.

them. To prepare squash blossoms, give them a very quick rinse under cool water, then gently pat dry. Trim away the stem and spiky outer green leaves (sepals) at the base of the flower and pull out the pistils standing up in the center of the blossom.

CHEF Several paper-thin slices of black truffle or raw vegetables — such as radishes, asparagus, fennel, or artichoke — would be lovely on top, adding a crisp textural contrast to the softer cooked vegetables in the pot.

SARA JENKINS, formerly of 50 Carmine, New York

Fried Artichokes with Taleggio

Personally, I think if you fry nearly anything and smother it with melted Taleggio, it's going to be delicious. And fried artichokes by themselves are pure heaven. So combining those two naturally produces a dish that is so outrageously tasty I'd almost be afraid to make it for a dinner party, lest I ate the whole thing before sharing it with any guests. That's why I tested this dish alone, in the privacy of my own kitchen. When I write that this dish serves six, keep in mind that number is relative to the greediness of the cook. Taleggio, a Northern Italian cow's-milk cheese, is one of those cheeses that tastes milder than you'd think from its aroma. It's a fairly salty, semisoft cheese with a washed orange rind that can develop some blue-green mold in spots, and it tastes a little like a dense, creamy improvement on American Muenster. Taleggio melts beautifully, so try it on any vegetable, or on pasta. Any Taleggio you buy will be great here, but for the real deal, look for a raw-milk (unpasteurized) Taleggio, which will cost more and have much more flavor. Choose a nice ripe one that oozes a little at the center. PREPARATION TIME: 45 MINUTES

SERVES 6

12 baby artichokes

Freshly squeezed juice of ½ lemon

Extra-virgin olive oil, for frying

Coarse sea salt or kosher salt and freshly ground black pepper

½ pound Taleggio cheese, thinly sliced

Chopped fresh flat-leaf parsley, for garnish

MELISSA'S TIP Baby **artichokes** are not babies so much as they are runts. They grow lower on the stalk at the same time that larger artichokes are growing above them. These smaller artichokes do not develop as much choke, which makes them infinitely easier to prepare. Trim all artichokes well, however, taking off every leaf that's not totally soft and yellow, since a tough or spiky leaf is no fun to eat. To trim a baby artichoke, trim the stem end at the base, then pull off all the tough green outer leaves. Finally cut off and discard the top third of the artichoke, and immediately place the trimmed artichoke in acidulated water (water with lemon juice in it) to keep it from turning brown.

1. Clean and trim the **artichokes** (see Melissa's Tip) and cut them in half lengthwise. Immediately place them in a bowl of water, acidulated with the lemon juice.

2. In a large pan over high heat, warm ¼ inch of olive oil until almost smoking. Pat the artichokes dry and fry them until nice and crispy outside and soft inside, 12 to 14 minutes. If necessary, lower the heat to finish softening the artichokes if they brown quickly. Season liberally with salt and pepper.

3. Preheat the broiler. Line the bottom of a baking dish with the **cheese** slices and broil until melted, about 2 minutes. Place the fried artichokes over the cheese and pop back in the oven to get everything nice and warm, about 2 minutes more. Sprinkle with parsley and serve.

JOSÉ ANDRÉS, Café Atlantico, Washington, D.C.

Elote Loco (Roasted Corn with Lime and Cheese)

This is my version of José Andrés's highly refined and embellished take on classic Mexican grilled corn, a street food that's usually served with any combination of mayonnaise, grated cheese, lime juice, and chile. But since nobody wants to be seen chomping away at a corn on the cob at an elegant restaurant, José uses miniature corncobs at Café Atlantico. I compromise by using easy-to-find regular-sized corncobs but removing the kernels so it's not messy to eat in front of your friends and acquaintances. It's an excellent combination of flavors and texture, at once salty, creamy, spicy from the chile, and sweet and juicy from ripe summer corn. I'm no purist, and frozen corn has its place in my kitchen, since it is certainly sweeter than starchy old corn sold out of season or days after picking. But this recipe relies on the fresh, lightly sweet, almost buttery flavor and the delightfully crisp texture of just-picked summer corn, and even I wouldn't dream of making this out of season. Head for farmstands for the best corn, and pick out plump, firm ears with well-developed kernels, dry, healthy silk, and fresh, green husks (if you nibble a thick husk tip, it should be sweet and crisp). Then, ideally, make this recipe the same day. **PREPARATION TIME: 30 MINUTES**

SERVES 6

6 ears corn, shucked

¾ cup chopped fresh cilantro

6 tablespoons freshly grated Parmesan cheese (1½ ounces)

6 tablespoons mayonnaise

3 tablespoons crème fraîche or sour cream

3 tablespoons freshly squeezed lime juice (from 1½ limes)

½ tablespoon pure chile powder (see Chef's Tip), or more to taste

CHEF'S TIP Chili powder, meant for use in chili con carne and other Tex-Mex dishes, has additions like garlic, cumin, and other spices that aren't needed here, so look for a pure chile product. You can buy varietal chile powders now, made from smoky chipotle, sweet ancho, or flavorful jalapeño peppers (you can order them from Penzeys Spices: 800-741-7787; www.penzeys.com), or make your own by grinding dried chiles in the small bowl of a food processor (just make sure you don't inhale any of the powder, and wash everything with soapy water to remove the chile oils afterward).

1. Arrange the corncobs on a baking sheet and place under the broiler, turning once, until browned, about 2 minutes. Wrap the entire pan with foil and let sit for 5 minutes to finish cooking. Remove the foil and let cool slightly before cutting the kernels from the cob.

2. To cut kernels off a corncob (something you've done if you or your child has ever had braces), first halve the ear crosswise, then stand it in a wide bowl and run a thin-bladed sharp knife downward along the cob, popping the kernels off into the bowl.

3. In a large serving bowl, toss the corn **kernels** with all the other ingredients, and serve.

MARK VETRI, Vetri, Philadelphia

Asparagus Flan with Parmesan

This is more decadent than you'd think, even for something as inherently rich as a flan. Dip your spoon into the center of the creamy asparagus custard and you'll find a perfectly runny golden egg yolk. To add yet another layer of lusciousness, Mark Vetri, one of Philadelphia's most renowned chefs, then tops the whole thing with an outrageous Parmesan cream sauce. I simplified both the overall technique and the sauce for this dish, but I didn't tinker with the cream-butter-and-eggs quotient, which for me is just about perfect.

PREPARATION TIME: 45 MINUTES

SERVES 4

ASPARAGUS FLAN

Coarse sea salt or kosher salt

1 bunch asparagus (about ¾ pound), trimmed

2 large eggs

¼ cup heavy cream

Freshly ground back pepper

Freshly grated nutmeg

2 tablespoons all-purpose flour

1 tablespoon unsalted butter, softened

4 large egg yolks

PARMESAN SAUCE

1 cup heavy cream

½ cup freshly grated Parmesan cheese, plus additional for garnish

A few drops of truffle oil (optional)

CHEF'S TIP You can substitute almost any vegetable for the **asparagus** in this recipe. Fennel, zucchini, and summer squash work well, as do winter squash and eggplant, though you should roast rather than blanch these last two or they might turn watery.

MELISSA'S TIPS If you have any extra asparagus **puree,** save it to use as a crostini topping. Simply mix it with a little chopped garlic, salt, and good olive oil, spread it on thinly sliced grilled or toasted bread, and there you have it.

1. Make the flans: Bring a large pot of salted water to a rolling boil. Blanch the **asparagus** in the boiling water until just tender, about 4 minutes. Drain and let cool. Place the asparagus in a blender and **puree;** add a little water if it is too thick to move around in the blender. Measure out 1 cup of the puree into a bowl and save any extra for another use. Add the whole eggs, cream, salt and pepper, and a sprinkle of nutmeg to taste. Whisk until just combined, then gently whisk the flour into the mixture.

2. In a large, covered skillet over medium-high heat, bring ½ inch of water to a boil. Use the butter to amply grease four 6-ounce glass or ceramic ramekins, and fill each halfway with the asparagus mixture. Gently place a raw **egg yolk** in the center of the puree and cover with the remaining puree.

Immediately place the ramekins inside the skillet, cover, and cook for 7 to 8 minutes, until just set.

3. While the flans cook, prepare the sauce. In a small saucepan over medium-high heat, bring the cream to a boil. Whisk in the Parmesan. Reduce the heat to low and simmer until thick, about 7 minutes. Stir in the truffle oil, if desired.

4. To serve, **unmold** each flan (see Melissa's Tips), spoon a pool of sauce around it, and serve with a little Parmesan cheese sprinkled on top. Alternatively, and more simply, place each ramekin on a saucer and serve in the mold with some sauce spooned over the top and a sprinkling of cheese.

As much as I adore the runny **egg yolk** in the center of this flan, if you would rather save that step and leave it out, the result will still be nearly as marvelous. And since no one but you knew the yolk was supposed to be there, no one but you will miss it.

To **unmold** the flans, place a plate over the top of one; turn over the ramekin, holding the plate flush against it, and use the back of a knife to rap sharply on the back of the ramekin; then gently lift off the ramekin, leaving the flan on the plate. Buttering the ramekins very well at the outset will make your life much easier when it comes time to unmold. Or, serve the flans in the ramekins for a stress-free alternative, which I highly recommend.

WALDY MALOUF, Beacon, New York

Three-Cheese Potato Gratin

This recipe is one of the handful in the book that needed no simplifying or changing. In fact, it's so simple that I would barely think to include it here—except it is absolutely the best potato gratin I've ever had. It's the definitive recipe, in my opinion. So even if it's more Mom than Chef, it still fits the theme of the book, in that it's the perfection of its form, the über-gratin. And the recipe does happen to come from a chef, so I say it's apropos. If you knew Waldy, you'd know that although he was trained in the classic French culinary tradition and has plenty of cheffy tricks up his white sleeve, he is, at heart, an all-American, meat-and-potatoes kind of guy. **PREPARATION TIME: 25 MINUTES, PLUS 60 TO 70 MINUTES BAKING**

SERVES 6

6 unpeeled garlic cloves

1 tablespoon butter, softened

1 1/2 cups heavy cream

1 1/2 cups chicken or vegetable broth, low-sodium if canned

1 sprig of fresh rosemary

1 sprig of fresh thyme

1/8 teaspoon freshly grated nutmeg

3/4 teaspoon salt

Freshly ground black pepper

4 medium baking potatoes, peeled

3/4 cup (3 ounces) grated Parmesan cheese

3/4 cup (3 ounces) grated Gruyère cheese

1/4 cup (1 ounce) grated aged goat cheese

CHEF'S TIPS Floury baking **potatoes** work best here, since the starch helps thicken the cream and chicken broth into a rich sauce.

MELISSA'S TIPS For Thanksgiving or other winter meals, substitute sweet **potatoes** in this recipe. Or use a combination.

CHEF You can substitute other **cheeses** for the ones I suggest. Blue cheese is terrific in place of the goat cheese if you want a jolt of flavor. For something milder, Cheddar works well, too. But try to use at least three to keep the different layers of taste.

1. Preheat the oven to 350°F. Slice one of the garlic cloves in half. Rub the cut sides all over the inside of a 1 1/2-quart shallow gratin or casserole dish. Brush the inside of the dish with the softened butter.

2. Smash the remaining 5 garlic cloves with the side of a knife and put them in a large saucepan. Add the cream, broth, rosemary, thyme, and nutmeg. Bring the mixture to a boil, then reduce the heat and let simmer for 15 minutes. Strain the mixture into a bowl, discarding the garlic and herbs. Stir in the salt and pepper.

3. Using a mandoline or food processor, or by hand, cut the **potatoes** into 1/8-inch-thick slices. Mix the Parmesan, Gruyère, and goat **cheese** together in a small bowl.

4. Cover the bottom of the gratin dish with an overlapping layer of a quarter of the potato slices. Pour a quarter of the

Fresh herbs are another nice addition. Chop them up and add them to the gratin with the potatoes. Cooked crumbled bacon is good, too. Or both.

MELISSA Leftover gratin is easily reheatable. You can nuke it for a minute or so or wrap it in foil and heat it in a 350°F. oven.

broth mixture over the potatoes, and sprinkle with a quarter of the grated cheese mixture. Continue layering the casserole in this manner until all the ingredients are used up. Using a spatula, press down hard on top of the gratin to compact it.

5. Bake the gratin until the top is crusty and golden brown and a knife easily cuts through the potatoes, about 60 to 70 minutes. Transfer the gratin to a rack and cool for at least 10 minutes before serving.

MARK LADNER, Lupa, New York

Farro with Spicy Cauliflower Ragù

Although this dish is supposedly about the cauliflower and farro, making it appear on the health-conscious side, don't be fooled. With the amount of cheese and butter Mark uses, it's decadent and incredibly satisfying, more like the whole-grain and vegetable version of macaroni and cheese than anything too salubrious. You can serve it with just about any roasted or pan-seared meat or fish, although it also makes an especially fine vegetarian entrée. PREPARATION TIME: 1 HOUR AND 15 MINUTES

SERVES 6

1 pound farro

Coarse sea salt or kosher salt and freshly ground black pepper

8 to 10 tablespoons unsalted butter

1 cauliflower, separated into florets, stems thinly sliced and kept separate

1 onion, sliced

1 sprig of fresh rosemary

1 teaspoon crushed red pepper flakes, or to taste

¾ cup (3 ounces) freshly grated Parmesan cheese

¾ cup (3 ounces) freshly grated Pecorino Romano cheese

MELISSA'S TIPS Farro is an ancient variety of wheat from the Mediterranean. Its hulled kernels have a nutty grain taste and delightful, nubby texture. It's terrific as a base for a grain salad, or try farro as a pasta alternative, topped with your favorite sauce. It is available at gourmet food shops, Italian specialty stores, and health food stores.

CHEF'S TIP The amount of **butter** you use is strictly up to you, but this dish should be on the rich side, so don't skimp. Or substitute a good olive oil for some of the butter.

1. Rinse the **farro** under cold running water until the water runs clear. Place the farro in a large pot with 6 cups of water and bring to a boil. Continue to boil until the farro is no longer crunchy, yet still has a little firmness to it, about 25 minutes, adding 1 tablespoon of salt during the last 10 minutes of cooking time.

2. Drain the farro, reserving the cooking liquid (or scoop the farro into a bowl using a skimmer or sieve, leaving the water in the pot). Season the drained farro with salt and pepper.

3. Meanwhile, make the ragù: In a large pan over medium heat, melt 2 tablespoons of the **butter.** Add the sliced **cauliflower** stems and the onion, and season with salt. Cook, stirring occasionally, until the onions are golden and the cauliflower has begun to caramelize, about 15 minutes. Lower the heat and add ½ cup of water. Simmer, scraping up any browned bits from the bottom of the pan, for 15 minutes. Add more water if the mixture begins to dry out.

4. Add the cauliflower florets, rosemary, red pepper flakes, and 1 cup of water, season with salt and pepper, and simmer, partially covered, until the florets are falling apart and the mixture has broken down into a rough sauce, about 30 minutes.

5. To serve, add the farro to the sauce along with 1½ cups of its cooking liquid and 6 to 8 tablespoons of butter. Cook, stirring, until steaming hot and well incorporated, about 5 minutes. Stir in the cheeses and serve at once.

MELISSA This ragù is a great way to eat **cauliflower.** It's excellent with the farro, or tossed with small pasta shapes or spätzle, and it also makes a fine topping for polenta and bruschetta.

FORTUNATO NICOTRA, Felidia, New York

Buckwheat Polenta with Porcini Mushrooms, Garlic, and Parsley

Combining nutty, full-flavored buckwheat flour with mild and sweet cornmeal to make polenta is typical in northern Italy, where it's called *taragna*, or *polenta nera*. It has a deeper color and flavor than regular polenta and is a nice change from the ordinary. It's also a dish that reflects the northern Italian and Istrian heritage of Felidia's owner, Lidia Bastianich. Aside from being a talented chef and expert on Italian cuisine, Lidia is also the matriarch of the Bastianich clan that includes her son Joe, who co-owns some of New York's finest Italian restaurants including Babbo, Esca, and Lupa. This recipe, however, was created by Fortunato Nicotra, Felidia's current brilliant chef de cuisine. He likes to pair the nutty polenta with sautéed fresh porcini, which are meaty and satisfying enough to serve as an entrée. PREPARATION TIME: 30 MINUTES, PLUS 20 MINUTES CHILLING TIME

SERVES 6

2 tablespoons unsalted butter

2 tablespoons coarse sea salt or kosher salt, plus additional to taste

1 bay leaf

1 cup instant polenta

½ cup buckwheat flour

Freshly ground black pepper

3 tablespoons extra-virgin olive oil

2 garlic cloves, sliced

4 cups (about ¾ pound) sliced porcini or other assorted wild and/or exotic mushrooms (see Chef's Tips)

Mascarpone, for serving (optional)

⅔ cup chopped fresh flat-leaf parsley, for serving

CHEF'S TIPS Use half milk and half **water** for a richer-tasting polenta.

Most Americans first experience porcini (also called boletes, or cèpes) dried, where their strong, woodsy taste is concentrated, and a slice or two can infuse a pot of sauce. But fresh porcini **mushrooms** are a seasonal delicacy that are worth the splurge. They are at their most flavorful in the fall. Look for fresh porcini wherever fancy mushrooms are sold (or order them from Marché aux Delices, 888-547-5471; www.auxdelices.com). Buy firm, flexible ones that don't seem to have dried out or developed damp spots. Clean the

1. In a medium saucepan, bring 3½ cups of **water** to a boil, and add the butter, salt, and bay leaf. In a small bowl, mix the polenta and buckwheat flour together, sifting the grains through your hand like sand through an hourglass. Slowly add the grains to the boiling water, stirring to avoid clumps. Stir until cooked through, about 5 minutes. Season with pepper and additional salt if necessary.

2. Discard the bay leaf and spoon the polenta into an 8-inch square cake pan. Chill in the refrigerator until set, about 20 minutes and up to 2 days (cover it if you are leaving it for more than 2 hours). Just before serving, preheat the broiler (to low if possible).

mushrooms by trimming away the bottom and wiping the cap and stalk with a damp towel.

MELISSA'S TIPS If porcini are out of season or out of your pocketbook range, you can use any **mushrooms** for this recipe. A good, not-too-hard-to-find mix might include shiitake, oyster, and cremini. Of course, chanterelles, black trumpets, and hen-of-the-woods would be fantastic if you could find any of them. And even white buttons are nothing to sneer at.

3. Prepare the **mushrooms:** In a wide skillet over medium-high heat, warm 1 tablespoon of the olive oil. Add half the garlic and sauté for 1 minute. Add half the mushrooms, a large pinch of salt, and several grindings of pepper and cook, stirring only occasionally, until soft and browned, about 3 to 4 minutes. Transfer to a plate and cover to keep warm. Repeat with another tablespoon oil and the remaining garlic and mushrooms.

4. While the mushrooms are cooking, broil the polenta. Brush the top with the remaining tablespoon of olive oil, then slide the pan under the broiler until the top is brown in spots and the polenta is heated through, about 3 minutes. Run the blade of a knife around the edges of the pan and turn the polenta out onto a cutting board. Cut into 24 rectangles. Serve the mushrooms over the polenta squares, garnished with **mascarpone,** parsley, and black pepper.

This earthy dish benefits from the rich creaminess of **mascarpone,** the smooth, buttery Italian cheese that's best known for its use in tiramisù. Serve a dollop of mascarpone on top of each portion, if desired.

Desserts

Warm Upside Down Brown Sugar
Cakes with Apricot Compote
KAREN DEMASCO, Craft and Craftbar

Caramelized Pineapple Cheesecake
on Almond Cake
NICOLE KAPLAN, Eleven Madison Park

Goat Cheese Cake with Thyme-
Macerated Raspberry Compote
CLAUDIA FLEMING, formerly of Gramercy Tavern

Rosemary Polenta Pound Cake and
Olive Oil Whipped Cream
CHRISTINE LAW, Postrio

Warm Chocolate Cakes with
Coffee Ice Cream and Cashew Brittle
DEBORAH SNYDER, Lever House

Cinnamon Plum Tart
GINA DEPALMA, Babbo Ristorante e Enoteca

Chocolate Peanut Butter Parfaits with
Caramelized Bananas
NICOLE KAPLAN, Eleven Madison Park

Meyer Lemon Pudding Cake with
Meyer Lemon Ice Cream
ANNE QUATRANO, Bacchanalia

Sticky Toffee Pudding with Toffee Sauce
DAVID CARMICHAEL, Oceana

Butterscotch Custards
KAREN DEMASCO, Craft and Craftbar

Chocolate Tart with a Cornmeal Crust
and Pear Compote
VICKI WELLS, Bolo

Peach and Blueberry Cobbler with
Vanilla Whipped Cream
LAUREN DAWSON, Hearth

Fresh Fig Tart with Parmesan Ice Cream
KOA DUNCAN, Bastide

Bing Cherry Compote with
Black Pepper Ice Cream
KAREN BARKER, Magnolia Grill

Layered Rhubarb Coupe with
Rhubarb Sorbet and Crème Fraîche
DAN BARBER AND MICHAEL ANTHONY,
Blue Hill at Stone Barns

Roasted Cinnamon Gelato with
Sherried Raisins
MEREDITH KURTZMAN, Otto Enoteca Pizzeria

Chocolate Marshmallow Mounds
CLAUDIA FLEMING, formerly of Gramercy Tavern

Vanilla Bean Kulfi with Blood Oranges
in Darjeeling Syrup
FLOYD CARDOZ, Tabla

Halvah Sesame Ice Cream Sundae
BILL YOSSES, Joseph's

Cornmeal Hazelnut Biscotti
KAREN BARKER, Magnolia Grill

KAREN DEMASCO, Craft and Craftbar, New York

Warm Upside Down Brown Sugar Cakes with Apricot Compote

What's nice about Karen DeMasco's recipe is that she deconstructs the upside down cake: instead of having soggy fruit that sometimes sticks to the bottom of the pan and not to the batter, she prepares the two parts separately. This gives you infinite options about what fruit to use, depending on the season and your mood; and how long to cook it, depending on what kind of texture you like (I like it slightly firm and not completely limp). For this recipe, however, my favorite fruit is apricot, since the tartness cuts the sweet, gooey richness of the brown sugar filling, which flows liberally from the center of the cake when you stab it. PREPARATION TIME: 45 MINUTES, PLUS 1 HOUR CHILLING AND 30 MINUTES BAKING

SERVES 6

APRICOT COMPOTE

4 cups sliced ripe apricots (about 12 apricots)

¼ cup granulated sugar

BROWN SUGAR TOPPING

1 cup packed dark brown sugar

¼ cup (½ stick) unsalted butter

¼ cup heavy cream

CAKES

1½ cups (3 sticks) unsalted butter, softened, plus additional for greasing the ramekins

¾ cup granulated sugar

¼ cup plus 2 tablespoons dark brown sugar

1 teaspoon pure vanilla extract

4 large eggs

1½ cups all-purpose flour

1 cup almond flour

1½ teaspoons baking powder

¾ teaspoon kosher salt or fine sea salt

FOR SERVING

Vanilla ice cream or whipped cream (optional)

CHEF'S TIPS You can prepare the apricot **compote** up to 2 days ahead. Chill the compote until ready to serve; let it come to room temperature for at least 20 minutes before serving.

When **apricots** are in season in the early to mid summer, there's nothing better. Small, fragrant apricots are preferable to the larger, blander ones that grocery stores often offer; if the apricots don't smell good enough to

1. Prepare the **compote:** In a medium saucepan over medium-high heat, cook the **apricots** and the ¼ cup granulated sugar until softened, about 6 minutes. Use within 2 hours or chill until ready to serve.

2. Prepare the brown sugar topping: Place the 1 cup brown sugar in a bowl. In a small saucepan over medium-high heat, bring the ¼ cup butter and the cream to a boil. Pour the mixture over the brown sugar and whisk until smooth. Let cool, then chill for at least 1 hour, and up to 1 day.

3. Preheat the oven to 325°F. Butter six 5-ounce **ramekins** and drop 1 tablespoon of the chilled brown sugar topping into the bottom of each one.

4. Make the cake batter: In the bowl of an electric mixer, cream the 1½ cups butter with the sugars and vanilla until fluffy and well combined, about 2 minutes. Add the eggs one at a time, beating well after each addition. Scrape down the bowl, add the all-purpose and **almond flours,** baking powder, and salt, and beat on low speed until just combined.

5. Divide the batter among the ramekins and place them on a baking sheet. Bake for 12 to 14 minutes, until the **cakes** begin to brown around the edges. Use a small spoon to sink a dollop of brown sugar topping into the center of each cake, then continue baking until the cakes are golden brown and firm to the touch, 16 to 18 more minutes. Transfer to wire racks and let cool slightly before unmolding each cake. Serve with apricot compote and, if desired, vanilla ice cream or whipped cream.

bother with, any ripe fruit will be great here. Plums are available into the fall, and raspberries are always a good choice—just sweeten to taste, and keep in mind that tender berries take only a minute to cook.

If you use a sweeter fruit, such as bananas, blueberries, peaches, or pears, try crème fraîche or sour cream as an accompaniment instead of ice cream or whipped cream.

MELISSA'S TIPS I have an assortment of **ramekins,** those little white custard or soufflé cups that usually have vertical ridges on the outside, and I use them often for individual baked desserts. The smaller-size ramekins hold about 5 ounces (150 milliliters), though they come in several different sizes (my large ramekins, which I use less often, hold 8 ounces/250 milliliters).

Almond flour is made from finely ground almonds and can be found at baking stores, some natural food stores, and Indian food shops. Store it in the fridge to prolong its shelf life. Or make your own by grinding 1 cup of sliced almonds in the food processor, pulsing on and off, until they're finely ground. The ground almonds won't quite have the same light texture as commercially prepared almond flour, but it will still make an amazing dessert.

CHEF The **cakes** can be made ahead and held at room temperature for up to 6 hours (don't unmold). Before serving, reheat them for 10 minutes at 350°F., then unmold them onto serving plates.

NICOLE KAPLAN, Eleven Madison Park, New York

Caramelized Pineapple Cheesecake on Almond Cake

Nicole Kaplan serves this cheesecake accompanied not only by the caramelized pineapple, but also by a pineapple soup, a scoop of coconut rum sorbet, and an almond tuile. I've pared it down to what I think are the essentials: her amazingly moist cheesecake set on top of a fluffy, marzipan-like layer, and the caramelized pineapple that will make you never order gelatinous strawberry cheesecake again. This is the perfect recipe for anyone who loves moist cream cheesecake but can't be bothered with using a water bath (even though they are really no big deal). In Nicole's recipe, the technique of baking the cheesecake on top of the almond cake insulates the cheese layer, so it won't be as likely to overcook and curdle. PREPARATION TIME: 45 MINUTES, PLUS 2 HOURS BAKING AND COOLING

SERVES 9

ALMOND CAKE

6 tablespoons unsalted butter, softened, plus more for greasing pan

1/3 cup plus 1 tablespoon granulated sugar

4 ounces (about 6 tablespoons) almond paste

1/4 cup cake or all-purpose flour

2 large eggs

1/4 vanilla bean, split lengthwise and scraped (see Melissa's Tips, pages 260–261)

2 teaspoons dark rum

CRÈME FRAÎCHE CHEESECAKE

1 3/4 cups (1 pound) cream cheese, at room temperature

1/2 cup granulated sugar

1/2 vanilla bean, split lengthwise and scraped

Pinch of kosher salt or fine sea salt

1 large egg plus 1 large egg yolk (see Chef's Tips, page 258)

1/3 cup crème fraîche

CARAMELIZED PINEAPPLE

1 pineapple, peeled, cored, and cut into 1-inch cubes (3 1/2 to 4 cups)

1 cup dark brown sugar

1/2 vanilla bean, split lengthwise and scraped

1/2 cup dark rum

MELISSA'S TIPS Almond paste is similar to marzipan but not as sweet. It varies in quality, and the cans in the grocery store tend to be overwhelmingly flavored with almond extract. So I like to use one a step up from that, such as Odense, which comes in tubes and is pretty easy to find. Or you can buy high-quality almond paste in bulk at baking-supply stores.

1. Preheat the oven to 350°F. Grease a 9-inch square cake pan.

2. Make the almond cake: Using an electric mixer, beat the butter, granulated sugar, and **almond paste** until completely smooth. This could take about 8 minutes—or even longer if the almond paste is dry. Beat in the flour until thoroughly combined. Add the eggs one at a time, beating until just combined after each addition. Mix in the vanilla and rum just until smooth. Spread the batter in the pan and bake for 20 to

22 minutes, until the cake springs back to the touch. Transfer to a wire rack to cool completely, at least 1 hour and up to 24 hours. (Cover the cake with plastic if keeping for more than 6 hours.)

3. Prepare the cheesecake: Reduce the oven temperature (or preheat) to 325°F. Using an electric mixer, beat the cream cheese and granulated sugar until light and fluffy. Beat in the vanilla seeds and salt. Add the egg and then the yolk, mixing until just combined after each addition. Mix in the **crème fraîche** until just combined.

4. Pour the cheesecake mixture over the top of the almond cake and bake for 30 minutes, or until the cake is softly set in the center (it will jiggle slightly). Let the cake cool on a wire rack for at least 1 hour, then chill for at least 4 hours, or overnight. For longer storage, **freeze** the cake (see Melissa's Tips).

5. For the **pineapple,** combine all the ingredients in a saucepan and cook over medium heat, stirring occasionally, until the fruit is just tender, about 10 minutes. Let cool slightly before serving.

6. To serve, cut squares of cake and serve with the warm pineapple on top.

Crème fraîche is a cultured French dairy product similar to sour cream, though with a tangier, richer taste and with the added bonus that it can be used to enrich sauces or soups and will not curdle when boiled. If crème fraîche is not available, you can use sour cream instead. Or you can make your own crème fraîche by combining 1 cup heavy cream with about 2 tablespoons yogurt or buttermilk, covering the container, and leaving the mixture in a warm place until thick and sour, about 12 hours (shake the container occasionally). You can refrigerate homemade crème fraîche for about a week—it will get thicker and tangier as it sits in the fridge.

This is a wonderful make-ahead recipe. It can be **frozen** for up to a week (just wrap it well) and served almost straight from the freezer. It will thaw in about 20 minutes after it's cut into squares. Or thaw the whole cake in the fridge overnight.

CHEF'S TIP The caramelized **pineapple** can be made in advance and refrigerated. Reheat it in a small pot or in the microwave just before serving. Extra pineapple is great over ice cream.

CLAUDIA FLEMING, formerly of Gramercy Tavern, New York

Goat Cheese Cake with Thyme-Macerated Raspberry Compote

I met Claudia Fleming when I was writing her chef's column for the *New York Times* back in 1999. But even by then, I already knew who she was and had been following her career for a long time. Before she started working at Gramercy Tavern (which is where she was when we first worked together), I lapped up her desserts at Luxe. I couldn't resist her flavor combinations. Chocolate with bay leaf and lemon verbena custards, to me, were and still are the height of pastry-chef brilliance.

Of course, when you idolize someone's desserts for that long, there's always a risk you won't actually like the person when you meet her. Not so with Claudia. We hit it off right away, over that first recipe we made for the *Times*, Rhubarb Rose Cobbler with Goat-Yogurt Rose Cream. So I was thrilled when a few weeks after the column came to an end, Claudia called and asked me to work on her book. Her original co-author, it turns out, was too busy on someone else's book to focus on Claudia's, and besides, she didn't really eat dessert. Obviously, this wasn't a problem with me.

There is a version of this goat cheese cake recipe in the cookbook Claudia and I wrote (*The Last Course*, Random House, 2001), but I've simplified and streamlined it here. Claudia served the cake with a hazelnut tart and a scoop of Concord grape sorbet. I've substituted another of her signatures, raspberry compote with lemon thyme, which is much easier to make. And if using both goat cheese and lemon thyme in one dessert sounds like too much, make it at least once and see for yourself why it's not. PREPARATION TIME: 35 MINUTES, PLUS 2 HOURS BAKING AND STANDING

SERVES 8

CHEESECAKE

1¼ cups plus 2 tablespoons (about 12 ounces) cream cheese, at room temperature

8 ounces fresh goat cheese, at room temperature

½ cup sugar

½ vanilla bean, split lengthwise and scraped (see Melissa's Tips, pages 260–261)

4 large eggs, at room temperature

1½ cups mascarpone

RASPBERRY COMPOTE

3 cups fresh raspberries

¼ teaspoon fresh thyme leaves, preferably lemon thyme

2 tablespoons sugar, or more to taste

CHEF'S TIPS Use an extremely fresh, mild **goat cheese** here. It should be clean and creamy tasting, with a slight tang, and should not taste barnyardy.

1. Preheat the oven to 325°F. In the bowl of an electric mixer fitted with the whisk attachment, combine the cream cheese, **goat cheese,** sugar, and vanilla bean scrapings. Beat until smooth and creamy.

2. Add the eggs and mix well. Add the **mascarpone** and beat until smooth.

3. Wrap the outside of an 8-inch springform pan with foil. Scrape the mixture into the pan and place it in the center of a larger baking pan. Pour enough very hot water into the baking pan to reach two thirds of the way up the side of the spring-form pan. Cover the entire baking pan with foil. Prick the foil in several places. Bake in the water bath for 1 hour, then lift the foil to allow the steam to escape. Replace the foil and return the cake to the oven to cook until just slightly jiggly in the center, about 50 minutes more.

4. Transfer the cake to a wire rack to cool completely before serving.

5. Just before serving, prepare the compote. In a blender or food processor, puree 1 cup of the raspberries with the **thyme** leaves and 2 tablespoons of sugar (or more if the berries seem tart). Let the mixture stand for 10 minutes. Toss gently with the remaining raspberries. **Serve** immediately.

MELISSA'S TIPS Mascarpone, a gentle, milky fresh cheese from Italy, works really well in the recipe because it's almost the antithesis of the goat cheese—luscious and subtle next to tart and earthy. But if you can't find it, heavy cream makes a fine substitute.

CHEF If you can find it, use **lemon thyme.** It gives the berries a particularly bright flavor.

MELISSA Other herbs can be substituted for the **thyme.** Basil is great with berries, as is mint or tarragon. Or leave out the herbs altogether. It will be a slightly less nuanced dessert, but perhaps less challenging, too.

CHEF This creamy cheesecake works really well when **served** with a crisp cookie on the side—kind of like what a graham cracker crust is supposed to do, but rarely does since it usually gets soggy. Shortbread cookies or ginger-snaps are good, or you can make the graham crackers from my Chocolate Marshmallow Rounds recipe on page 257, which are a perfect complement.

MELISSA Although the berries need to be prepared just before serving, the cheesecake can be made a day or two ahead and refrigerated. Bring it to room temperature, then unmold it immediately before serving for the best texture.

CHRISTINE LAW, Postrio, San Francisco

Rosemary Polenta Pound Cake and Olive Oil Whipped Cream

Olive oil whipped cream. It's strange, I'll admit. But I always like to test chefs' wackier recipes because, for all the weird, unappetizing conceits, there are a few brilliant gems that I'll make again and again. Like this. The olive oil gives the cream a thicker, slicker texture and a slightly savory flavor that pairs well with sweets, especially those with berries or chocolate. In addition to this delightful pound cake recipe (which you can also use in the rhubarb coupe recipe on page 252), I love it with the warm chocolate cakes on page 229.

PREPARATION TIME: 1 HOUR, PLUS 20 TO 30 MINUTES BAKING

MAKES 6 INDIVIDUAL CAKES OR 1 SMALL LOAF

POUND CAKE

½ cup sugar

Grated zest of 1 lemon

½ cup (1 stick) unsalted butter, softened, plus additional to grease pans

½ teaspoon finely chopped fresh rosemary

¼ teaspoon freshly ground black pepper

2 large eggs

2 tablespoons crème fraîche

1 teaspoon freshly squeezed lemon juice

¼ cup all-purpose flour

¾ teaspoon baking powder

⅛ teaspoon kosher salt or fine sea salt

¼ cup plus 3 tablespoons finely ground polenta or cornmeal

Coarsely ground polenta or cornmeal, for dusting

OLIVE OIL WHIPPED CREAM

½ cup heavy cream

½ cup crème fraîche

¼ vanilla bean, split lengthwise and scraped (see Melissa's Tips, pages 260–261)

1½ teaspoons sugar

1 tablespoon extra-virgin olive oil

FOR SERVING

1 teaspoon lavender salt (see Melissa's Tips)

CHEF'S TIPS Grinding the sugar and lemon zest together helps release the essential oils in the citrus.

1. Preheat the oven to 350°F. Prepare the pound cake: Using a mortar and pestle or food processor, **grind** together the sugar and lemon zest. Using an electric mixer, cream the butter with the sugar–lemon mixture, rosemary, and pepper on medium speed until smooth. Add the eggs, one at a time, scraping down the bowl frequently. Add the crème fraîche and lemon juice and mix well.

RECIPE CONTINUES

2. In a medium bowl, whisk together the flour, baking powder, and salt. Stir in the finely ground polenta. Add the dry ingredients to the batter and mix on low speed just until incorporated. (Do not overmix.)

MELISSA'S TIPS This recipe makes enough cake for 6 and uses either **ramekins** or a small **loaf pan,** which you may or may not own. Double the recipe if you'd rather bake a standard loaf—just increase the baking time to 40 to 45 minutes.

3. Butter six 5-ounce **ramekins** or one 4-cup **loaf pan** and coat with a fine layer of coarse polenta or cornmeal. Spoon the batter into the ramekins and bake for 20 to 25 minutes, until the cakes are golden and the center springs back when touched. Or bake the 4-cup loaf for about 30 minutes. Let cool on a wire rack before unmolding. The cakes will keep, refrigerated, for up to 5 days.

4. Preheat the broiler.

CHEF You must use an intense brand of **olive oil** (I like Tenutadi Capezzana or Frantoia Barbera, but any good strong oil will work), or the whipped cream won't have enough flavor to make it interesting.

5. Prepare the olive oil whipped cream: Using a whisk or electric mixer, whip together the heavy cream, crème fraîche, and vanilla pulp until the cream starts to thicken but is still pourable. Continue whipping while gradually adding the sugar, followed by the **olive oil.** Whip just until soft peaks form.

MELISSA You can buy **lavender salt** at some gourmet stores or order it online from Faerie's Finest (562-983-8397; www.faeriesfinest.com). Or, make your own by grinding ¼ teaspoon dried lavender flowers and ¾ teaspoon *fleur de sel* with a mortar and pestle or in a clean electric coffee grinder.

6. Invert the cakes onto a baking sheet and toast under the broiler, watching carefully to be sure they don't burn, until the outsides are golden and slightly crispy, about 4 minutes. (Alternatively, you can use a toaster oven.) Or, cut the whole cake into slices and toast those. Sprinkle the toasted cakes with a pinch or two of **lavender salt** and **serve** immediately with the olive oil whipped cream.

Serve this with plenty of fresh, seasonal berries if you like.

DEBORAH SNYDER, Lever House, New York

Warm Chocolate Cakes with Coffee Ice Cream and Cashew Brittle

There is some debate as to who invented the molten chocolate cake, with its oozing center of chocolate lava. But ever since Jean-Georges Vongerichten popularized it in New York in the 1990s, it's been tiresomely ubiquitous on upscale restaurant menus. Thankfully, Deborah Snyder's version is a little different. With its soft, creamy center and intense chocolate taste, it's closer to the richest, fudgiest brownie ever. Deborah serves the cakes with homemade coffee ice cream and cashew brittle. Since it's easy to buy good coffee ice cream (or any other flavor you prefer), I skipped that recipe, but I included the brittle. It's not only unusual, it's also particularly delicious and not hard to make. But store-bought peanut brittle will work just as well here—I love the brittle from See's Candies (800-347-7337; www.seescandies.com). Or just leave it out altogether and serve these lovely cakes with regular whipped cream or Olive Oil Whipped Cream (page 227). Really, that's all they need. PREPARATION TIME: 45 MINUTES, PLUS 20 TO 25 MINUTES BAKING

SERVES 8 (PLUS 1 FOR THE COOK!)

CASHEW BRITTLE

2 tablespoons light corn syrup

3 tablespoons unsalted butter, sliced

½ cup granulated sugar

¼ teaspoon kosher salt or fine sea salt

¼ teaspoon pure vanilla extract

2 cups (8 ounces) roasted cashews

CHOCOLATE CAKES

1½ sticks (6 ounces) unsalted butter, plus additional for the ramekins

Granulated sugar, for the ramekins

¼ teaspoon coarse sea salt, plus additional for the ramekins

10 ounces bittersweet chocolate, chopped

5 large eggs

¾ cup plus 2 tablespoons packed dark brown sugar

1½ teaspoons pure vanilla extract

¾ cup all-purpose flour

2 tablespoons unsweetened cocoa powder

¼ teaspoon baking soda

FOR SERVING

Coffee ice cream

MELISSA'S TIPS For something that your guests have definitely never had, skip the **brittle** and pair this cake with the Roasted Cinnamon Gelato on page 254. Make a little extra of the sherried raisins (one and a half times the recipe is perfect) to use as a garnish.

1. Line a rimmed baking sheet with parchment paper or a nonstick liner, or oil it well. Pour the corn syrup into a medium saucepan, then add, in this order, the butter and granulated sugar. Place the pan over medium-high heat and cook, swirling as necessary for even browning, until the mixture is a deep amber caramel (spoon a little onto a white plate if you're

RECIPE CONTINUES

not sure), about 7 minutes. Immediately pull the pan off the heat and stir in the salt and vanilla (stand back—the mixture may spit). Add the nuts and stir vigorously so they are thoroughly coated (pop the pan back over the heat for a few seconds if needed to soften the caramel). Turn the nuts out onto the prepared baking sheet and spread them into a single layer. Let cool.

2. Break up the nuts by coarsely chopping the **brittle.** Store in an airtight container in a cool, dry place for up to a month.

3. Prepare the cakes: Preheat the oven to 375°F. Brush nine 5-ounce ramekins with softened butter, then sprinkle them with granulated sugar to coat the bottoms; shake out excess sugar. Place a tiny pinch of coarse sea salt in the bottom of each ramekin. Place the ramekins in a roasting pan.

4. Bring an inch of water to a boil in the bottom of a double boiler or in a saucepan with a metal bowl suspended over it. Melt the **chocolate** and the $1\frac{1}{2}$ sticks of butter together over simmering water. Let cool.

5. Using an electric mixer, whip together the eggs, brown sugar, and vanilla on high speed until they have tripled in volume, about 3 minutes.

6. In a mixing bowl, sift together the flour, cocoa, baking soda, and the $\frac{1}{4}$ teaspoon salt. Working gently to avoid deflating the eggs, fold the cooled chocolate mixture into the egg mixture, and then fold in the dry ingredients.

7. Ladle the **batter** into the ramekins, filling them about two-thirds full. Place the roasting pan holding the ramekins on the oven rack, then carefully pour very **hot tap water** into the pan so that it comes halfway up the sides of the ramekins. Cover the pan with **foil** and bake until the cakes are set and just springy on the top, about 20 minutes. Let the cakes rest in the pan for a few minutes, then run an offset spatula around their sides and unmold them onto dessert plates. If the first cake seems too soft to unmold, return the ramekins to the oven for another 5 minutes (minus the water bath). Serve warm, with cashew brittle and coffee ice cream.

GINA DEPALMA, Babbo Ristorante e Enoteca, New York

Cinnamon Plum Tart

While everyone else in Babbo's dining room is inhaling Mario Batali's pastas, I usually hold back a little, saving room for Gina DePalma's brilliant desserts. This one is a clever take on a classic fruit tart, which Gina spices with cinnamon—both in the custard and in the cookie-like crust. She usually pairs it with an exotic homemade gelato, such as sage, but I like it best plain, and preferably still a little warm from the oven. PREPARATION TIME: 50 MINUTES, PLUS 2 HOURS AND 20 MINUTES CHILLING AND BAKING

SERVES 8

CRUST

1½ cups all-purpose flour, plus more for dusting

3 tablespoons granulated sugar

½ teaspoon kosher salt or fine sea salt

½ teaspoon ground cinnamon

6 tablespoons (¾ stick) unsalted butter, chilled and cut into cubes

1 large egg yolk (see Chef's Tip, page 258)

3 tablespoons ice water

FILLING

6 tablespoons (¾ stick) unsalted butter, softened

⅓ cup confectioners' sugar

½ teaspoon ground cinnamon

Pinch of kosher salt or fine sea salt

2 large egg yolks

½ teaspoon pure vanilla extract

1½ pounds large round purple or red plums (5 or 6 plums, 4 cups sliced)

2 tablespoons light brown sugar

1 tablespoon freshly squeezed lemon juice (from ½ lemon)

MELISSA'S TIPS If you don't like **cinnamon,** you can leave it out of both the crust and filling with no harm done. Or substitute an equal measure of ground ginger.

1. Make the crust: In a food processor, combine the flour, granulated sugar, salt, and **cinnamon,** and pulse to combine. Add the butter and pulse until it disappears into tiny beads. In a small bowl, whisk together the egg yolk and ice water and add to the flour mixture, pulsing until it starts to come together. Gather the dough together to form a ball, flatten it into a disk, wrap it in plastic, and chill in the refrigerator for 1 hour.

2. When the dough has chilled, roll it out on a floured surface to fit a 9-inch tart pan with a removable bottom. Trim any excess from the top using the rolling pin. Cover the crust with plastic and chill in the refrigerator for 20 minutes.

3. Preheat the oven to 375°F. Line the crust with foil and fill with dried beans or pie weights. Bake for 15 minutes, then

RECIPE CONTINUES

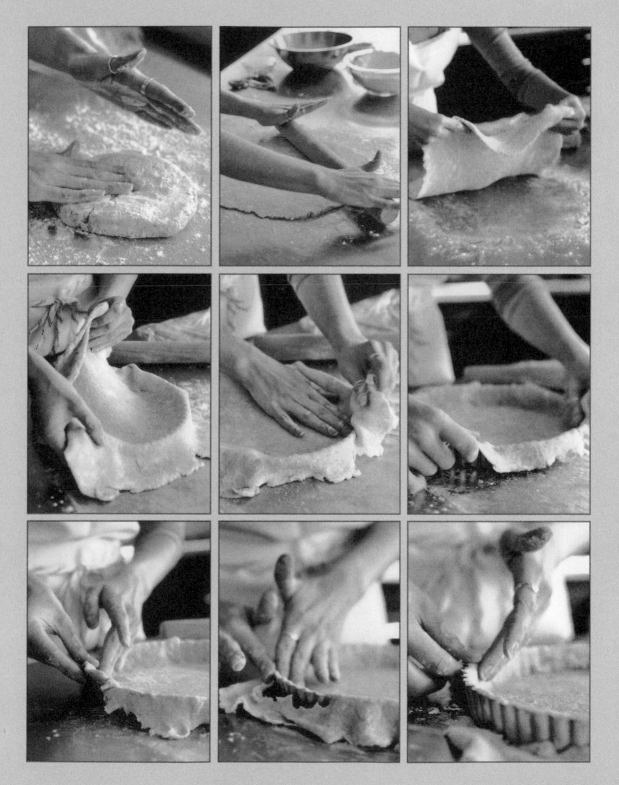

remove the beans and foil and bake for 10 more minutes. Transfer the pan to a wire rack and let cool. Reduce the oven temperature to 325°F.

4. Prepare the filling: In an electric mixer fitted with the paddle attachment, cream together the butter, confectioners' sugar, cinnamon, and salt. Beat in the egg yolks and vanilla, scraping down the sides of the bowl.

5. Cut the **plums** in half, remove the pits, and slice thin. Toss the plum slices in a bowl with the brown sugar and lemon juice.

6. To assemble the tart, spread the filling evenly on the bottom of the crust. Arrange the plum slices in concentric circles over the filling, and dribble any plum juices over the tart. Bake for 40 to 55 minutes, turning the tart back to front after 25 minutes to ensure even browning. The crust and filling should be golden brown, and the plums, tender and bubbling.

CHEF'S TIP Use ripe, juicy **plums,** preferably in a range of colors. Peaches will also work, in season.

MELISSA Whipped cream or crème fraîche is excellent with this tart, as is ice cream. If you want to go all out, serve it with the Meyer Lemon Ice Cream on page 238.

NICOLE KAPLAN, Eleven Madison Park, New York

Chocolate–Peanut Butter Parfaits with Caramelized Bananas

Streamlining this dessert was one of the big challenges in this chapter—not because Nicole Kaplan's original dessert is particularly baroque, but it does have nearly half a dozen components, and they are all delicious. So picking which ones to nix was tough. Her version included covering the peanut butter parfait with a hard chocolate shell so the result is almost like a Reese's Peanut Butter Cup that you put in the freezer (if you have never done this, go and do it now). Her dessert also features peanut brittle, spiced caramel, and tapioca. I simplified the parfait recipe, replaced the somewhat persnickety chocolate shell with an easygoing fudge sauce, and kept the chocolate sablés and caramelized bananas. It's still time-consuming compared to many of the other recipes here, but so worth it if you love chocolate, peanut butter, and bananas combined in a dessert that is not the least bit cloying. PREPARATION TIME: 1½ HOURS, PLUS AT LEAST 6 HOURS FREEZING, 30 MINUTES CHILLING, 15 MINUTES BAKING

SERVES 6

PEANUT BUTTER PARFAITS

3 large eggs, separated

1 tablespoon light or dark brown sugar

1 cup whole milk

⅓ cup peanut butter, chunky or smooth (see Melissa's Tips)

½ teaspoon kosher salt or fine sea salt

½ cup granulated sugar

1 cup heavy cream, whipped to soft peaks

CHOCOLATE SABLÉS

1½ cups all-purpose flour

1 cup unsweetened cocoa powder

Pinch of kosher salt or fine sea salt

14 tablespoons (1¾ sticks) unsalted butter, softened

½ cup plus 1 tablespoon granulated sugar, plus additional for sprinkling

1 large egg

1 large egg yolk (see Chef's Tips, page 258)

CHOCOLATE SAUCE

3 ounces unsweetened chocolate, chopped

4 tablespoons (½ stick) unsalted butter

1 cup granulated sugar

2 tablespoons light corn syrup

Pinch of kosher salt or fine sea salt

½ cup heavy cream

1 teaspoon pure vanilla extract

CARAMELIZED BANANAS

2 bananas, peeled and sliced

2 tablespoons granulated sugar

1. Make the parfaits: Place the egg whites in a clean bowl of an electric mixer fitted with the whisk attachment. In another bowl, whisk the egg yolks with the brown sugar.

RECIPE CONTINUES

2. In a saucepan over medium-high heat, warm the milk until it is steaming. Whisk the **peanut butter** into the milk until dissolved. Whisking constantly, gradually add some of the hot milk mixture to the egg yolks to warm them. Continuing to whisk constantly, add the yolks to the saucepan and cook over medium heat, stirring with a wooden spoon, until the mixture thickens, about 3 minutes. Immediately pour this custard into a clean bowl. Add the salt and let cool.

3. Beat the egg whites until very foamy, then slowly begin adding the granulated sugar, a tablespoon at a time. When the sugar has all been added, continue to beat (if necessary) until the meringue is fluffy and glossy and holds stiff peaks.

4. Using a whisk, mix a little of the egg whites into the peanut butter mixture to lighten it. Gently fold the rest of the whites in, working quickly to avoid deflating them. Fold in the whipped heavy cream. Fill six 5-ounce ramekins with this mixture, cover them with plastic wrap, and **freeze** for at least 6 hours and up to 3 days.

5. Make the sablés: In a bowl, whisk together the flour, **cocoa,** and salt. In the bowl of an electric mixer, cream together the butter and sugar. Add the egg and the yolk, mixing on medium-low speed until incorporated. Gradually add the dry ingredients until the dough is just combined.

6. Working with half the **dough** at a time, roll it out as thin as possible between sheets of plastic wrap or wax paper (you'll have about a 10 by 14-inch rectangle for each half of the dough). Repeat with the other half of the dough. Place the rolled dough on a flat baking pan and refrigerate until firm, at least 30 minutes.

7. Preheat the oven to 325°F. Line two baking sheets with parchment or wax paper or a nonstick liner. Cut the rolled dough out into 3-inch rounds and place them on the baking sheets. Sprinkle about ½ teaspoon of sugar over the top of each cookie. Bake until firm and dry, about 15 minutes. Transfer the pans to wire racks and let cool. The **cookies** can be stored in an airtight container for up to 1 week.

8. Make the **chocolate sauce:** In a double boiler set over simmering (not boiling) water, combine the chocolate and butter. Cook the mixture, stirring occasionally, until the chocolate melts. Add the sugar, corn syrup, and salt, and cook until the sugar dissolves, about 5 minutes. Add the cream and continue to cook, stirring often, until it is quite smooth, about 10 more minutes. Stir in the vanilla. Serve immediately or rewarm over simmering water before serving.

9. Just before serving, prepare the bananas: Preheat the broiler and line a baking sheet with a nonstick liner. Lay the banana slices out on the baking sheet in a single layer and sprinkle them with the sugar. Place the pan under the broiler and broil, watching carefully, until the sugar is caramelized, 1 to 2 minutes.

10. To serve, place a cookie on each dessert plate. Dip the bottoms of the ramekins into very hot water for a few seconds, dry them so they don't drip, then turn the parfaits out on top of the cookies. Drizzle with chocolate sauce, top with caramelized bananas, and serve.

MELISSA You can, of course, substitute store-bought chocolate wafers for the homemade. Nabisco's Famous work well, though they are sweeter and less refined than Nicole's elegant sablés.

Ditto for the **chocolate sauce.** Or leave it out altogether and serve this with shaved chocolate on top instead. To make chocolate shavings, use a vegetable peeler or simply grate chocolate coarsely in the food processor (just be careful not to overprocess, or it might melt).

ANNE QUATRANO, Bacchanalia, Atlanta

Meyer Lemon Pudding Cake with Meyer Lemon Ice Cream

Using Meyer lemons in place of regular lemons gives these citrusy cakes a more delicate and perfumed flavor. Once baked, the cakes separate into two layers: a light, foamy base topped with silky lemon curd. At Bacchanalia, Atlanta's number-one restaurant according to *Zagat,* Anne serves them with Meyer lemon ice cream, but purchased lemon sorbet or ice cream is nearly as enjoyable. If you want to gild the lily, however, I've also included Anne's recipe. PREPARATION TIME: 30 MINUTES, PLUS 23 MINUTES BAKING

SERVES 8

Meyer Lemon Ice Cream

PREPARATION TIME: 20 MINUTES, PLUS 3 1/2 HOURS CHILLING AND CHURNING

MAKES ABOUT 1 1/4 QUARTS

3 1/2 Meyer lemons (or 3 regular lemons and 1/4 orange, see Melissa's Tips), zested and juiced

2 1/2 cups whole milk

1 1/2 cups heavy cream

1 cup sugar

6 large egg yolks (see Chef's Tips, page 258)

1/2 teaspoon pure vanilla extract

Pinch of kosher salt or fine sea salt

MELISSA'S TIPS The Meyer lemon is a particularly sweet, fragrant variety of lemon that originated in China and was brought to California. Look for them in gourmet grocers or you can order a 5-pound box from Melissa's (800-588-0151; www.melissas.com). You can also just substitute regular lemons with a squeeze of orange added for sweetness. In the cake recipe, instead of 1/3 cup Meyer **lemon juice,** you can use 1/4 cup regular lemon juice plus 2 tablespoons freshly squeezed orange juice.

1. In a saucepan over medium heat, combine the **lemon** zest, milk, cream, and 1/2 cup of the sugar. Stir until the sugar dissolves, heat until steaming, then turn off the heat and let steep for 10 minutes.

2. In a large bowl, whisk together the egg yolks and remaining 1/2 cup of sugar. When the milk mixture has steeped, rewarm it to just below a simmer. Whisking the egg yolks constantly, gradually add the hot milk mixture. Return the liquid to the pot and stir constantly over low heat until the custard has thickened enough to coat a wooden spoon, 3 to 5 minutes.

3. Add the lemon juice, vanilla, and salt. Strain through a fine-mesh sieve, let cool to room temperature, then refrigerate for at least 3 hours or up to 2 days. Freeze in an ice-cream maker according to the manufacturer's directions.

Meyer Lemon Pudding Cakes

6 tablespoons (¾ stick) unsalted butter, at room temperature, plus additional for greasing the ramekins

¾ cup sugar

1 tablespoon Meyer or regular lemon zest

¼ teaspoon kosher salt or fine sea salt

6 large eggs, separated

⅓ cup all-purpose flour

3 cups whole milk

⅓ cup freshly squeezed Meyer lemon juice, from 2 to 3 Meyer lemons (see Melissa's Tips)

Meyer Lemon Ice Cream or lemon sorbet or ice cream, for serving

1. To prepare the cakes, preheat the oven to 350°F. Butter eight 5-ounce ramekins and place them in a roasting pan. Using an electric mixer fitted with the paddle attachment, cream the butter with ½ cup of the sugar, the lemon zest, and salt until well blended. Add the egg yolks one at a time, beating well after each addition. Reduce the speed and mix in the flour. Gradually mix in the **milk** and then the **lemon juice.**

2. In a clean bowl, using the electric mixer fitted with the whisk attachment, beat the egg whites to soft peaks. Slowly add the remaining ¼ cup of sugar and beat until stiff. Using a rubber spatula, fold the whites into the yolk mixture in three additions.

3. Divide the batter among the prepared ramekins. Place the pan in the oven and carefully pour very hot tap water into the roasting pan until it comes halfway up the sides of the ramekins. Cover the pan with foil and bake until the cakes are puffed and firm to the touch, about 23 minutes. Transfer the ramekins to a wire rack and let cool slightly. (Alternatively, you can let the cakes cool completely and keep at room temperature for up to 6 hours, then rewarm in a 300°F. oven for 3 to 4 minutes and proceed.)

4. To serve, run a thin knife or offset spatula around the sides of the cakes and invert them onto dessert plates. **Serve warm** with ice cream or sorbet.

MELISSA If the batter seems curdled as you mix in the **milk** and **lemon juice,** just keep mixing—it will work out beautifully once it's baked.

CHEF'S TIP Although these cakes are excellent at room temperature, they are at their best **served warm** from the oven.

DAVID CARMICHAEL, Oceana, New York

Sticky Toffee Pudding with Toffee Sauce

At Oceana, David Carmichael serves this traditional British sweet with sophisticated bells and whistles, like pomegranate foam and black walnut ice cream. But even in its simplest, most nursery-like state, it's a worthy dessert that's sure to be a resounding hit. PREPARATION TIME: 1 HOUR, ABOUT 17 OR 47 MINUTES BAKING TIME

SERVES 12

CAKE

5 tablespoons unsalted butter, softened, plus more for greasing ramekins

1 cup coarsely chopped pitted dates

1 teaspoon pure vanilla extract

1 teaspoon baking soda

2 cups all-purpose flour

1 teaspoon baking powder

¼ teaspoon kosher salt or fine sea salt

1¾ cups granulated sugar

1 large egg

TOFFEE SAUCE

2 cups dark brown sugar

11 tablespoons (1⅜ stick) unsalted butter

1 cup plus 2 tablespoons heavy cream

3 tablespoons dark rum

MELISSA'S TIPS If you want to add an edgy element, replace ⅓ cup of the **dates** with coarsely chopped candied ginger.

1. Preheat the oven to 325°F. Grease twelve 5-ounce ramekins, a quart-size soufflé dish, or an 8-inch cake pan.

2. Make the cake: In a small saucepan, combine the **dates** and 1 cup water, and bring to a boil. Take the pan off the heat and stir in the vanilla and baking soda. Set aside.

3. In a bowl, whisk together the flour, baking powder, and salt.

4. Using an electric mixer, cream the granulated sugar and the 5 tablespoons of butter together on low speed until just combined. Add the egg and mix on low speed until smooth. Add half of the flour mixture, and mix until just combined. Mix in all of the date mixture. Add the remaining flour mixture and finish mixing by hand, using a rubber spatula.

5. Spoon the mixture into the mold(s) and place on a baking sheet. Bake until the tops are golden and the edges begin to pull away from the sides of the pan but the center is still a bit wobbly, 15 minutes for individual puddings, 40 to 45 minutes for one large one.

6. While the puddings bake, prepare the toffee sauce: In a medium saucepan, combine the brown sugar, butter, and cream with ¼ cup water, and bring to a boil. Reduce the heat to medium-low and simmer for about 10 minutes, until the sauce resembles thin custard. Turn off the heat, stir in the **rum,** and keep warm.

7. As soon as the cakes come out of the oven, immediately pour as much of the toffee sauce onto the cakes as they will absorb. Use a paring knife to release the cakes from the side of the mold(s) and poke a few holes in the center to get extra sauce down inside. Return the pudding(s) to the oven for 1 to 2 minutes. Transfer to a wire rack and let cool somewhat, then **serve** warm with vanilla ice cream and any remaining sauce.

Instead of using **rum** in the toffee sauce, you can substitute your favorite liquor— Scotch or Irish whiskey work particularly well.

CHEF'S TIP This gooey dessert is great **served** with vanilla ice cream or crème fraîche.

KAREN DEMASCO, Craft and Craftbar, New York

Butterscotch Custards

The genius of this recipe is that Karen DeMasco uses plenty of salt and both caramel and brown sugar for the deepest, most intense butterscotch flavor imaginable. If you've never made caramel before, don't be intimidated. It's really not any harder than melting butter, and the good thing is that sugar is cheap enough that if you do mess it up (by overcooking it, usually), you can always make it again. PREPARATION TIME: 30 MINUTES, PLUS 1½ to 2 HOURS BAKING AND COOLING, AND 4 HOURS CHILLING

SERVES 8

2 cups heavy cream

1 cup whole milk

¼ cup dark brown sugar

¾ cup granulated sugar

6 large egg yolks, lightly beaten (see Chef's Tips, page 258)

1 teaspoon pure vanilla extract

¾ teaspoon kosher salt or coarse sea salt

MELISSA'S TIPS Burning sugar to make caramel is just about as easy as, well, burning anything. However, you do want to be in control of how dark the **caramel** gets, and in this recipe it only needs to be golden brown. Just watch carefully and use a light-colored pot, or take the pan off the heat and spoon some syrup onto a white plate to check the color.

I use **vanilla** extract so much that it makes sense to steep my own, since I can produce a big batch more affordably that way and it is more intensely flavored. To do this, pack a tall jar with fresh vanilla beans—the more the merrier. Fill the jar with brandy or vodka and let macerate for at least 2 weeks, though a month is better. Leave the vanilla beans in the jar and top up with a little brandy whenever it runs low. It will last for years; mine is at eight and counting.

1. Preheat the oven to 300°F. In a medium saucepan over medium heat, bring the cream, milk, and brown sugar to a simmer, stirring until the sugar dissolves.

2. In a separate saucepan over medium-high heat, simmer the granulated sugar with ¼ cup water, swirling the pan occasionally, until the mixture is a golden **caramel,** 10 to 12 minutes. Slowly whisk some of the cream mixture into the caramel to stop the cooking (stand back; the liquid may spit), then continue to whisk over low heat to dissolve any caramel bits that have hardened. Whisk the caramel into the rest of the cream mixture.

3. Whisk the warm caramel cream into the egg yolks along with the **vanilla** and salt. Pour the mixture through a fine-mesh strainer set over a bowl.

4. Pour the custard into eight 5-ounce **ramekins** or an 8- or 9-inch glass loaf pan and place the custard(s) in a larger roasting pan (see Melissa's Tips on page 228). Place the pan on the oven shelf, then pour enough very hot tap water into the pan to come about halfway up the sides of the ramekins.

Cover the pan with foil and bake until just set around the edges, 40 to 50 minutes for individual custards, 30 to 45 minutes for one large custard, lifting a corner of the foil after 15 and 30 minutes to vent the steam, then reclosing the foil. Transfer the ramekins to a wire rack and let them cool to room temperature before chilling in the refrigerator until set, at least 4 hours and up to 3 days.

CHEF'S TIP The **cooking time** will vary depending on the shape of your dishes, so keep a close eye on the puddings. They are done when they are firm around the edges and slightly jiggly in the middle.

VICKI WELLS, Bolo, New York

Chocolate Tart with a Cornmeal Crust and Pear Compote

Sharing the spotlight with any celebrity chef can be hard for a pastry chef, but Vicki Wells certainly holds her own next to Food Network darling Bobby Flay. Like his recipes, hers use bold flavors and interesting ingredient combinations. Here, she pairs chocolate, cornmeal, and pears in a truffle-like tart. Although at Bolo Vicki makes individual tarts, I turned her recipe into one larger dessert that is easier and less time-consuming, and no less impressive to eat. PREPARATION TIME: 35 MINUTES, PLUS 1 HOUR CHILLING AND 20 MINUTES BAKING

SERVES 10

CORNMEAL CRUST

½ cup (1 stick) unsalted butter, softened

¾ cup plus 2 tablespoons sugar

1 egg yolk (see Chef's Tips, page 258)

½ cup plus 3 tablespoons all-purpose flour

⅓ cup cake flour

¼ cup yellow cornmeal (see Melissa's Tips, page 264)

½ teaspoon kosher salt or fine sea salt

CHOCOLATE FILLING

2 tablespoons whole milk

1½ cups heavy cream

4 tablespoons sugar

½ vanilla bean, split lengthwise and scraped (see Melissa's Tips, pages 260–261)

2 ounces bittersweet chocolate, chopped (about ⅓ cup)

3 egg yolks

2¼ teaspoons unsweetened cocoa powder

Large pinch of kosher salt or fine sea salt

PEAR COMPOTE

2 tablespoons unsalted butter

4 ripe pears, preferably Bosc, peeled, cored, and cut into 1-inch cubes

2 tablespoons sugar

1 vanilla bean, split lengthwise and scraped

2 tablespoons pear brandy or cognac

MELISSA'S TIP Because cake flour has less protein than regular all-purpose flour, it makes baked goods especially delicate. In this recipe, Vicki uses a combination of **flours,** which produces a tender crust with enough structure to support the rich chocolate filling. If you don't have any cake flour on hand, you can substitute all-purpose, or, even better, use 3 tablespoons of cornstarch and the rest all-purpose flour, which will approximate the protein percentage of cake flour.

1. Make the cornmeal crust: In the bowl of an electric mixer fitted with the paddle attachment, cream the butter for 1 minute. Add the sugar and beat until light and fluffy. Beat in the egg yolk until smooth. Add the **flours,** cornmeal, and salt, and mix until the dry ingredients are just incorporated. (Alternatively, prepare the dough in a food processor by pulsing together the dry ingredients, then pulsing in the butter and, finally, the egg yolk, until the dough comes together.) Pat the dough into a disk, wrap it in plastic, and chill until firm, at least 40 minutes and up to 3 days.

2. On a floured surface, roll out the dough to ⅛ inch thick and fit it into a 9-inch tart pan with a removable bottom. Fold the overhanging dough back over the sides to reinforce them, and use any extra dough to **patch** tears in the bottom, if necessary. Chill until firm, at least 20 minutes and up to 24 hours (wrap the dough in plastic if you are storing it for more than an hour).

CHEF'S TIP Patch any holes in your tart shell and bake the tart on a **rimmed baking sheet** to avoid the risk of custard running down into your oven.

3. Preheat the oven to 350°F. Set the tart pan on a **rimmed baking sheet** and bake until the shell is golden brown, about 15 minutes. Reduce the oven temperature to 300°F.

4. Make the chocolate filling: In a saucepan over medium heat, combine the milk, cream, 2 tablespoons of the sugar, and the vanilla pod and pulp. Heat until it reaches a bare simmer, then remove the pan from the heat and add the chocolate, stirring until it melts.

5. In a bowl, whisk the egg yolks with the remaining 2 tablespoons of sugar, the cocoa powder, and salt. Whisk the egg yolk mixture into the chocolate mixture, then pour the filling through a fine-mesh strainer into the tart shell. Bake the tart on the baking sheet until the custard is almost set but still a little jiggly at the center, 18 to 20 minutes. Let cool on a wire rack.

6. Prepare the compote: In a skillet over medium heat, melt the butter. Add the pears and cook, stirring, until they are just beginning to soften and release their juices, 1 to 2 minutes, depending on ripeness. Add the sugar and vanilla pod and pulp and cook until the pears are tender, 2 to 4 minutes. Pour the brandy into the pan and cook for another 2 minutes. Transfer to a bowl and let cool to room temperature.

7. Serve slices of tart with pear compote on the side.

LAUREN DAWSON, Hearth, New York

Peach and Blueberry Cobbler with Vanilla Whipped Cream

Hearth is one of those restaurants where I always want to order everything on the menu. Although the food seems simple, it usually transcends the typical. Like this cobbler. It sounds, perhaps, like every other cobbler. But it is frankly better than most, with a crispy biscuit topping and fruit that's just sweet enough. Lauren bakes individual cobblers and tops them with homemade ice cream. I adjusted the recipe to make one large dish, which is quicker to assemble and better for serving family style. And you won't be left with six ramekins to scour. PREPARATION TIME: 25 MINUTES, PLUS 20 MINUTES RESTING AND 1 HOUR BAKING

SERVES 6

4 cups ripe peaches, pitted and cut into 1-inch cubes (about 6 peaches, or 1¾ pounds)

1 cup blueberries

½ cup plus 2 tablespoons sugar, or more to taste

2 cups plus 1 tablespoon all-purpose flour

10 tablespoons (1¼ sticks) unsalted butter, chilled and cubed

2 teaspoons baking powder

½ teaspoon kosher salt or fine sea salt

¾ cup whole milk

1 cup plus 3 tablespoons heavy cream

1 egg yolk (see Chef's Tips, page 258)

½ vanilla bean, split lengthwise and scraped (see Melissa's Tips, pages 260–261)

MELISSA'S TIPS If you like, substitute raspberries for the **blueberries** and add another tablespoon of sugar.

CHEF'S TIPS Don't make this more than a few hours ahead, or the biscuit topping will get soggy. And definitely don't refrigerate it.

1. In a bowl, gently toss the peaches and **berries** with ½ cup of the sugar and 1 tablespoon of the flour. Let sit for at least 20 minutes, then taste and add a little more sugar if the fruit seems too tart.

2. Preheat the oven to 325°F. Prepare the topping: In the bowl of an electric mixer fitted with the paddle attachment, combine the remaining 2 tablespoons of sugar and 2 cups of flour with the butter, the baking powder, and salt. Mix at medium-low speed until the butter is in small pebbles. Slowly pour in the milk and mix until the dough just comes together. (Alternatively, using a food processor, pulse together the dry ingredients, then pulse in the butter until the mixture is in small pebbles. With the motor running, pour in the milk and process until the dough just comes together.)

3. Pour the fruit into a 9 by 13-inch cake pan or gratin dish, and spoon the dough on top, leaving some space between the spoonfuls of dough. Whisk 3 tablespoons of the cream with the egg yolk and brush this glaze over the dough.

4. Bake until the top is firm and golden brown, 50 minutes to 1 hour. Let cool slightly before serving.

5. Just before serving, using a whisk or electric mixer, whip the remaining cup of **cream** with the vanilla pulp until it holds soft peaks. **Serve** with the cobbler.

MELISSA You can sweeten the whipped **cream** to taste with superfine sugar or honey.

CHEF Cobbler tastes best warm from the oven but also reheats well—put it in a 325°F. oven for 10 minutes before **serving.**

KOA DUNCAN, Bastide, Los Angeles

Fresh Fig Tart with Parmesan Ice Cream

Parmesan ice cream falls into the same category as olive oil whipped cream (see page 227) — that savory-sweet crossover grouping that also includes, more prosaically, chocolate-covered pretzels and strawberries steeped in balsamic vinegar. But paired with Koa Duncan's caramelized fresh fig tart, the result is a dessert that also plays the part of a cheese and fruit course. Of course, the tarts are just as tasty — and far less risqué — served with a dollop of crème fraîche instead. Or, for a similar impact without the work of making ice cream, serve the tart with shavings of good Parmigiano-Reggiano on top. PREPARATION TIME: 1 HOUR AND 20 MINUTES, PLUS 33 MINUTES BAKING, 4 HOURS CHILLING AND COOLING

MAKES 6 TARTS AND 1 PINT ICE CREAM

PARMESAN ICE CREAM

5 large egg yolks (see Chef's Tips, page 258)

3 tablespoons sugar

2 cups whole milk

2 tablespoons corn syrup

½ cup (about 1½ ounces) grated Parmesan cheese

APRICOT CREAM

3 large eggs

5 large egg yolks

½ cup apricot fruit butter or jam

3 tablespoons sugar, plus up to 5 tablespoons additional, to taste

4 tablespoons (½ stick) unsalted butter

FIG TARTS

1 pound puff pastry, thawed

1 pint ripe Mission figs, stemmed and quartered lengthwise

2 tablespoons unsalted butter, melted

About 1 tablespoon sugar, for sprinkling

MELISSA'S TIPS I think this shocker **ice cream** is lovely with the fig tarts, but feel free to substitute a dollop of crème fraîche or sour cream. Or serve both and let your guests choose. Vanilla ice cream works well, too, and is far less challenging.

CHEF'S TIPS Look for imported **Parmigiano-Reggiano** for this recipe; it's worth seeking out.

1. Prepare the **ice cream:** In a bowl, whisk together the egg yolks and sugar. Place a mesh sieve over a medium bowl.

2. In a saucepan over medium heat, combine the milk and corn syrup, and heat until steaming. Take the pan off the heat and stir in the **Parmesan.** Either use a hand-held blender or transfer the mixture to a standing blender, and blend until smooth. Return the Parmesan mixture to the pan if you used a stand blender, and put the pan over low heat to gently warm it (do not let it boil).

3. Whisking constantly, add a little of the hot liquid to the yolks to warm them. Slowly pour the yolks into the milk, still whisking constantly. Continue to cook over low heat, stirring, until the mixture thickens enough to coat the back of a wooden spoon, 2 to 3 minutes. Immediately pour through the sieve and let cool. Refrigerate until chilled, at least 3 hours, then freeze in an ice-cream maker according to the manufacturer's instructions.

4. Prepare the **apricot cream:** In the base of a double boiler (or in a saucepan with a metal bowl suspended over it) heat an inch of water until simmering. In the top of the double boiler, whisk together the eggs, yolks, **apricot butter or jam,** and 3 tablespoons of the sugar. Whisk these ingredients constantly over the simmering water until the apricot cream is as thick as pudding, 8 to 10 minutes. Whisk in the butter and add more sugar to taste (you might end up adding as much as 5 more tablespoons if you're using a tart butter, or just 1 more tablespoon if you're using jam). Let cool, then press a piece of plastic wrap directly onto the surface of the apricot cream and refrigerate until chilled, at least 2 hours.

5. Prepare the tarts: Preheat the oven to 400°F. Roll the **puff pastry** out to ⅛ inch thick—you should have about a 16 by 9-inch rectangle. Place the pastry on a baking sheet and chill it in the refrigerator for 10 minutes. Cut out six 4-inch circles of pastry. Spray a **heavy baking sheet** with nonstick cooking spray and put the pastry rounds on top. Then spray the bottom of another heavy baking pan and place it directly on top of the puff pastry to weight it. Bake the puff pastry between the pans until light brown, about 15 minutes. Transfer to a wire rack and let cool. Keep the oven at 400°F.

6. To assemble, spread a layer of apricot cream over each pastry round. Arrange the figs on top of the apricot cream. Brush melted butter over the figs, then sprinkle the top of each tart with about ½ teaspoon of sugar. Return to the oven until the tops of the figs begin to caramelize, about 18 minutes. Serve warm with small scoops of the ice cream.

MELISSA This recipe makes extra **apricot cream,** which is great on toast, in yogurt, or anywhere you might use lemon curd. You could also use 2 pounds of puff pastry and 2 pints of figs and make 12 tarts—there will still be enough ice cream to garnish each tart with a scoop.

CHEF Taste the **apricot butter or jam** to determine how much sugar you'll need—the cream should not be cloying. Make sure to find a really high-quality brand for this; it will make a huge difference.

MELISSA Since homemade **puff pastry** is usually not an option, I use purchased frozen pastry here. Just make sure to choose a good, all-butter brand (such as Dufour, available from baking and gourmet stores). It makes all the difference. Thaw the frozen puff pastry in the fridge overnight before using.

You will need two **heavy baking sheets** that fit into each other for this recipe.

KAREN BARKER, Magnolia Grill, Durham, North Carolina

Bing Cherry Compote with Black Pepper Ice Cream

Maybe it's because she's originally from Brooklyn, or maybe it's that I'm unendingly sweet-toothed, but whatever the reason, Karen Barker's desserts always seem to resonate with me. Like many of her recipes, this one is based on a classic: cherries jubilee. But instead of the fire coming from a showy display of pyrotechnic flambéing, here it comes from the flavor, with the addition of crushed black peppercorns.

PREPARATION TIME: 30 MINUTES, PLUS 4½ HOURS CHILLING AND FREEZING

SERVES 6

BLACK PEPPER ICE CREAM

1¾ cups half-and-half

1½ cups heavy cream

7 large egg yolks (see Chef's Tips, page 258)

¾ cup sugar

⅛ teaspoon kosher salt or fine sea salt

¾ tablespoon crushed black peppercorns

2 teaspoons pure vanilla extract

BING CHERRY COMPOTE

2½ cups pitted Bing cherries

¾ cup dried sour cherries

¼ cup freshly squeezed orange juice (1 large orange or 1½ small oranges)

3 tablespoons sugar

⅛ teaspoon kosher salt or fine sea salt

Freshly ground black pepper

3 tablespoons brandy

1½ teaspoons cornstarch

MELISSA'S TIPS If you don't want to make homemade **ice cream,** use vanilla ice cream and grind a little more pepper on top of the cherries.

CHEF'S TIPS You can crush the **peppercorns** with a mortar and pestle, if you have one. Or wrap them in a clean towel and smash them with a frying pan, mallet, or heavy can or jar.

MELISSA Bing cherries are the familiar large, dark red, sweet cherries available in midsummer, but any other variety of sweet cherry, such as the Lambert, is also great here. To pit cherries, crush them slightly with the side of a chef's knife and pull out the pit (wear a big, preferably red apron for this

1. Prepare the **ice cream** base: In a saucepan over medium heat, bring the half-and-half and cream to a simmer. In a mixing bowl, whisk together the egg yolks, sugar, and salt. Slowly whisk a bit of the hot cream into the yolks to temper them, then whisk the yolk mixture into the pot. Cook over low heat, stirring, until the mixture is thick enough to coat the back of a wooden spoon, about 5 minutes. Strain into a bowl and let cool completely.

2. Chill the base thoroughly (for at least 4 hours and up to 24), then whisk in the **pepper** and vanilla. Freeze in an ice-cream machine according to the manufacturer's instructions.

3. Prepare the compote: In a saucepan over medium heat, bring the **Bing cherries,** dried cherries, orange juice, sugar, and salt to a simmer. Simmer, stirring, until the cherries soften and release their juices, about 5 minutes. Add a few twists of black pepper. In a small bowl, mix together the brandy and cornstarch, and add it to the cherry mixture. Cook, stirring, until the cherry juices thicken, about 3 minutes. Remove from the heat and let cool. Refrigerate if not using within a few hours (it will keep for 2 days).

4. Serve the ice cream topped with cherry compote.

messy job). Or use a cherry-pitting device—mine is a metal one that works like a hole puncher. If you cook or bake with cherries a lot, you might want the type of cherry pitter that violently yet neatly guillotines cherries and spits them, pitted, into a container.

CHEF I like to **serve** a couple of scoops of the ice cream with this compote, accompanied by a crisp cookie, such as my Cornmeal Hazelnut Biscotti on page 264. The pepper in the ice cream brings out the pepper in the biscotti, and vice versa.

DAN BARBER AND MICHAEL ANTHONY, Blue Hill at Stone Barns, Pocantico Hills, New York

Layered Rhubarb Coupe with Rhubarb Sorbet and Crème Fraîche

At Blue Hill at Stone Barns, chef and quasi-farmer Dan Barber rears his own chickens and grows fifty different kinds of heirloom tomatoes, all his own herbs, and esoteric vegetables like skirret (a delicate, white root vegetable). Given his mania for all things local (twenty yards away from the kitchen door is about right), it's obvious that wild rhubarb, which grows like a weed, features prominently on the menu in season. In this recipe, Dan, along with co-chef Michael Anthony, stews it with just enough sugar to take off the edge, then layers it in a glass with homemade pound cake, sorbet, and sabayon. I have streamlined the process—substituted crème fraîche for the sabayon, and purchased pound cake for the homemade—but the combination of texture and flavors is still completely Stone Barnian. Even with supermarket rhubarb.

PREPARATION TIME: 45 MINUTES, PLUS OVERNIGHT CHILLING AND FREEZING

SERVES 8

2 cups dry white wine

1¼ cups packed light brown sugar

2½ pounds rhubarb, trimmed and cut into
  ½-inch slices (about 8 cups)

¼ cup granulated sugar

1 cup crème fraîche

¼ cup heavy cream

8 slices pound cake, cut into ½-inch cubes

CHEF'S TIP Because **rhubarb** is botanically a vegetable, and a tart one at that, there's a temptation to load it with sugar to make it more like a fruit. But I like to play up its tartness and keep the sugar to a minimum. I find that way it works really well combined with sweet garnishes, and its natural pectin makes it great for jam.

MELISSA'S TIPS Rhubarb goes from firm to mush in a heartbeat, so **simmer** it gently and keep an eye on the compote, straining out the whole rhubarb pieces while they're still a tad firmer than you'd like—they will finish cooking as they cool.

1. In a saucepan, combine the wine and brown sugar and bring to a simmer. Add the **rhubarb** and reduce the heat to medium-low. **Simmer** gently until the rhubarb is tender but not falling apart, 8 minutes. Use a slotted spoon to transfer 2 cups of the rhubarb to a heat-proof measuring cup for the compote. Refrigerate until serving time.

2. Add the granulated sugar to the remaining rhubarb and liquid in the pan and bring to a boil. Let simmer vigorously until the rhubarb has fallen apart, about 10 minutes. Let cool, then strain through a mesh sieve (you will have about 3 cups liquid). Chill until very cold, at least 4 hours, or overnight. Freeze in an **ice-cream machine** according to the manufacturer's directions.

3. Lightly whip the crème fraîche with the heavy cream until thick. To assemble, place the **pound cake** cubes in the bottom of 8 parfait or wine glasses. Next, layer in the compote, then a scoop of sorbet. Top with a dollop of the whipped cream and serve.

If you don't have an **ice-cream machine,** use purchased strawberry sorbet for a strawberry–rhubarb coupe. If in season, you could also add some fresh, sliced strawberries to the rhubarb. Or, turn the rhubarb into a granité: Pour the mixture into a metal pan or bowl and freeze, stirring every 20 minutes or so, until you get a slushy, icy mixture with large frozen flakes.

Store-bought **pound cake** works really well in this recipe, as do crumbled shortbread cookies. But if you feel like baking, try the rosemary polenta pound cake recipe on page 227. The slightly gritty texture is a great match with the slippery rhubarb compote.

MEREDITH KURTZMAN, Otto Enoteca Pizzeria, New York

Roasted Cinnamon Gelato with Sherried Raisins

Gelato guru Meredith Kurtzman's roster of flavors is not only surprising, it is also extraordinary. She knows exactly how to balance ingredients to create a clean, pure taste even in the most outrageous-seeming varieties, such as olive oil–*fleur de sel,* or her sheep's-milk ricotta gelato. This one, with cinnamon and sherried raisins, seems relatively straightforward on the surface, but there's a lot going on beneath it. First of all, Meredith roasts the cinnamon sticks before infusing them in the custard; not only does this give the gelato an intoxicating scent, it also brings out the essential oils of the spice, which lends a particularly silky texture. Though you won't recognize it, she also adds six coffee beans, which accentuate the earthy flavor of the cinnamon. A touch of orange zest adds brightness, and simmering the sherry until syrupy keeps the gelato from becoming icy, while the alcohol keeps it from freezing too solidly and helps maintain a creamy texture. This may well become your favorite gelato flavor. It's certainly one of the most unique. PREPARATION TIME: 25 MINUTES, PLUS 1 TO 3 HOURS STEEPING AND OVERNIGHT CHILLING AND FREEZING TIME

MAKES 1½ QUARTS

GELATO

6 cinnamon sticks

3½ cups whole milk

½ cup heavy cream

½ vanilla bean, split lengthwise and scraped (see Melissa's Tips, pages 260–261)

6 coffee beans, crushed

Grated zest of 1 orange

1½ cups sugar

10 large egg yolks (see Chef's Tips, page 258)

½ teaspoon pure vanilla extract

½ teaspoon kosher salt or fine sea salt

SHERRIED RAISINS

1 cup medium-dry sherry

¾ cup golden raisins

CHEF'S TIP Using whole **cinnamon sticks** adds a strong cinnamon flavor and doesn't result in a grainy mouthfeel, which happens if you flavor gelato with ground spices. I actually like to use cassia bark, from India, as opposed to true cinnamon. Cassia has a sweet, complex flavor profile, although it is usually labeled as cinnamon in this country. Look for an Indian origin on the label, if possible.

1. Make the gelato base: Roast the **cinnamon sticks** on a baking sheet in a 350°F. oven until very fragrant, 10 to 15 minutes. (Alternatively, place the cinnamon sticks in a dry cast-iron pan and toast lightly over medium-high heat until very fragrant, about 5 minutes.)

2. In a medium saucepan over medium heat, bring the milk and cream to a simmer. Add the toasted cinnamon sticks, vanilla pod and pulp, coffee beans, and orange zest. Turn off the heat and let steep for at least 1 or up to 3 hours. Strain the liquid through a fine sieve and discard all the solids.

3. Return the infused milk mixture to the saucepan, add ¾ cup of the sugar, and bring to a simmer over medium heat. In a bowl, whisk the egg yolks with the remaining sugar. Whisk a little of the hot milk mixture into the yolk mixture to temper it. Whisking constantly, pour the tempered egg mixture into the saucepan. Cook, stirring constantly, until steam rises from the mixture, about 2 minutes. Immediately strain through a fine-mesh sieve into a heat-proof bowl. Stir in the vanilla extract and salt and let cool. Chill for at least 6 hours or overnight.

4. Prepare the **raisins:** In a small saucepan, bring the sherry to a simmer. Turn off the heat, add the raisins, and let soak for 1 hour. Strain the raisins, reserving the liquid. Return the liquid to the saucepan and simmer over medium heat until syrupy, about 3 minutes; you will have about ⅓ cup. Return the raisins to the sherry and refrigerate for at least 1 hour and up to 1 month.

5. Scrape the chilled gelato base into the bowl of an ice-cream machine, and add the chilled raisins with their liquid. Churn until just beginning to firm up. Transfer to the freezer and freeze for 1 hour or until hardened.

MELISSA'S TIP If you don't like **raisins,** or at least don't want them in your ice cream, just leave them out. The cinnamon gelato can happily stand on its own.

CLAUDIA FLEMING, formerly of Gramercy Tavern, New York

Chocolate Marshmallow Mounds

Of course, Claudia makes her own graham crackers, which she originally used for the most outrageous graham cracker crumb crust imaginable. Recently, she came up with the idea to use them to make a version of homemade Mallomars. Claudia loves taking classic childhood favorite desserts and re-creating them in a more sophisticated way. I've simplified her technique for making meringue so that you don't have to use a candy thermometer, and I don't bother tempering the chocolate for the coating. This means the cookies don't hold up for more than about two or three days. But believe me, no matter how many you make, they won't last that long anyway. PREPARATION TIME: 1 HOUR AND 10 MINUTES, PLUS 18 MINUTES BAKING AND AT LEAST 6 HOURS CHILLING AND DRYING

MAKES 30 COOKIES

GRAHAM CRACKERS

1 cup (2 sticks) unsalted butter, softened

¼ cup firmly packed brown sugar

¼ cup granulated sugar

¼ cup honey

2 cups all-purpose flour

½ cup whole-wheat pastry flour

1 teaspoon kosher salt or fine sea salt

½ teaspoon ground cinnamon

MARSHMALLOW TOPPING

¾ teaspoon powdered unflavored gelatin

2 large egg whites

⅓ cup plus 1 tablespoon granulated sugar

1 teaspoon pure vanilla extract

Pinch of kosher salt or fine sea salt

CHOCOLATE COATING

4 ounces extra-bittersweet chocolate (see Chef's Tips)

1 teaspoon flavorless oil such as canola

MELISSA'S TIPS The **graham crackers** can be baked 2 days ahead and stored in an airtight container.

Graham crackers are traditionally made with graham **flour,** a specific grind of whole wheat flour. But whole-wheat pastry flour, which is a finer grind, makes a better cookie here, and, let's admit it, we're making a cookie, not a health cracker. Whatever kind of whole-wheat flour you buy, bear in mind that the whole grain contains oils that cause whole-wheat flour to go rancid if stored for too long. So keep it in a good plastic container in the freezer to maximize its shelf life, and taste a pinch to be sure it isn't bitter.

1. Make the **graham crackers:** Using an electric mixer, cream the butter and the sugars until smooth, about 1 minute. Add the honey and beat until well combined.

2. In a medium bowl, whisk together the **flours,** salt, and cinnamon. Mix the flour mixture into the butter mixture in two batches, scraping down the sides of the bowl between additions. Mix until the dough is well combined. Scrape the dough onto a piece of plastic wrap and form it into a log 1¼ inches in diameter. Chill until firm, at least 4 hours and up to 2 days.

RECIPE CONTINUES

When beating **egg whites,** there must be no fat in them, either in the form of a bit of egg yolk or a greasy bowl, as this will keep them from becoming fluffy. To separate eggs without getting any yolks in the whites, set up a clear or white bowl or glass to break the white into, so that you can be sure there are no traces of yolk in it. Also have ready a bowl for all the whites after they are checked, and a bowl for the yolks. Cold eggs are easier to separate since the whites and yolks are less runny when chilled. Break the eggs against a flat surface to reduce the likelihood of the shell puncturing the yolks, then gently transfer the yolk from one half of the shell to the other, letting the white fall into the glass or bowl. The chalazae are the white stringy bits that attach the yolk to the white—they can be added to either the white or the yolk without making any difference.

Beating **egg whites** slowly and adding the sugar very gradually (starting when the whites have reached a thick, foamy stage) will incorporate air into the meringue in the most stable way possible, making the whites less liable to deflate as you work with them. Egg whites whip up best at room temperature, so take yours out of the fridge at least 20 minutes before you start.

Semisweet and bittersweet **chocolate** (the terms tend to be used interchangeably) can contain anywhere from 35 to 60 percent cocoa solids, while extra-bittersweet chocolate is 66 to 80 percent. For this recipe, extra-bitter provides the necessary contrast to the sweet marshmallows, so seek out as close to 72 percent as you can find. Michel Cluizel is one of my favorites.

3. Preheat the oven to 325°F. Slice the dough into ⅛-inch-thick coins and transfer them to a baking sheet. Prick each cookie two or three times with a fork and chill for 20 minutes. Then bake until golden brown, about 18 minutes, and transfer to a wire rack to cool.

4. Make the marshmallow topping: In a small bowl, mix the gelatin with ½ tablespoon cold water and let sit for 5 minutes, then stir in 1 tablespoon boiling water to melt the gelatin.

5. In a metal bowl (use an electric mixer bowl if possible) set over a saucepan filled with 1 inch of boiling water, combine the **egg whites** and ⅓ cup of the sugar. Cook, whisking constantly, until the sugar dissolves. Transfer the mixture to an electric mixer and beat with the whisk attachment until cool to the touch. Add the remaining tablespoon of sugar, the dissolved gelatin, vanilla, and salt, and continue to beat until thick and fluffy. Using a pastry bag, a Ziploc bag with a corner cut off, or a spoon, pipe or spoon blobs of the marshmallow mixture on top of the graham crackers and let dry for 1 hour.

6. Melt the **chocolate** either in the microwave or in a small metal bowl set over a saucepan filled with 1 inch of simmering water. Stir in the oil. Dip each cookie in the melted chocolate and let dry for at least 1 hour at room temperature (or 10 minutes in the refrigerator) before serving.

FLOYD CARDOZ, Tabla, New York

Vanilla Bean Kulfi with Blood Oranges in Darjeeling Syrup

Kulfi is an Indian frozen dairy confection that is at least as delicious as ice cream, though it is, miraculously, prepared without eggs or churning. Instead, kulfi is made simply by cooking down milk (or milk and cream) until it becomes so thick it is almost chewy—like a cross between ice cream and fudge. Sweetened, flavored (common varieties are pistachio, almond, and mango), and reduced, the milk is then frozen, usually on a stick to be sold as street food on hot days. While some recipes for kulfi call for sweetened condensed milk, Floyd cooks down the milk himself, which gives him more control over the sweetness, avoids the fillers in most canned condensed milk, and allows him to achieve a heady vanilla-bean flavor. PREPARATION TIME: 1 HOUR AND 45 MINUTES, PLUS AT LEAST 4 HOURS FREEZING

SERVES 4

KULFI

1 1/3 cups heavy cream

1 cup whole milk

1/4 cup sugar

1 vanilla bean (preferably Tahitian), split lengthwise and scraped (see Melissa's Tips)

Pinch of kosher salt or fine sea salt

BLOOD ORANGES

1/2 cup sugar

1 sprig of fresh rosemary

1 bag or 2 teaspoons Darjeeling tea

1/4 teaspoon rosewater

2 blood oranges

MELISSA'S TIPS This **kulfi** is so simple and incredible that you might want to make a double recipe—just continue to reduce the doubled recipe until you have about 1 1/2 cups. Since it is very rich and satisfying, 3 tablespoons per serving is plenty!

Vanilla beans are the seedpods of a type of orchid. Both the pod and the tiny black seeds inside are full of intense flavor. Pastry chefs usually split the pods lengthwise with a sharp knife, then use the tip of the knife to scrape out the pulp, and use both pulp and pod, straining out the pod once its flavor has infused into the dessert. If there is no

1. Make the **kulfi:** In a heavy-bottomed saucepan over medium heat, combine the cream, milk, sugar, and **vanilla** pod and pulp. Bring to a simmer, then reduce the heat and cook on low, stirring often, until the mixture has been reduced by a third (you'll have about 3/4 cup total), about 1 hour and 15 minutes. Stir in the salt and let cool. Remove the vanilla pod. Divide the kulfi among 4 small ramekins. Cover the surface directly with plastic wrap and freeze for at least 4 hours and up to 4 days.

2. Make the **oranges:** In a saucepan, combine the sugar with 1/2 cup water. Bring to a simmer, stirring until the sugar has dissolved. Add the rosemary and tea and let cool. Strain the cooled syrup into a bowl and add the rosewater.

3. Supreme the oranges: Use a serrated knife to slice the top and bottom off each orange, exposing the fruit. Stand an orange on its base and cut the rest of the peel off, working with the curve of the fruit, so that the segments are free of all peel, pith, and membrane. Holding the orange over the bowl of syrup (so that its juices are added to the syrup), slice the segments free and let them fall into the bowl. Repeat with the other orange.

4. To serve, dip the base of each ramekin of kulfi into scalding hot water, dry with a towel, then run a knife around the inner edge. Invert the kulfi onto shallow dessert or pasta bowls. Spoon the oranges and their syrup over and around the kulfi, and serve immediately.

straining option, then you can just use the seeds and save the pods for another purpose, such as vanilla sugar. (To make vanilla sugar, slowly dry the pods in a low oven, then add them to your sugar container.) Look for plump, moist vanilla beans rather than shriveled, hard ones. Keep vanilla beans wrapped in plastic in the refrigerator, and don't worry if they develop a white musty coating—it's not mold.

CHEF'S TIP Vanilla beans grown in different places have different flavors. In this recipe I prefer the fruity and floral flavor of Tahitian vanilla beans, though of course Bourbon or Mexican vanilla beans are also good.

MELISSA If blood **oranges** are unavailable, regular oranges make a fine substitute.

BILL YOSSES, Joseph's, New York

Halvah Sesame Ice Cream Sundae

Halvah comes from an Arabic word meaning sweetmeat, or confection. But halvah as we know it in the United States is a flaky, sticky, utterly addictive (I think) candy made mostly from sesame seeds. And it's a perfect match for creamy desserts like Bill's sundae. Here, Bill uses every form of sesame imaginable to create a suave sesame ice cream and a velvety tahini and honey sauce that are layered into a sundae garnished with crumbled halvah and sesame brittle. To streamline this, I replaced the homemade brittle with those familiar sesame crunch candies you can get in delis and candy stores. The result is a celebration of sesame that is far more than the sum of its parts. PREPARATION TIME: 45 MINUTES, PLUS AT LEAST 3½ HOURS CHILLING AND CHURNING

MAKES ABOUT 1 QUART ICE CREAM

SESAME ICE CREAM

8 large egg yolks (see Chef's Tips, page 258)

¾ cup sugar

3 cups whole milk

1 cup heavy cream

2 teaspoons sesame oil

2 teaspoons pure vanilla extract

¼ teaspoon kosher salt or fine sea salt

CARAMEL SAUCE

½ cup sugar

TAHINI SAUCE

½ cup heavy cream

⅓ cup tahini

1½ tablespoons honey

FOR SERVING

6 ounces (¾ packed cup) halvah, crumbled

8 sesame crunch candies, broken into pieces

MELISSA'S TIPS If you don't want to make the sesame **ice cream,** store-bought vanilla ice cream layered with halvah sauce and crumbled halvah will still make an excellent sundae.

1. Make the **ice cream:** In a bowl, whisk the egg yolks with ¼ cup of the sugar. In a saucepan, bring the milk, cream, and remaining ½ cup of sugar to a boil. Whisking constantly, pour a little of the hot milk into the yolks to warm them. Then drizzle the yolk mixture into the saucepan, whisking constantly. Cook over medium-low heat, stirring, until the custard is thick enough to coat the back of a wooden spoon, about 5 minutes.

2. Transfer the custard to a bowl and stir in the **sesame oil, vanilla,** and salt. Let cool, then refrigerate for at least 3 hours or overnight. Freeze in an ice-cream maker according to the manufacturer's instructions.

3. Make the caramel sauce: Place the sugar in a small, heavy saucepan over medium heat and swirl until all the sugar is melted. Let the sugar cook until it is a deep amber caramel, about 4 minutes. Pour in ½ cup of water (be careful, it will spit) and whisk until smooth, about 1 minute. Keep warm or reheat before serving.

4. Make the **tahini sauce:** Pour the cream into a saucepan and cook until steaming. Add the tahini and honey and cook, whisking constantly, until smooth and frothy, about 1 more minute.

5. Serve scoops of the sesame ice cream drizzled with caramel and tahini sauce, with crumbled halvah and sesame candy scattered on top.

MELISSA Sesame, like most oily seeds and nuts, is prone to going rancid. Taste **sesame oil** and **tahini** and discard if it starts to develop a bitter aftertaste. Keep your tahini in the fridge to prolong its shelf life. It's also a good idea to stir up tahini every so often, since it separates like peanut butter; and the longer it's left, the more difficult it becomes to reincorporate the oil into the cementlike ground sesame beneath.

CHEF'S TIPS Whenever I can, I add **vanilla** extract off the heat, since heat tends to mitigate the flavor of the vanilla. So for ice cream, I always stir the extract into the custard after cooking it.

Homemade ice cream is so fresh tasting, but since it has no preservatives in it, it's best eaten within a few days. After a week or so, it will lose its luxurious texture and might begin to taste like your freezer.

MELISSA This **tahini sauce** is one of the easiest, most unusual creamy dessert sauces imaginable—I love it on ice cream, plain or chocolate cakes, waffles, or crepes (especially with bananas).

KAREN BARKER, Magnolia Grill, Durham, North Carolina

Cornmeal Hazelnut Biscotti

In this biscotti recipe, Karen Barker's inimitable mark is the addition of a healthy dose of freshly ground black pepper. She developed the recipe to serve with the Bing Cherry Compote on page 250, but they can stand on their own, or be served with purchased ice cream, sorbet, or fresh fruit. Everyone will be so impressed with these cookies that no one will mind if the rest of dessert is prefab. PREPARATION TIME: 35 MINUTES, PLUS 35 MINUTES BAKING AND 25 MINUTES COOLING

MAKES 1 1/2 DOZEN BISCOTTI

¾ cup all-purpose flour, plus more for dusting

½ teaspoon baking soda

½ teaspoon baking powder

3½ ounces (¾ cup) skinned, lightly toasted, finely chopped hazelnuts (see Melissa's Tips)

¼ cup stone-ground yellow cornmeal (see Melissa's Tips)

⅛ teaspoon kosher salt or fine sea salt

Freshly ground black pepper

½ cup sugar

4 tablespoons (½ stick) unsalted butter, at room temperature

Finely grated zest of 1 orange

1 large egg

½ teaspoon vanilla extract

MELISSA'S TIPS To toast and skin **hazelnuts,** spread them on a baking sheet and put them in a 350°F. oven, tossing once, until they are browned and fragrant, about 15 minutes. Let them cool, then rub the nuts with a cloth towel to remove their bitter skins.

The flavorful crust of these biscotti depends on gritty, sweet-tasting yellow **cornmeal.** I buy fresh stone-ground cornmeal every few months and smell and taste it before using, as it can go rancid pretty quickly. Storing it in the freezer will prolong its shelf life . . . if you have room in your freezer, that is.

CHEF'S TIPS I always **zest** citrus directly over the bowl I will be putting it in (in this case, the mixing bowl with the butter), which is neater and ensures that none of the flavor is lost.

1. Preheat the oven to 350°F. Line a baking sheet with parchment or wax paper or a nonstick liner. Whisk together the flour, baking soda, and baking power. Stir in the **hazelnuts, cornmeal,** salt, and a few twists of black pepper.

2. Using an electric mixer, cream the sugar, butter, and orange **zest** until light and fluffy. Add the egg and vanilla and mix well, scraping down the sides as you go. Add the dry ingredients and mix on low speed until just combined.

3. On a floured surface with floured hands, roll the dough into a log about 12 inches long. The dough will be somewhat sticky. Place the log on the prepared baking sheet.

4. Bake for about 20 minutes, until the log is golden brown and fairly firm to the touch. Remove from the oven and let cool for 20 to 25 minutes. **Slice** the log into ½-inch-thick diagonal slices, arrange them on the prepared pan, and bake for another 15 minutes, until lightly brown and toasted. Cool completely and store in an airtight container.

acknowledgments

As I know all too well, any book, but especially a cookbook, is a collaborative effort. Even when you write it yourself there are still so many people who helped in numerous and sometimes hidden ways. In other words, I've got a lot of thanking to do:

My first debt is to all the amazingly talented chefs who let me interrupt their recipes in these pages. Many, many thanks to all of you. Obviously, without your often baroque brilliance and generosity there'd be no book!

Chris Pavone, my first editor at Clarkson Potter, deserves thanks for reading my mind. He and I both came up with the concept for this book, simultaneously and separately. Five years later, here it is. Chris also thought up the incomparable title. Thank you, Chris, for editing me, encouraging me, fighting for me, and buying me many rounds of drinks while we pretended to work.

Pam Krauss, the editorial director at Clarkson Potter and a fellow Brooklynite with a shopping fetish nearly equal to my own, took over editing *Chef, Interrupted* when Chris left. Thanks, Pam, for always noticing my shoes and typos and for being so darn cool.

Concerning the lovely look of this book, I had absolutely nothing to do with it and owe all of that glory to the talented folks who know about such things: Tina Rupp, the photographer; Toni Brogan, the food stylist; and Tiziana Agnello, the prop stylist, made the photo shoot both fun and productive, with a gorgeous result. Jane Treuhaft stitched text and photos together and made everything look integrated and fresh.

Cocktail maven David Wondrich not only supplied the "Mixologist Interrupted" recipes for this book, he also supplies me with nearly as much homemade punch as I can drink on a regular basis. Thank you for looking after my health, Dave, and of course thanks to Karen and Marina just because I adore you all and you are constantly supportive of my various endeavors.

I owe Janis Donnaud, my agent, much gratitude for many things, this book just one on a long list. So it's nice to have a public forum to say, "thanks for everything." Thanks, Janis, for not only being on my side, but for always being one step ahead of (read: smarter than) everyone else, especially me.

Another regular thankee is Zoe Singer, my recipe tester, recipe editor, and mostest companion/assistant, for her general braininess, goofiness, and for putting up with my slow speed when we go running in the park. Every day is a better day when I get to work with Zoe. And thanks for being my friend, too.

Ditto about being my friend and tolerating my slow pace to Ana Deboo, who also copyedited this entire manuscript and talked me out of trashing it midway. I still miss you, Ana. Thanks, you know, for everything . . .

When Zoe was away for that hot summer of intensive testing, Elizabeth (Betsey) Thomas stepped in to save the day and my deadline. Thanks, Betsey, for all the hard work, and for teaching me my new favorite expression for when something doesn't taste very good.

I don't know if I should thank them or vice versa, but while I was working on this book, my sister Amy and brother-in-law David ate most of the food that we tested—an essential task and a great help. Thanks to you both for, you know, arriving at my kitchen with empty Tupperware and plenty of opinions about which recipes worked and which ones tasted like, well, ask Betsey.

Finally, thanks to my foodie parents, Rita and Julian Clark, for exposing me to amazing food from my earliest childhood. That's where it all started, and may it continue for a very long time . . .

index

conversion chart
EQUIVALENT IMPERIAL AND METRIC MEASUREMENTS

American cooks use standard containers, the 8-ounce cup and a tablespoon that takes exactly 16 level fillings to fill that cup level. Measuring by cup makes it very difficult to give weight equivalents, as a cup of densely packed butter will weigh considerably more than a cup of flour. The easiest way therefore to deal with cup measurements in recipes is to take the amount by volume rather than by weight. Thus the equation reads:

1 cup = 240 ml = 8 fl. oz.   ½ cup = 120 ml = 4 fl. oz.

In the States, butter is often measured in sticks. One stick is the equivalent of 8 tablespoons. One tablespoon of butter is therefore equivalent to ½ ounce/15 grams.

LIQUID MEASURES

Fluid Ounces	U.S.	Imperial	Milliliters
⅛	1 teaspoon	1 teaspoon	5
¼	2 teaspoons	1 dessertspoon	10
½	1 tablespoon	1 tablespoon	14
1	2 tablespoons	2 tablespoons	28
2	¼ cup	4 tablespoons	56
4	½ cup		120
5		¼ pint or 1 gill	140
6	¾ cup		170
8	1 cup		240
9			250, ¼ liter
10	1¼ cups	½ pint	280
12	1½ cups		340
15		¾ pint	420
16	2 cups		450
18	2¼ cups		500, ½ liter
20	2½ cups	1 pint	560
24	3 cups		675
25		1¼ pints	700
27	3½ cups		750
30	3¾ cups	1½ pints	840
32	4 cups or 1 quart		900
35		1¾ pints	980
36	4½ cups		1000, 1 liter
40	5 cups	2 pints or 1 quart	1120

SOLID MEASURES

U.S. AND IMPERIAL MEASURES		METRIC MEASURES	
Ounces	Pounds	Grams	Kilos
1		28	
2		56	
3½		100	
4	¼	112	
5		140	
6		168	
8	½	225	
9		250	¼
12	¾	340	
16	1	450	
18		500	½
20	1¼	560	
24	1½	675	
27		750	¾
28	1¾	780	
32	2	900	
36	2¼	1000	1
40	2½	1100	
48	3	1350	
54		1500	1½

OVEN TEMPERATURE EQUIVALENTS

Fahrenheit	Celsius	Gas Mark	Description
225	110	¼	Cool
250	130	½	
275	140	1	Very Slow
300	150	2	
325	170	3	Slow
350	180	4	Moderate
375	190	5	
400	200	6	Moderately Hot
425	220	7	Fairly Hot
450	230	8	Hot
475	240	9	Very Hot
500	250	10	Extremely Hot

Any broiling recipes can be used with the grill of the oven, but beware of high-temperature grills.

EQUIVALENTS FOR INGREDIENTS

all-purpose flour—plain flour
baking sheet—oven tray
buttermilk—ordinary milk
cheesecloth—muslin
coarse salt—kitchen salt
cornstarch—cornflour
eggplant—aubergine

granulated sugar—castor sugar
half and half—12% fat milk
heavy cream—double cream
light cream—single cream
lima beans—broad beans
parchment paper—greaseproof paper
plastic wrap—cling film

scallion—spring onion
shortening—white fat
unbleached flour—strong, white flour
vanilla bean—vanilla pod
zest—rind
zucchini—courgettes or marrow